The Philosophy of Antonio Negri
Volume Two

D1527724

Also available

The Philosophy of Antonio Negri: Resistance in Practice
Edited by Timothy S. Murphy and Abdul-Karim Mustapha

The Philosophy of Antonio Negri

Volume Two

Revolution in Theory

Edited by

Timothy S. Murphy

and

Abdul-Karim Mustapha

Pluto Press

LONDON • ANN ARBOR, MI

First published 2007 by Pluto Press
345 Archway Road, London N6 5AA
and 839 Greene Street, Ann Arbor, MI 48106

www.plutobooks.com

Copyright © Timothy S. Murphy and Abdul-Karim Mustapha 2007

The right of the individual contributors to be identified as the authors of this work has been asserted by them in accordance with the Copyright, Designs and Patents Act 1988.

British Library Cataloguing in Publication Data
A catalogue record for this book is available from the British Library

Hardback
ISBN-13   978 0 7453 2610 8
ISBN-10   0 7453 2610 2

Paperback
ISBN-13   978 0 7453 2609 2
ISBN-10   0 7453 2609 9

Library of Congress Cataloging in Publication Data applied for

10 9 8 7 6 5 4 3 2 1

This book in printed on paper suitable for recycling and made from fully managed and sustained forest sources. Logging, pulping and manufacturing processes are expected to conform to the environmental regulations of the country of origin.

Designed and produced for Pluto Press by
Chase Publishing Services Ltd, Fortescue, Sidmouth, EX10 9QG, England
Typeset from disk by Stanford DTP Services, Northampton
Printed and bound by Antony Rowe Ltd, Chippenham and Eastbourne, England

Contents

Editors' Acknowledgements

Like the first volume of *The Philosophy of Antonio Negri*, this one has been in the works for many years, so our first words of thanks must go to our endlessly patient contributors. We are very grateful to Pluto Press and especially David Castle for their long-term commitment to this very large project. We would also like to thank Sebastian Budgen for suggestions regarding the contents of the volume and Ted Stolze for his translation of Pierre Macherey's essay. And since our editorial collaboration has again taken place electronically, each of us has separate personal acknowledgements to make.

Timothy S. Murphy would again like to thank Abdul-Karim Mustapha for his foresight in getting this project rolling and generating so much of its momentum, and Steve Wright for his unflagging interest in these books and for his willingness to discuss critically many of their elements over the past several years. The everyday energy necessary to complete this labor, like so many others, came from Julie (along with Iris and Daisy). He would like to dedicate this book to the memory of his brother, Kevin John Murphy (1965-2006).

Abdul-Karim Mustapha would like to thank Timothy S. Murphy for the spirit of mind to see this project through in all the years it has been in the making, and for his commitment to enriching both the content and the effectivity of Negri's philosophy in general. He would also once again like to thank Guiseppe Cocco, Yann Moulier-Boutang, Antonella Corsani, Bruno Karsenti, Maurizio Lazzarato, François Matheron, and Charles Wolfe. Lastly, he would like to thank Bruce, Debra, Avi and Ellie Feinberg for cultivating a world of grace and hope, Bruce Speight for his tenacity and wit, Joyce Payne for her pedagogy of perseverance, Stephen, Louise and Mark Garrell for their immeasurable scope of the world, José Rabasa and Catherine Durand for continuity, and his wife Robin Felice for all things possible and her sensitivity to the poetic and metaphysical in all that seems impossible. He would like to dedicate the book project to his late grandmother L. Duro MacRae, his late grandfather Alhaji M. Sanusi Mustapha, his late uncle Ibn Muktarr Mustapha, and to his daughter and the promises of the world that is hers.

Pierre Macherey's contribution originally appeared in French in *Cahiers Spinoza* 4 (1983), and was later reprinted, with substantial revisions, in

Macherey's book *Avec Spinoza* (Paris: Presses universitaires de France, 1992). It is translated here by permission of Presses universitaires de France.

Miguel Vatter's contribution originally appeared in *Kairos: Revue de philosophie* 20 (2002), and it is reprinted here by permission of *Kairos* and the author.

Introduction: A Free Man's Wisdom ...

Timothy S. Murphy and Abdul-Karim Mustapha

This book is the companion to our previous volume, *The Philosophy of Antonio Negri: Resistance in Practice*, published by Pluto Press in 2005. The essays in that volume focus primarily on the theoretical and practical contributions that Antonio Negri has made to radical activism over the course of his long and varied career: his conceptions of the socialized worker, the refusal of work, immaterial labor and constituent power, as well as his critiques of the Leninist party form and Althusser's notion of history as a 'process without a subject', among many other things. The essays in this volume, *Revolution in Theory*, focus primarily on Negri's originality and influence both as an innovative historian of philosophy and as a systematic philosopher, the author of a surprising new 'constitutive' ontology that has become increasingly controversial over the past few years. We frankly admit that this division of subjects we have devised, both within this volume and between the two, is somewhat tendentious and open to dispute, since on the one hand Negri's activism has always been informed by his philosophical background and the novel conceptions to which that led him, and on the other, Negri's philosophical work has always developed directly out of his passionate engagement in practical political activity (or, more recently, his equally passionate interest in the many singular social and political movements currently under way around the globe). We doubt that there is any single, definitively coherent and consistent arrangement to be made of the essays we have included in these two volumes, essays which represent a very broad spectrum of critical responses to an equally broad selection of the elements that constitute the singular multiplicity that is Negri's work. Nevertheless, the material constraints of book production have compelled us to divide our project into two volumes, and each individual volume into sections composed of the essays that we feel resonate most strongly with one another.

Although Negri's work is singular, its correlative multiplicity means that it is not without precedents in and debts to the history of philosophy, and not without important ramifications for contemporary philosophy. The sections into which this volume is divided address these debts and ramifications, as we shall explain below. One of Negri's favorite propositions from Spinoza's *Ethics* is the famous claim that 'A free man thinks of nothing less than of death, and his wisdom is a meditation on life, not on death' (Spinoza 1985:

E IV P67, 584), which could well describe Negri's own philosophy as readily as it does Spinoza's. If his work is not strictly a philosophy of life or vitalism, as some critics claim, it is at very least a philosophy of living labor and constituent power directed against the dead labor of accumulated capital and constituted power. The general perspective and tone of affirmation that his thought shares with that of Gilles Deleuze represent another aspect of this 'wisdom', in that Spinoza conceives of death as the decomposition of the relation that constitutes the body, and thus death can come not only to individuals but to social movements, nation states and constitutions, but such decomposition is no cause for regret or melancholy. On the contrary, the finitude of all such bodies is a constantly renewed challenge for us to construct new bodies, new constitutive relations, a new common on the plane of immanence that is human history. One consequence of this affirmation is Negri's preference, which he raises to the level of a methodological principle, for looking ahead, into 'time-to-come', rather than backward in continual self-criticism, a choice that has attracted and repelled readers in equal measure. We will leave the question of whether or not Negri really is Spinoza's 'free man' to the judgment of our readers—but we strongly recommend that, before deciding, they read his 'Author's Preface to the English Language Edition' of *Marx Beyond Marx*, which stages itself as a dialogue between a 'free man, the author of *Marx Beyond Marx*', and a prisoner, which Negri was when the translation was originally published. The dialogue concludes with the 'free man' admonishing the prisoner, who had complained of experiencing the capitalist 'world as a prison', '[D]on't pretend to total impatience when you know very well that theory allows you to cope' (Negri 1991a: xv–xvii). If theory can allow us too to cope with the world, then perhaps Negri's philosophy can offer us at least a hint of what a 'free man's' life, a life of immanent creation, might be like.[1]

Unlike *Resistance in Practice*, which we divided into two sections focused on Negri's work in the historical context of 1970s Italy on the one hand and on contemporary critiques, displacements, and applications of his ideas on the other, this volume is divided into three sections according to the subjects addressed by our contributors. The first section, 'Extensive Engagements', examines Negri's lifelong relationships to the major figures in the history of philosophy whose ideas have influenced his in significant and widely acknowledged ways, namely Spinoza, Marx, and Machiavelli. In the opening essay, Pierre Macherey examines Negri's reading of Spinoza in *The Savage Anomaly* in order to identify its fundamental and recurring gesture, which he suggests characterizes Negri's philosophical (and political) work as a whole: the identification of a (logical, phenomenological, historical) crisis that interrupts the calm deduction of a philosophical system and drives thought ahead of itself in search of a resolution that would be constitutive and open instead of dialectical and teleological. Jason Read takes up Macherey's insight regarding the crisis in order both to deepen it with respect to Negri's account of Spinoza and also to extend it to encompass an examination of Negri's reading of Marx. In so doing Read more fully explicates Negri's gesture as a powerful methodological instrument for reinventing both the practice of philosophy and the philosophy of praxis. The final essay in this section, by Miguel Vatter, confronts Negri's account of constituent power, which underpins his influential work on empire and the multitude, with Hannah Arendt's countertheory of the relation between state and revolution, in order to bring to light Negri's reliance on a contentious and partial reading of Machiavelli's distinction between virtue and fortune.

The second section, 'Intensive Encounters', examines the intersections, interferences and antagonisms between Negri's work and other philosophical perspectives whose influences on him are both more recent and more 'local' than those of Machiavelli, Spinoza and Marx, but which nevertheless help to situate and clarify Negri's thought in relation to other contemporary philosophical currents. This section opens with Judith Revel's essay, which takes up the challenge of accounting for Negri's relatively recent open engagement with the philosophical legacy of Nietzsche. Revel poses the necessary question of why and how Negri adopted (and adapted) concepts and strategies drawn from Nietzsche's great French disciples Michel Foucault and Gilles Deleuze, rather than those approaches that gave rise to the major Italian current of Nietzsche interpretation represented by Gianni Vattimo and Massimo Cacciari. Alberto Toscano critically examines Negri's use of a concept of biopolitics which he derives, rather tendentiously, from the late work of Foucault. Toscano intervenes with great care to differentiate Negri's 'epochal' use of the concept both from Foucault's microphysical interpretation and from the parallel philosophical projects of Paolo Virno and Giorgio Agamben. Ted Stolze's concluding essay in this section introduces English-language readers to an aspect of Negri's thought that has aroused intense suspicion and hostility—when it has been noticed at all: his unexpected engagement with religion and theology in the wake of his experience in prison. While recent works by Alain Badiou and Giorgio Agamben have brought the tools of contemporary continental philosophy to bear on the reading of biblical texts, Negri anticipated them by 20 years with his atheist and Marxist meditation on the Book of Job (soon to appear in English translation) as a parable of materialist resistance to suffering.

The third section, 'Constitutive Ontology', presents responses to and assessments of Negri's ongoing attempt to construct a viable ontology in the wake of both the Marxist critique of metaphysics as an exorbitantly mediated form of repressive ideology and the deconstructive critique of metaphysics as the incessantly repeated gesture than encloses thinking within a specular system of binary essences. Mahmut Mutman approaches Negri's metaphysical project by means of a nonlinear set or 'constellation' of pointed questions posed from the margins of Negri's discourse and cutting transversally across it, questions that seek to deconstruct the residual binarisms on the basis of which Negri's ontological claims continue to operate. Alex Callinicos, one of Negri's most relentless yet careful critics, views Negri's 'flight into ontology' as a belated attempt to salvage his philosophical categories and activist strategies, which represent at best creative misreadings of Marx, from the generalized catastrophe experienced by the global left at the end of the 1970s. In the book's final essay, Charles T. Wolfe asks whether Negri's constitutive ontology is really a version of the age-old doctrine of materialism as he sometimes claims, and comes to the conclusion that if so, it must be a materialism not of nature but of artifice, not of atoms but of relations (and thus language), and not of orderly and predictable growth but of radical new production, indeed innovation, particularly in its emphasis on human temporality. Wolfe's conclusions bring the book full circle, back to a new formulation of the crisis that continually drives thought ahead of itself, which Macherey saw as Negri's characteristic philosophical gesture.

Although some of these arguments may strike hard-headed activists as so much other-worldly or at best superstructural hair-splitting that bears little or no relation to political practice, we would remind them of what Marx writes in his second thesis on Feuerbach: 'Man [*Mensch*] must prove the truth, i.e., the reality and power, the this-worldliness of his thinking in practice' (Marx 1970b: 121). Negri has faced up to the challenge of practice throughout his life as a philosopher–activist, with more or less success as situations have unfolded, and he continues to face it with every new concept he posits and every new stand he takes. The this-worldliness of his thinking, which is to say the radical immanence of both his philosophy and his activism, leaves him with no transcendent ideological refuge from the defeats he has experienced, but only his own extraordinary theoretical creativity, his 'free man's wisdom'—and the common bonds of the movements to which he has always devoted that creativity.

NOTE

1. We apologize for the gender bias in the language of this paragraph (and also a later one), but it is there in our sources and our chain of allusions depends upon it.

Part I

Extensive Engagements

1
Negri's Spinoza:
From Mediation to Constitution
Description of a Speculative Journey

Pierre Macherey

Translated by Ted Stolze

Antonio Negri's book on Spinoza, *The Savage Anomaly* (Negri 1991b), is above all remarkable for the extraordinary interpretive power of a reading that is itself 'savage', a reading that manages to breathe new life into a thought, so as not only to actualize thought but to make it effectively present. Negri is an extraordinary storyteller or narrator of philosophy, because for him a speculative enterprise is not reducible to a theoretical system whose form would be definitively fixed and whose place would be irremediably confined to the established order of philosophical reflection, but is itself in movement, a philosophy in action, a philosophy of practice that is itself practice, process, or history: therefore it can only be understood according to the meaning of its immanent development, starting from the project that haunts it and confers upon it its innovative character. In order to grasp such an effort—literally the *conatus* of a concrete reflection—it must be followed to the limit at which it unveils that which constitutes its essence, by dramatizing the succession of moments that lead to it and highlight its progression, which is also its truth. What is eternally true in Spinoza's philosophy, the source from which it draws its necessity, is this passage that leads it beyond its initial organization, its 'first foundation', toward a 'second foundation', in which it realizes all the power[1] it bears in itself, through a movement of transgression that also reverses it in itself. One could say 'Spinoza beyond Spinoza', as Negri has elsewhere written 'Marx beyond Marx' (Negri 1991a).

To limit ourselves to these formulations, there is something profoundly Hegelian in Negri's approach, and in his effort to make the synchronic standpoint of the system depend on the diachronic standpoint of the process, that is, to present the true 'not only as substance but also as subject'. By restoring to the system its internal procession, for which the result is nothing if it is abstracted from the movement in which it is itself engendered, and by making an immanent and productive relation out of the connection between philosophy and history, doesn't Negri still find himself within a dialectical perspective, for which an effective thought is not reducible to a fixed and autonomous form, without antecedent or consequent, but consists in going beyond such a form, which it throws back into the past in order to project itself toward a future meaning (and it is only through this movement that it manages to make itself present to itself)? But here a first problem appears: for Spinoza's effort, according to Negri, is going to separate him from every dialectical reference that could be reinscribed within the Hegelian order of a 'thought of mediation', in order to switch him over to the standpoint of 'constitution', which is irreducible to such an assimilation. Thus, Spinoza must be dragged away from the bad path of the thinkers of mediation and the doctrines of *potestas*—Hobbes/Rousseau/Hegel—and put back into his authentic genealogy—Machiavelli/Spinoza/Marx—which situates him, on the contrary, on the side of the thought of *potentia* endowed with a new logic of constitution. But to make this rupture and the process through which it is realized comprehensible, does Negri no longer need to refer to Hegel at all? Does he really manage to 'rescue' Spinoza from Hegel?

To try to respond to this question, we must retrace Spinoza's itinerary, as Negri describes it, from the beginning, from the *Short Treatise* to the *Political Treatise*, an itinerary whose successive stages end up being arranged along a trajectory—even if it is discontinuous—that goes beyond the system inside it to the point of making explicit the 'philosophy of practice' whose promise it secretly carried within itself from the beginning, and which, according to Negri, constitutes its profound truth.

The point of departure for this journey is given by 'the utopia of Spinoza's circle', which is the object of the second chapter of *The Savage Anomaly*, in which Negri examines the *Short Treatise*, the *Treatise on the Emendation of the Intellect*, the *Principles of the Cartesian Philosophy*, and the *Metaphysical Thoughts*, a collection of texts written between 1660 and 1663. Negri explains how, through these texts, Spinoza inscribes his enterprise within an ideological context imposed by the society of his age—Holland in the second half of the seventeenth century, in which new forms of capitalism are elaborated—and by the position he himself occupies in it, through the intermediary of his 'circle'—that of a cultivated merchant, whose education and preoccupations have placed him at the crossroads of the diverse traditions of Judaism, Renaissance humanism, Scholasticism, and Cartesianism. These elements will initially fuse into a substantialist ontology with a pantheistic character, which can be reinterpreted within the perspective of Neoplatonism. It is here that Spinoza must begin: 'Pantheism must be traversed. That is the only way to get beyond it' (Negri 1991b: 28).[2] For this fusion of disparate elements is provisional: instead of achieving an indissociable unity, it will create the conditions of a tension internal to this primitive schema, in which a mysticism and a rationalism coexist, and thus provoke its crisis. A breakthrough is attempted in the *Treatise on the Emendation of the Intellect*, which constitutes 'an initial attempt to go beyond the original pantheistic horizon' (Negri 1991b: 28), by sketching 'a sort of phenomenology of the idea' (Negri 1991b: 35), the aim of which is to develop the ontology of productivity in the form of a theory of knowledge, and endeavoring to wrest Being from its causal depth in order to carry it up to the surface where it achieves its effects. But this effort fails, and the *Treatise on the Emendation of the Intellect* ends without being completed, 'in full idealism' (Negri 1991b: 39). This impasse has the significance of a symptom:

> This is the crisis of the *Treatise on the Emendation of the Intellect*. It is located in this slippage between the productivity of knowledge and the capacity to demonstrate this productivity at work. It is determined around the fact that the idea of truth (defined in the intensive and extensive totality of pantheistic ontology) does not have the capacity to elaborate itself definitively as a phenomenological function; it does not have the capacity to present itself definitively as a physical power. (Negri 1991b: 37)

The pantheistic ontology bears within itself the promise of a theory of Being as power, hence of a 'strategy of constitution' (Negri 1991b: 35), but at the same time it prevents this promise from being fulfilled and blocks this strategy. Hence the need for a critical reflection, whose moment is represented by the *Principles of the Cartesian Philosophy* and *Metaphysical Thoughts*, which in a way prepare the passage from the pre-Spinoza to the first Spinoza: faced with the 'crisis of the method' (Negri 1991b: 41), these works insist on the 'materialist potentialities' (Negri 1991b: 42) of the ontology, and through a radical critique of universals they exclude every element of transcendence from knowledge. According to Negri, 'it is the highest exposition of the utopia of Spinoza's circle … in the form of an ontological paradox' (Negri 1991b: 43). Then the moment has come for the doctrine to return onto itself, in an effort of refounding [*refonte*] that will give rise to the 'first foundation' of the first and second parts of the *Ethics*.

I shall add only one remark to the presentation of this first stage of Spinoza's journey: straightaway the conditions of a 'crisis' are given in Spinoza's philosophical enterprise; the latter proceeds on the basis of its internal contradiction, that is, its own project is elaborated to the extent that it provides itself with the means of escaping this contradiction, which will give rise to the necessity of new crises, and the latter in their turn will be the conditions of its progress. Can the movement that begins here be interpreted in terms of a dialectic? For that to be the case, a negativity would have to work its way into the movement's process, taking the place and function of a middle term. Hence the question, which we can pose without at present having the means to answer it: What could play the role of the middle term in the theoretical development analyzed by Negri? Does this process undergo such a mediating intercession, or is it a motorless and hence nondialectical development? Yet what would be the alternative to a dialectical description of the process as Hegel theorizes it? Wouldn't it be a teleological schema, along the lines of the passage from power to action in an Aristotelian type of thought, that introduces the necessity of a movement without making it proceed through a mediation, to the extent that it tends to do nothing other than realize what it carries in itself from the start? Now it seems that it is indeed in this sense that Negri turns Spinoza into a kind of precursor to himself, by means of this initial crisis that, tearing him from himself, projects him ahead of his own origins, and thus makes him anticipate his later progress, the need for which is thus formulated in this way from the start. By considering the following moments of Spinoza's enterprise, Negri will enable us to witness many other crises: but will the latter be anything other than a repetition of the first crisis, whose unresolved tension animates the theoretical process to the very end by conferring on it a kind of finality and unity? Negri's interpretation lends itself to such an objection to the extent that it presents the trajectory followed by Spinoza not only as an uneven journey traversed by heterogeneous determinations but as an itinerary that begins at one point—that of a crisis—in order to wind up at another point—again that of a crisis, indeed, the repetition of the same crisis. By examining the rest of his analysis, we are going to see if Negri's interpretation confirms this objection or if, on the contrary, it provides the means to rule it out.

In the third chapter of his book, Negri describes the 'first foundation' of Spinoza's system as it is set out in the first two parts of the *Ethics*: it corresponds to the labor of constructing a first '*Philosophia*', drafted and revised between 1661 and 1665, which strives to synthesize the pantheism of Spinoza's circle by developing an ontology of productivity to its extreme limit. Presenting the composition of the *Ethics* in this way involves not only resituating it somewhere within the development of a theoretical process but also showing how the composition itself is traversed by the movement that impels the process, which allows several 'theoretical layers' (Negri 1991b: 48) or levels to be distinguished within it. This movement is double: it is the internal history of Being that, by crossing successive layers, follows the itinerary of its liberation in order to discover, in the last books of the *Ethics* (whose composition Negri dates to the years 1670–75), the highest expression of its power, human practice, whose properly ethical reality is constituted and not mediated. It is also the history of the reflection of Being within Spinoza's thought, which to that extent modifies the theoretical perspective of its analysis and extricates it from the pantheistic presuppositions that previously conditioned its unfolding: 'In Spinoza's theoretico-practical experience the *Ethics* is a philosophical *Bildungsroman*, and the changes of the theoretical *Darstellung* are superimposed on it' (Negri 1991b: 48). Thus, the process of knowledge coincides exactly with the development of its content, whose productivity it mimics in a certain way. But for such an interpretation to be possible, this development would have to be capable of being measured with the help of the markers of a chronological succession, allowing us to differentiate absolutely the moments of before and after. By recognizing in the first two parts of the *Ethics* the function of a 'first foundation', preceding the 'second foundation' which the subsequent parts will realize in a later moment, Negri assigns to them a homogeneous theoretical content, even if it is not systematic, since it opens onto a perspective of crisis. This homogeneous theoretical content is what authorizes us to read these first two parts as if they formed a set, a sort of first *Ethics* or an *Ethics* within the *Ethics*, whose standpoint will have to be eliminated so that, under other conditions, the discourse that refounds it may be formulated.

What characterizes the first two parts of the *Ethics* and assigns them the function of a singular moment in the process of Spinoza's thought? It is the fact that they are inhabited, marked by a problematic of mediation, which can only disappear on the occasion of a theoretical crisis and caesura, for which the *Theological–Political Treatise* will later provide the means. On what clue does Negri rely in order to detect the traces of such a problematic? He finds it in the interposition of the attribute between substance, which expresses the absolute causality of being, and the mode, which expresses its effective reality or the result of this productivity. The attribute's intercession is required for the passage from an intensive ontology of *natura naturans* to an extensive ontology of *natura naturata* to be possible. For this passage to occur, there must be the 'mediation' of a principle of articulation and organization that permits us to differentiate the infinite without altering its univocity. 'The attribute is therefore the agent of the organization of the infinite toward the world. It is the key to the degrading, emanating, or, better, fluent determination of being' (Negri 1991b: 53–4). 'Therefore, posing criteria for the organization of spontaneity means exercising some kind of mediation, bearing some kind of transcendence or, at least, some kind of difference' (Negri 1991b: 55). But this attempt at mediation doesn't succeed, to the extent that it contradicts the productivity of Being to which it pretends to offer the means of realizing itself. In fact, it submits Being to an abstract order, which has no meaning except from the standpoint of the understanding, and reduces ontological speculation to logical conditions posed in and for consciousness. This kind of argument, and the notion of attribute that sustains it, will have to disappear for Spinoza to manage, at the end of a second foundation, to liberate Being from such a theoretical constraint and provide it with an ethical realization, within the horizon of the new problematic of constitution.

> The attribute would have to organize the expansivity of being, but actually it only reveals it. The attribute would have to direct the ordering of all the powers, but actually it simply puts them in relation. This claim carries with it an idea of ought, of ontological normativity, but this is not demonstrated, it is only stated, hypostatized. From this perspective, outside of this first stage of the *Ethics*, the figure of the attribute will be progressively eliminated. To the extent that the *Ethics* opens to the constitutive problem as such, the function of the attribute will become more and more residual. (Negri 1991b: 59)

Obviously, in order to be able to speak of such an elimination, the succession of parts of the *Ethics* must be interpreted from a strictly chronological perspective, in which what is said afterward is separate from what is said before, according to the irreversible order of a progressive development that advances only by deviating from its point of departure.

In the presentation given here of the notion of the attribute, there is something quite striking: it confirms what Hegel himself proposed.[3] For Hegel, substance, attribute, and mode are the moments of a gradual process in the course of which the Absolute realizes itself: this process, as it is organized on the basis of their succession, is a movement of degradation, which converts the initial Being of substance into the ultimate effects in which it exhausts itself, those that correspond to modal reality; this takes place through the intermediary of the attributes that are the condition of passage from one to the other. The analysis proposed by Hegel coincides with Negri's on at least these two points: it presents the relation of substance to mode through the intermediary of the attribute on the model of an evolving process, in which the function of the concepts is assigned to them by the order of their succession, according to a cyclical development in which the attribute occupies the position of the middle term, hence of mediation. On the other hand, this process, as it is thus mediated by the attribute, represents the passage from substance to mode as a sort of movement of emanation, successively bringing to light everything that at the start was enclosed within the primitive absolute, according to a process of reasoning inspired by Neoplatonism. For this analysis to be defensible, one must admit the following: on the one hand, the attribute comes before the mode and after substance, following an order of passage that is the key to its theoretical fecundity or sterility; on the other hand, the attribute must assume the responsibility of delivering substance from the unity that initially ties it intimately to itself, by explaining it within abstract categories borrowed from the reflective labor of the understanding, which confers on them their characteristic of exteriority. According to Hegel, the process thus expounded is a caricature of the dialectical process, because it lacks the immanent negativity that would make the progressive movement of its implementation coincide with the process of a return to itself, and in itself, of substance, having thus become subject. According to Negri, on the contrary, we are dealing here with an authentic dialectic, in the sense that the dialectic is defined by a subordination of the real to the search for mediations that permit it to be organized; but it is precisely for this reason that Spinoza's conception is lacking with regard to its own internal requirements, which are those of an effective 'constitution' of the real that is completely free in relation to such a dialectical manipulation. Despite starting from common premises, these analyses thus lead to opposite conclusions: Hegel condemns *en bloc* the inadequacies of Spinoza's system, whereas Negri is led to distinguish successive theoretical levels in this system, the first of which must be crossed in order to reach the second. But these two seemingly antagonistic forms of reasoning—since Hegel attributes to the dialectic a theoretical privilege that Negri, on the contrary, rejects—rely on very similar interpretations of the notion of attribute, to which they assign an intermediary position between substance and the modes, and which they thus restrict to a reflective and subjective content, given outside of Being and within knowledge alone.

If we return to the text of the *Ethics*, we see that this interpretation poses a certain number of problems. As Martial Gueroult has shown, the notion of attribute does not intervene in the economy of the demonstrative reasoning after that of substance in order to reflect the content of substance in a form that would be external to it, but rather precedes it: infinite substance is itself 'constituted' on the basis of the infinite attributes. On the other hand, if the attributes 'express' the essence of substance, it is not in the sense of an arbitrary and subjective manifestation belonging specifically to consciousness or to knowledge and having only an ideal or formal function. When Negri sets aside the realist or objective explanation of the notion of attribute, he makes this surprising remark: 'This interpretation anticipates (too early, in fact) results that we, too, will arrive at later' (Negri 1991b: 58). In other words, if the attributes are not the forms through which the absolute is reflected in the understanding, according to the interpretation adopted by both Hegel and Negri, then the discourse of the *Ethics* can no longer be reduced to the conditions of an evolving unfolding, in which each notion is supposed to come in its place, that is, in its time, without being able to anticipate this constraint or to suppress it. On the other hand, in order to be able to distinguish successive theoretical levels in the text of the *Ethics*, disposed in relation to one another according to a progressive order, the attributes must be restricted to this mediating function that they fulfill so badly, or so well, so as to conclude from this obstacle the inadequacy of Spinoza's standpoint in philosophy, as Hegel does, or—as Negri does—the necessity of going beyond this spontaneous standpoint of the first foundation and transforming it into a new standpoint in which there will no longer be room for attributes or any kind of mediation.

But for this new foundation to be carried out, a crisis must open up in the very development of the system. This is how Negri reads the second part of the *Ethics*: as the development, the rise of an internal tension through the clash of two incompatible perspectives.

> When the discussion focuses on the mode and the analysis turns to the singularity with the love that a revolutionary ascetic brings to it, to the movement, and to the struggle that is expressed by it, the enigma of the mediation of spontaneity must itself be problematized ... . The spontaneity of the process is no longer able to present the centrifugal force of the substance and the centripetal force of the mode as superimposed and closely fitting elements. Their relationship is now the problem. The world is a paradox of alternation and coincidence: Substance and mode crash against each other and shatter. (Negri 1991b: 61–2)

This critical threshold is reached around 1663–64 when Spinoza, moving from Rijnsburg to Voorburg, discovers the impossibility of reconciling the pantheistic utopia of his circle with the analysis of the world according to the real constitution of its power: the time has thus come for the 'real Spinoza' who takes the place of the 'Spinoza of ideology' (Negri 1991b: 70). The real Spinoza is the one who rejects the dialectical project of a search for mediations and the enterprise of manipulating the real, an enterprise that, on the contrary, characterizes the bourgeois utopia of *potestas* and obstructs the development of a materialist thought of *potentia*.

> Making an ideology out of the Spinozian utopia, transforming it in accordance with bourgeois thought, is possible only if the fullness of the Spinozian conception of the thing, of things, of modality and substance is

limited, diluted until it is reduced to a shadow, a duplication of reality—
and not the true and immediate reality. (Negri 1991b: 72)

But at the point we have reached, this conception of the thing remains
trapped in an alternative that tears it apart, without any possibility of
reconciliation.

No, substance and mode are not opposed as reality and unreality, as
intellect and imagination. They are not situated in an emanationist
derivation. Rather, they constitute a polarity. The crisis consists of the
discovery of the impossibility of a linear and spontaneous mediation of
this polarity. It consists precisely of the crisis of the constitutive force, of
the internal tension of the utopia itself. (Negri 1991b: 77)

Thus, the theoretical caesura that is going to prepare the refounding [*refonte*]
of the system is itself preceded by this internal crisis of the utopia, having
matured at the heart of the discourse of the *Ethics* through the development
of the contradictory tendencies that have haunted it from the start. 'From
this perspective, why would anyone be astonished by the fact that, in the
middle of the elaboration of the *Ethics*, Spinoza quits everything and begins
his political work ... now it is history that must refound ontology ... '
(Negri 1991b: 84).

This 'caesura of the system' is carried out by the *Theological–Political
Treatise*, which Negri thinks 'plays an extraordinarily central role in
the development of Spinoza's thought as a whole' (Negri 1991b: 91). It
represents, in fact, a consideration of the modal reality of the world as
it is first experienced by the imagination: this confrontation implies a
rupture in relation to the previous intellectualist tradition. 'Here, in effect,
the theological and physical bases of Books I and II of the *Ethics* are put
aside' (Negri 1991b: 91) at the same that 'a new logic' (Negri 1991b: 92)
is elaborated that describes the historically constitutive function of the
imagination: the first six chapters of the *Treatise* not only demystify the
latter from an immediately critical perspective, but they show, through the
genesis of political institutions, that the imagination is itself a power that
is productive of the real.

Therefore, two levels can be identified: a first, static level on which the
imagination proposes a partial but positive definition of its own contents
and a second, dynamic level on which the movement and effects of the
imagination are validated as a function of the ethical constitution of the
world. The political raises the theological to the level of truth. And here
the problem of 'false consciousness' is posed in modern terms! (Negri
1991b: 94–5)

If the imagination is productive, this is because it is not only part of the order of appearance: the modal reality within which it intervenes is thus not a degraded form of absolute Being but the expression of its infinite power. So the metaphysical perspective inherited from Neoplatonism, which limited its horizon to the pantheistic ideology, is effectively reversed:

> The *Theologico-Political Treatise* is the point on which Spinozian metaphysics is transformed. Stating that politics is a fundamental element in the Spinozian system, therefore, is correct, but only keeping in mind that politics itself is metaphysics. It is not a decorative addition, but the soul of metaphysics. Politics is the metaphysics of the imagination, the metaphysics of the human constitution of reality, the world. (Negri 1991b: 97)

Politics intervenes not on philosophy but within philosophy, from the inside: it adjusts its course, which it pursues in the direction of a new problematic required by the theoretical crisis that it has opened up. Thus, the *Theological–Political Treatise* must be read after the *Ethics*, as its continuation, even if the latter corresponds to a complete reorientation of its project. By the same token, it appears that the discourse of the *Ethics*, beneath its manifest content, was already inhabited by a political concern, even if unacknowledged; and this concern incited it to go beyond the limits imposed by its initial problematic: if politics is rediscovered within metaphysics, this is insofar as metaphysics is pushed outside itself by this project of refounding that works on it and transforms a pantheistic ontology into an ethics of practice. This is what allows Negri to write that 'Spinoza's true politics is his metaphysics' (Negri 1991b: 114), because it is on this basis that 'a new metaphysical scenario' (Negri 1991b: 102) is elaborated, consisting in 'the materialist foundation of an ethical horizon' (Negri 1991b: 101).

The question posed earlier seems to arise again here: Does the process described by Negri allow for a middle term, which would restore a metaphysical character to it? For political speculation effectively occupies this place of the middle term in the development of philosophical discourse, vis-à-vis which it thus plays the role of an incitement or a motor. 'We have been following a process, and we have arrived at an intermediate point' (Negri 1991b: 106). But this means that the *Theological–Political Treatise* is itself torn apart by the debate that it has helped to reveal: like the *Ethics*, it appears as a kind of *Bildungsroman*, that is, it is organized according to the progressive course of an intellectual itinerary that proceeds by internal rupture, and thus bears in itself the mark of the theoretical rupture whose agent and representative it is. After the first ten chapters of the *Treatise*, which express the need for a modal constitution resting on a phenomenology of the imagination, follow five chapters of 'crisis', which interrupt its progress and situate it within the intermediary situation assigned to it:

But the philology of being has not yet succeeded in reaching its goal; the strategic goal, that is, is not realized by the end of the philological part of the *Theologico-Political Treatise*. Traces of dualism and a tiresome problematical quality still remain. (Negri 1991b: 106–7)

In fact, according to Negri, chapters 11 to 15 of the *Treatise* represent a point of stoppage in its movement of innovation to the extent that, through the twist that they give to the notion of natural right, they seem to return to the abstract conception of the universal. This is the 'paradox' of the *Theological–Political Treatise*: 'In the middle of a laborious constitutive excavation the research is blocked and tactically turned back, precisely on a point where everything was predisposed so that it might proceed' (Negri 1991b: 108). In the final chapters of the *Treatise*, then, Spinoza must efface the traces of this regression by abandoning the dialectical and mediating problematic of the contract in order to orient himself toward 'a collective constitution of reality' (Negri 1991b: 106) that completely renovates the question of the relations between the individual and community. However, this supercession will only be effective ten years later, at the moment when Spinoza, at the end of his life, writes the *Political Treatise*: 'For the moment, though, we are still far short of this conclusion' (Negri 1991b: 114). *The Theological–Political Treatise* opens up a crisis in philosophical discourse, but it doesn't provide the means to overcome it. Thus, 'we are in the midst of the metaphysical interruption' (Negri 1991b: 118). Political speculation is only what reveals this caesura, which is why the metaphysical debate once again begins, and it is through the reprise of the discourse of the *Ethics* that it must pursue its forward march. 'Politics is the soul of the crisis and of Spinoza's philosophical development. But its solution, the renewed engagement and the realization of the constitutive pressure, send us necessarily to ontology' (Negri 1991b: 119).

The moment has come, therefore, for the 'second foundation', analyzed by Negri in the seventh chapter of his book, which is devoted to the last three parts of the *Ethics*. This is the moment when the passage from the problematic of mediation—characteristic of the doctrine of the contract as well as the doctrine of attributes—to the problematic of constitution, which is situated within a 'materialist horizon' (Negri 1991b: 128), is actually carried out.

The first stage of the *Ethics*, in this situation, is not critiqued: It is simply overthrown. The possibility that this could be read as the problematic scaffolding for a 'superficial' (that is to say, materialistic) refiguration and a practical reconstruction of the world is realized. If the first stage of the *Ethics* presents two options, here the choice has been made: only the 'upward path', the constitutive path, is viable .... The second stage of the *Ethics*, in its conclusive configuration (at least that which is handed down to us in the *Posthumous Works*), elaborated between 1670 and 1675, is the emblem of this project .... With the second foundation of the *Ethics*, *natura naturata* wins a total hegemony over *natura naturans*. What could be the work of the devil if not this? (Negri 1991b: 129)

Then, in fact, the savage anomaly and excessiveness of Spinoza's thought, which has broken every attachment with the philosophical traditions from which it arose, bursts forth and projects itself forward toward this 'philosophy of the future' whose promise it carries within itself.

It is in the third book of the *Ethics* that this new thought begins to take shape: with the theory of the passions, the elements that are indispensable for the realization of the new constitutive project are going to 'fuse'. Here Spinoza goes against every current of the thought of his century that introduces into the definition of the passions a criterion of mediation and thus subordinates them to a rational norm that goes beyond them: the bourgeois ideology of developing capitalism substitutes for the traditional finalism of religion a new form of exploitation of human existence, which folds the latter into the constraints of an economic and political organization external to its own tendency.

> Passional ambiguity is resolved through the mediating role of appropriation, the appropriation in an ordered social scheme that over-determines passionality—here we have the dialectic in its true form, a process of mediation that constructs nothing because its norm is implicit, it is constructed, it is a 'formal cause' and not an 'efficient cause'. Transcendence dominates mediation, if only in logical and transcendental forms; appropriation is 'legitimated' (subordinated to the universal), it is diverted and mystified in its own definition. (Negri 1991b: 132)

On the contrary, by founding his conception of human existence on a dynamic of desire as the expression of a *potentia*, that is, a natural power, which escapes the mediation that would impose upon it an artificial order of *potestas*, that is, a power in the juridico-political sense of the term, Spinoza invalidates this dialectic of the passions that seeks to transcend its immanent necessity in a system of abstract rationality. So 'we have finally reached a basis for the reconstruction of the metaphysics that has immeasurably expanded our perspective, both in logical and ethical terms' (Negri 1991b: 135): for, breaking with the ideology of possessive individualism that Macpherson has elsewhere described (Macpherson 1962),[4] 'the constitutive and expansive materialism of power, therefore, demands a collective determination' (Negri 1991b: 136). At this point there is no longer room to search for mediations, as contract theorists do, in order to reconcile the interests of the individual and those of society, which means, in fact, to submit the first to the second: 'the denial of the concept of mediation itself resides at the foundation of Spinozian thought' (Negri 1991b: 140), in the sense that it is, in the principle of its refoundation in a doctrine of human freedom, the ultimate expression of the productivity of infinite Being. The affirmation of natural power culminates, then, not in a dialecticized order but in the dissolution of every mediation.

At this point of rupture the second foundation is initiated with the theory of *conatus* that, assuring the passage from Being to the subject, carries out a veritable doctrinal conversion: 'the versatility of the metaphysical being is transformed into the exuberance of the ethical being' (Negri 1991b: 151), according to a movement that is more projective or propulsive than progressive. For the dynamic that begins here spreads outside of every teleological presupposition: it is carried ahead of itself, not in order to win over little by little a preexisting space that would be progressively opened up to it, and that at the end of its effort it would wind up completely conquering, but in order to develop to the maximum, under the antagonistic conditions imposed by the socialization of the affects, the productivity of causal Being from which it proceeds.

> Here the critical being, the conflictual being, the antagonistic being becomes key to both greater ontological perfection and greater ethical freedom. The powers developed here are never flattened or diminished but, rather, are stimulated to grow and expand in keeping with the power of antagonism itself, of life. (Negri 1991b: 153)

This propagation is carried out through the movement of *cupiditas*, in which the subject's affirmative essence is expressed, without any negativity being interposed between power and the material forms of its actualization: 'in fact, with respect to constitutive power, there exists only the tension of the dynamic essence, not the dizziness of any type of externality' (Negri 1991b: 155–6). Thus, substance is expressed in its modes, not by the artifice of a mediating *Aufhebung*, but through a constitutive process that is given to itself as the space it fills absolutely, without reference and relation to a void or to a nonbeing on which it would set about progressively to realize the ends that are proper to it. For the *cupiditas*, which is the form the *conatus* takes in the appetite of a subject endowed with consciousness, 'is not a relationship, it is not a possibility, it is not an implication: It is a power, its tension is explicit, its being is full, real, and given' (Negri 1991b: 156). We see in what sense one can speak here of liberation: it consists not in an indeterminate choice of possibilities allowing the finite subject to go beyond the limits of its own existence, following an intentional movement that would extricate it little by little from its initial conditions, but in the radical affirmation of its causal power, which tends to realize all its effects insofar as the latter are constitutive of its own being.

It is here that, according to Negri, the *Ethics* really begins, in the strict sense of the term.

> The horizon of power is the only metaphysical horizon possible. But since this is true, only ethics (as a science of liberation, of the practical constitution of the world) can adequately investigate it. The active infinity has until now been presented as power; now the active infinity must be organized by ethical action. However, since ethical action is constituted by the same power that defines the infinite, the infinite will not simply be 'organized' by ethical action, as an object by a subject. It will, rather, present itself as a structural organization of the ethical, of the subject and the object in their adequateness—infinity, expression of infinite power, organization of power: interchangeable elements in the vast perspective of human behavior. (Negri 1991b: 156)

Let us understand that liberation is not a manipulation of reality by a subject that, by its own initiative, would be positioned outside of the organization that it imposes and that is imposed on it: it is the direct expression, without mediations, of the ontological power that defines the subject in itself by constituting it not as an independent individual element but as taking part in the relational and collective system in which its action is dynamically inscribed. '*Cupiditas* is a mechanism of liberation' (Negri 1991b: 157): this formula signifies precisely the elimination of every teleological relation between the subject and its ideal possibilities, the movement that it really follows, which proceeds in the opposite direction of the power that effectively constitutes it in the affirmation of the values in which it identifies its own existence.

At this turning point between the third and fourth parts of the *Ethics*, Negri remarks that 'the metaphysical horizon constructed in part I is reintroduced here' (Negri 1991b: 157), but this is in order to observe that the latter is profoundly modified: the categorical articulation that constituted the notion of attribute 'is put to the side' at the moment when human practice realizes 'the absoluteness of the relationship between substance and modality'. For an essential displacement is then brought about, which assigns to human action a central position within ontology. The whole question is to know if this modification continues a movement that already began at the moment when substance was defined as such, or if it initiates an original constitutive process, which tends to identify itself with the profound truth of Spinoza's project. By adopting the thesis of the 'second foundation', Negri apparently situates himself on the side of this second hypothesis, which makes human practice as such the foundation of a new theoretical construction and no longer only the prolongation, effect, or result of a causal development whose conditions had been posited prior to its intervention. But doesn't this amount to inverting the lessons derived from the analysis of the *conatus* on the basis of a reading of the third part of the *Ethics*? If human practice, as subjective practice, is at the center or foundation of an ethics of liberation that reveals to the world its own essential nature, doesn't it take on the value of a kind of absolute beginning, thus isolating itself from the reality on which it acts?

Now the fourth part of the *Ethics* 'opens the system into the world of contingency, of the possible, of practice in relation to a science of contingency and possibility' (Negri 1991b: 157). We must ask ourselves if this 'science' guarantees the autonomy of a properly human project, creative of possibilities and constituting its actor as a true subject, or if on the contrary it reintegrates it into the causal power of productive Being, nature, of which it is only a particular determination. Paradoxically, Negri seems to return here to a dialectical conception of human action, the latter being no longer only the product of a necessary movement that includes and directs it and in which it inscribes its own operations, but holding the power to go beyond the conditions that limit it and to project itself in the direction of a temporal development that carries it beyond what it is.

> Spinoza's revolutionary conception of being succeeds in comprehending the negativity that constitutes contingency and possibility: It comprehends the negativity as an element of the organization of the existing being at its margin, as a subordinate level of the expansive being, and therefore as a space vacated by positivity, as something to construct in order to integrate the infinite. Contingency is the future, it is the indefinite that human practice, as *potentia*, integrates into the positive infinity. (Negri 1991b: 157)

To include, to integrate the negative within the positive is to posit the latter in a recurrent way 'as a space to be occupied', whose preestablished existence seems to condition the project that will ultimately come to fulfill it: isn't this precisely the contrary of what the analysis of the *conatus* had led us to affirm? In reality, according to Negri, the fourth part of the *Ethics* doesn't merely continue the third part, but constitutes in relation to it 'a powerful leap forward, which reformulates the constitutive project at a very high level of power: It is the proposal of a permanent reopening of being' (Negri 1991b: 159). Thus, by projecting itself onto the terrain of liberation, the constitutive power of Being undergoes a veritable mutation: it becomes precisely practice, subjectivity, an opening onto a world of possibilities or an ethical world in which it tends consciously and voluntarily to be realized. It is a question then of 'accentuating the potentiality of being', that is, not 'the definition of a state but rather of a dynamic, not a result but a premise' (Negri 1991b: 159). Does this mean that the previous ontological construction—that of the first and second parts of the *Ethics*—had only a static significance, essentially distinct from the dynamic that begins here? But if, as proposition 4 of the fourth part of the *Ethics* states, 'it is impossible that a man should not be a part of Nature, and that he should be able to undergo no changes except those which can be understood through his own nature alone, and of which he is the adequate cause' (Spinoza 1985: *E* IV P4, 548), then it is clear that this power he bears is not the one that he himself ideally posits as an individual or collective subject, since the condition for him to begin to be liberated is precisely the renunciation of this illusion of autonomy.

However, the difficulty we have just raised is perhaps resolved by the following consideration: at the point to which, following Negri, we have accompanied him, Spinoza is found still in mid course, and the new constitutive schema that he is in the process of elaborating hasn't completed its transformation, which explains the contradictory context in which it is inscribed. 'The situation of the system determined here is one of crisis' (Negri 1991b: 164). In fact, the conditions of a true genesis of sociality, which must give its material horizon to the process of liberation, are still only sketched formally: 'the political problem, as a constitutive problem, is deferred, to be treated later in the *Political Treatise*' (Negri 1991b: 164). In anticipation of this later elaboration, the movement that carries Being to an absolute expression of its power presents itself as the projection in the direction of a possibility, by means of an anticipation of its content which necessarily throws its determination out of balance. Now this imbalance also characterizes Spinoza's situation, and his own position vis-à-vis the historical reality with which he is confronted: that of a market society.

> There is the fact that with this dissymmetry of the constitutive process, with its limiting itself on the predominantly gnoseological horizon, Spinoza pays the price (in anticipation) for this actual dissymmetry in history. The revolution and its margin, yesterday; the crisis and its

margin, today: The concreteness of the revolutionary trajectory is not recognizable to the eye of theory. The society that Spinoza is faced with is not dominated by a global constitution of production. Forcing the image of liberation on a theory founded on production, then, requires dealing with a rupture from reality. And it is this rupture that, folded back on the form of the argumentation of the *Ethics*, determines this and other gaps, this and other deferments. Society is still a perspective, a goal for the research and the transformation. (Negri 1991b: 164)

The effective constitution of the real is to some extent suspended, because the material conditions of its production are not yet gathered together: the morality of generosity in which it is provisionally found to be expressed constitutes merely its virtual realization, its promise.

Time is extended in hope. The prison of the world is destroyed, its bars and its mechanisms of closure are broken open. The world is a flat present, predisposed to and capable of grasping the tension of the ethical being, as a full project tending toward the future. (Negri 1991b: 167)

Does the fifth part of the *Ethics* bring about a new conversion, leading the possible back to the real of which it is the determinate manifestation? Now if, at this level, there is, according to Negri, 'dislocation of being', it is in this sense that 'Spinozian pantheism coincides precisely and entirely with this sense of contingency' (Negri 1991b: 168), which apparently means that it is, on the contrary, on the side of the possible that Spinoza's project finally orients its progression. But can one still speak in this regard of a progression? And isn't what we now see instead a return to previous positions? In fact, Negri refuses to consider the last part of the *Ethics* as a culmination that would give the theoretical research its definitive closure. On the contrary, he reads in it a return of the crisis that from the beginning had marked the system and had ceaselessly incited it to renew its speculation.

The fact is that part V of the *Ethics*, much more so than parts III and IV, is grafted onto the initial trunk of Spinoza's investigation, onto the terrain of the first foundation. There is the keen sense that the procedure of drafting part V was conducted during several different phases, that it indeed preceded, to a great extent, the drafting of parts III and IV. All this is demonstrated by the reappearance, certainly residual but no less effective, of metaphysical scenarios that seemed to have been completely rejected and discarded from the system's development. (Negri 1991b: 169)

Far from effacing the marks of the theoretical caesura that made it possible, the second foundation reproduces in its very discourse this tearing whose alternative it prolongs or repeats through the tension of dissymmetrical theoretical levels. This tension rests, according to Negri, on a dissociation of the ethical project, which gives rise concurrently to an ascetic and purely intellectual ethics of the soul that 'is the reawakening of the utopia of the first foundation', and a materialist, constitutive ethics, an ethics of the body that 'confirms the positivity of the second foundation' (Negri 1991b: 171). But in order to distinguish, and oppose, these two trajectories we must set aside the principle according to which the soul is, and is nothing other than, the idea of the body—and the principle of this coinciding has been grounded from the beginning in the doctrine of the attributes. By refusing to recognize a constitutive function in the attributes, and by deducing from this refusal the unavoidable necessity of their withering away, Negri himself has thus provided the presuppositions of the dilemma, of the circle in which, provisionally at least, he encloses Spinoza's reflection. But the two ethics that he situates as alternatives in relation to one another are, in fact, according to the very terms used by Spinoza, only two complementary formulations of one and the same affirmation, which has specifically eliminated every possibility of contradiction or opposition from his discourse.

By isolating an ascetic requirement, which he isolates on the basis of an analysis of the notion of the 'intellectual love of God', Negri pursues a double operation. On the one hand, he confers on this requirement, beyond its apparent residual function, a value of anticipation, preliminary to the achievement of the constitutive process, which must be pursued beyond the *Ethics* itself:

> The ascetic spirit, one could say, is a completion and an overdetermination of the imagination and its functions that are constitutive of reality. It is a justification, an extrinsic motivation of the ethical process, which is employed until the ethical process has reached the solidity of the immediate relationship between essence and existence, or their identity, which has no justification other than itself. (Negri 1991b: 174)

On the other hand, he assigns to this requirement a genuinely dialectical significance by interpreting it as 'the last attempt to play the game of the contradiction' (Negri 1991b: 174): by momentarily obstructing the movement of authentic liberation, by a final repetition of the crisis that animates Spinoza's entire speculative journey, he starts the progression over again and prepares the way that is going to lead, after the *Ethics*, to the *Political Treatise*. But by attributing to this dialectic such a residual or propadeutic function, and by making the specter of mediation, which he must nevertheless finally exorcise, return at the end of the unfolding of the process of liberation, doesn't Negri himself also play the game of the dialectic, which assigns to theoretical research a unique orientation, gradually bringing it together with the goal in which it must finally be accomplished? No doubt Negri is perfectly consistent with himself when he refuses to enclose the 'second foundation' within the circle of a perfectly consistent system, and when he shows that it leads to 'the ineluctable need of an alternative truth' (Negri 1991b: 176), this alternative being none other than that of opposing historical forces, whose conflict obscures the last pages of the *Ethics*; but when he interprets this ultimate hesitation as the anticipation of a later resolution by this philosophy of the future whose necessity, or rather whose possibility, would somehow be inscribed in it, he revives the theme of negativity and the teleology that the latter inspires, even if he says he has set them aside.

In returning in 1675 to political reflection with his *Political Treatise*, which he will leave unfinished at his death in 1677, Spinoza concludes by attaining this truth that, recursively, gives meaning to his entire enterprise: 'politics is the fabric on which constitutive human activity principally unfolds' (Negri 1991b: 186). Essentially, the culmination of the constitutive project in fact situates human freedom in the midst of modal reality, certainly not 'as a power within a power [*tanquam imperium in imperio*]', but within the framework of the complex network of relations it maintains with all of nature, all of whose power it recovers for its own benefit. So 'the aporias we find in part V of the *Ethics* along these lines are definitively dissolved' at the moment when 'the subject and efficient cause tend toward an identity' (Negri 1991b: 189). It is understood that the project of liberation could not go beyond this synthesis that designates at one and the same time its accomplishment and its limit, in the form of a doctrine of free necessity. But this doctrine cannot assume the completely integrated form of a harmonious system: to the end it must affirm a critical and revolutionary vocation by developing the opposition between power and Power [*pouvoir*], *potentia* and *potestas*. 'Therefore, the problem we are left with does not deal with impossible processes of pacification but instead opens up to a dangerous process of the construction of being' (Negri 1991b: 194). Thus Negri's interpretation constantly preserves an ambivalence in the text it analyzes, from which it also derives what is essential to its force of suggestion: the breach that, from the beginning, tears apart Spinoza's project and propels it ahead of each of its momentary realizations will not finally be enclosed within the miracle of a resolution. The philosophy of the future that Spinoza's thought bears within itself, and toward which it bears its entire immanent movement, remains perpetually yet to come: vis-à-vis its current formulations, it maintains a value of interrogation that postpones or suspends its definitive achievement. In this regard, the points of suspension with which the text of the *Political Treatise* ends have an exemplary significance.

Likewise, the difficulty that stopped us a moment ago also seems to be overcome. In introducing a subjective dimension into ontological reality, ethics doesn't alter the latter's objectively necessary character at all. Insofar as ethics leads ontological reality 'by the hand' to a politics, it cannot be enclosed within the narrow limits of an individual morality but, on the contrary, opens up onto a collective construction of society, which invalidates a strictly voluntaristic conception of freedom.

> If society inheres in being, it is constituted by being in being: No miracle solution can be substituted for the mechanism (both double and unique) of the ontological dislocation and of the collective constitution on the physical, material horizon of the world. (Negri 1991b: 194)

Human practice, then, holds no privilege that would isolate it within common nature, but the power that properly belongs to it is rooted in the causality of the productive Being of which it is itself an expression. This expression is necessarily conflictual, which prevents it from being absorbed into a unified order that would be somehow transcendent. 'In its progression, which though not linear is nonetheless continuous, the Spinozian machine grinds up the bourgeois ideological horizon, making all of its contradictions spring up again' (Negri 1991b: 196). To the absolutism of state power, it opposes the freedom of collective power, which derives its legitimacy from its own immanent development. For 'the constitutive process dislocates being onto always higher levels of perfection only through antagonism. The State, the sovereignty, and the limitlessness of Power are then filtered through the essential antagonism of the constitutive process, of power' (Negri 1991b: 199). Thus what is effaced is the artificial distinction between right and fact, civil society and the state, which are, on the contrary, confounded in the global movement of constitution, without any mediation being required in order to unify it. But that doesn't mean that the elements of the social totality are reconciled all in one blow, harmonized in a homogeneous and stable whole, by an artificial constraint that would hinder their free development; they are deployed in the extensiveness of an expanding body, in the conquest of its own domain, which constantly invents new forms of existence in the course of struggles in which negativity doesn't play the role of legitimation. This expansion is the authentic political production of reality.

On this point Negri is certainly right: there is no room here for a dialectic of Hegel's sort, proceeding from this immanent and continuous movement that progressively transforms negation into the negation of the negation, according to the recursion of a teleology. But does that mean that a thought of Spinoza's sort must invalidate every kind of dialectic? Wouldn't it instead constitute an incentive to reconsider the functioning and the status of the dialectical process, with the aim of extricating it from a finalist conception? To end with this question is to confirm the critical and revolutionary position of this philosophy that, contrary to the interpretation that has often been given it, doesn't lead to a dogmatic doctrinal lesson whose definitively true content would no longer have to be recognized and assimilated as such, but rather is characterized by the radical questioning of all forms of speculative evidence. One can say, therefore, that Spinoza's philosophy really leads nowhere, to the extent that it doesn't provide the revelation of a completed meaning on which it would close down its own project, from a perspective that would necessarily be teleological. Thus, instead of the itinerary followed by a thought that little by little reaches its ends by discovering that part of truth it exclusively holds, Spinoza's philosophy describes an uneven journey by way of which, from rupture to rupture, this thought returns on itself, not in order to conclude with the ultimately regained unity of its message, but in order to open up to the endless contestation that the real opposes to it.

NOTES

1. Translator's note: Here and in most other places in this chapter, Macherey uses the French word *puissance* as the translation of Negri's *potenza*. He only uses the French word *pouvoir*, which corresponds to Negri's usage of *potere*, in one place, which is marked by the inclusion of the French word in brackets.
2. Translator's note: References in this translation of Macherey's essay to Michael Hardt's English translation of *The Savage Anomaly* (Negri 1991b) have often been slightly modified to conform more precisely to Macherey's quotes from the French translation.
3. Translator's note: For much of the rest of his essay, Macherey refers implicitly to the critical account of Spinoza's philosophy contained in Hegel's *Lectures on the History of Philosophy* (Hegel 1995), volume 3, pp.252–90.
4. Translator's note: Negri wrote a preface to the 1973 Italian translation of Macpherson's *Political Theory of Possessive Individualism*, which was included as an appendix to the original Italian publication of *The Savage Anomaly* in 1981.

2

The *Potentia* of Living Labor: Negri and the Practice of Philosophy

Jason Read

> But only where theory does not deny practice and practice does not deny theory is there character, truth, and religion. Spinoza is the Moses of modern freethinkers and materialists.
>
> —Ludwig Feuerbach,
> *Principles of the Philosophy of the Future*

A cursory survey of the writings of Antonio Negri presents one with an expansive plurality of topics covered. Negri's writing addresses topics from Spinoza's ontology and political philosophy to works on Marx, the history of political thought, globalization, and the changing conditions and politics of labor. This broad survey of topics by one writer is itself remarkable. What is perhaps more provocative, however, is that within these different books on apparently unrelated themes, there appears a series of concepts, or words—*potentia*, living labor, constituent power, and immaterial labor—which seem to connote or designate a series of interrelated problems. These problems could, at least provisionally, be situated at the intersection of labor and power: the materiality of a creative power that constitutes the world, not through some power of transcendence, but which creates the world by being entirely immanent to it. Thus, it is not simply the breadth of topics covered, ontology, politics, sociology, etc., which makes Negri an impressive, singular—and ultimately challenging—figure in contemporary philosophy and political thought, but the indication that beneath these seemingly disparate researches there is a unity of a philosophical political project.

But what exactly is this unity? It is in answering this question that some of the traditional ways of understanding the intersection of philosophy and politics fall short of the challenge of Negri's thought. One possibility is to understand Negri's thought as developing an ontology of immanence and power, drawn from the weighty tomes of Spinoza, which is then applied to politics and society. On the other extreme, it is possible to understand Negri as a thinker who interprets philosophy through a history of the sociopolitical transformations of labor—an ontology 'applied' to the messy realities of politics or a historicization of the fundamental transformations of ontology. While these two interpretations are possible, they miss the point, in that they situate the different spheres of inquiry in a relation that is both hierarchical and one-directional: philosophy determines politics or politics determines philosophy. Negri's thought transforms both the philosophy of politics, proposing a new understanding of power and labor, but also a new politics of philosophy, a new way of doing philosophy, of situating philosophy in relation to politics, economics, and other forms of knowledge.

What this means can best be grasped by a brief comparison with Louis Althusser. As Althusser argued, Marx's writings are not to be understood as a new *philosophy of praxis*, a philosophy that would elevate praxis to the place that previous (idealist) philosophies had elevated reason or knowledge, but as a new *practice of philosophy*, a new way of doing philosophy. As a term for analysis, 'philosophical practice' refers less to the concepts produced or positions taken than to the particular manner each philosopher has of writing, broaching questions, and producing concepts. It is on this level that Marx's radical break can be measured. For Althusser, this new way of doing philosophy was characterized by the extreme heteronomy of philosophy, its determination and transformation by other forms of practice: economic, political, etc.

> ... [P]ractice is what philosophy, throughout its history, has never been able to incorporate. Practice is that other thing, on the basis of which it is possible not only to knock philosophy off balance, but also to begin to see clearly into the interior of philosophy. (Althusser 1990a: 249)

Althusser insists on the fundamental difference between the 'philosophy of praxis' and the 'practice of philosophy', arguing against philosophers such as Antonio Gramsci and Jean-Paul Sartre, who saw praxis as not only the central concept of Marx's philosophy, but as a way to restore the rift between philosophy and Marxism, speculation and practice. Negri's position is irreducible to either term of the opposition; it is best defined as *developing a new philosophy of praxis through a new practice of philosophy*. In other words, a philosophy of praxis, of the constitutive dimension of human activity, cannot simply be developed speculatively, as a pure movement of thought, but must be developed through a continual encounter with its constitutive conditions and limitations, with the materiality of the world. 'Discontinuity and untimeliness are the soul of theoretical practice, just as the crisis is the key to the development of the real' (Negri 1996: 53). This is the unity of his thought, a disjunct unity in which philosophical speculation must continually open itself to historicity and materiality, and the challenge that Negri poses to philosophy.

In the following pages I shall outline this challenge by focusing on Negri's interpretation of Spinoza and Marx, obviously only small parts of Negri's corpus. In doing so I shall outline Negri's philosophy of praxis, *potentia*, living labor, or constituent power, and show how this concept is developed through a passage of discontinuity that passes through politics, metaphysics, and history in order to reassemble them in a forceful new articulation of materialist philosophy.

PART ONE: PARS DESTRUENS–PARS CONSTRUENS

The gap, or the disjuncture—that is, thought's relationship to praxis—is articulated by Negri through a reading and a rearticulation of the relation between the destructive, negative, or critical moment of thought (*pars destruens*) and the creative or affirmative moment in a praxis of thinking (*pars construens*) in Spinoza. The relation of a simultaneous destruction and creation, maintained in their paradoxical unity, is the unstable maintenance of thought at the limit of the concept, and at the edge of praxis, or invention. *Pars destruens* is a total destruction of the presuppositions of thought, the received thoughts and ideas. It is through this destruction that thinking can engage with *pars construens*, a creation or invention, and thus a praxis and poetics without guarantee.[1] Developing a link between the seventeenth-century practice of critical doubt and social practice, Negri writes: 'Doubt is a social practice destructive of things, not simply of spectres and unreal ideas—destructive to the extent that it affirms liberty' (Negri 1989: 160). Unlike Descartes, who follows the path of radical doubt to the point that it brings him back to the same place, the same fire, nightclothes, and sheet of paper, Spinoza's critical practice makes it possible to invent. It is a practice, a tension of thinking that risks itself in the creation of the new (Negri 1991b: xv).

The relation between *pars destruens and pars construens* is not something which Spinoza's thinking or texts directly offer to a casual or passive reading; it demands a strategy of reading, and an engagement with the limits and divisions of the text. Negri's reading of Spinoza combines a complex conjunction of interpretive practices. Negri investigates both the historical conditions and the textual articulation of Spinoza's writing, but not through the conventional dialectic of historical context and herme-neutically recuperated meaning. Central to Negri's reading is the assertion that Spinoza's thought cannot be reduced to a simple reflection of the historical period of its articulation, that in some sense Spinoza's thought is a 'philosophy of the future': but this irreducibility is not a matter of a simple transcendence of those conditions, or Spinoza's 'discovery' of some 'universal' truth. The irreducibility of Spinoza's thought to its conditions is founded on its relationship to what Negri identifies as the 'crisis' (Negri 1991b: 266). Historically, at the time of Spinoza's writing, the crisis is the tension between the emerging developments of scientific and productive forces, and the organization of the 'market', as the organizing and mediating force of the social (Negri 1991b: 20). This crisis is identified historically in the recession and wars of the late 1600s, all of which indicate the impossibility of a smooth transition from feudalism to capitalism, that is, the impossibility of subordinating the new productive forces of science and technology to the old values and order. This crisis is more than a precondition for interpreting Spinoza's thought, and thus more than a simple context, for at least two reasons. The first is the complexity of Spinoza's response to this crisis, the manner in which the historical antagonism of productivity and order becomes a problem and a tension internal to Spinoza's project. The second reason is that this 'crisis' is not a totally discrete event limited to the time of Spinoza's writing, but is extended and displaced, in its repetition, to include the present. The relation, division, or even antagonism between the multiplicity of immanent relations of constitution and production, what Marx called the forces of production, and the mediating orders of law, state, and market, or what Marx called the relations of production, is the crisis without stasis that is history and historicity. The crisis that Spinoza confronts continues to define the present, in that the present is still defined by this tension, by the difficulty of subordinating the new productive forces to the relations of production.

This thought of the crisis frames the various textual tensions and divisions that Negri explores and articulates in his reading of Spinoza. For Negri, Spinoza's text is divided in both its metaphysics and politics between a Neoplatonist tendency toward the affirmation of a transcendent order in the first foundation of the *Ethics*, and a materialist philosophy of constitution as organization in the second foundation.[2] The development of the relationship *pars destruens–pars construens* has as its enabling condition this crisis, and the destruction of any transcendent mediation of this crisis, and of transcendence altogether.

> ... [T]here are in effect two Spinozas, if only we were able to succeed in suppressing and subduing the suggestions or the apologies that erudite history produces, if we were able to situate ourselves on the solid terrain of the critical and historiographic consciousness of our own times, these two Spinozas would come to life in full play. (Negri 1991b: 4)

If the crisis makes possible a reading of the tensions and divisions of Spinoza's text, then Spinoza also makes possible a reading of the crisis; that is, Spinoza makes possible a reinvestigation and a rethinking of the ontological, subjective, and political dimensions of the contradiction between 'relations and forces of production' (Negri 1991b: 223). Spinoza makes possible an ontological understanding of production: production is not simply relegated to the economic sphere, but becomes the manner in which praxis changes itself and its own conditions. Production becomes the path to liberation.

According to Negri, Spinoza's *Ethics* opens onto a fundamental paradox, a paradox that stems from the absolute affirmation of substance as infinite being, and as the power of existence. The paradox is the tension between two grounds of ontology: two ways of conceiving the relation between unity and multiplicity, or between substance and the modes. 'In Spinoza a decision is never made between two perspectives: the dynamic one, for which substance is a force, and the static one, for which substance is pure linear coordination' (Negri 1991b: 79). This paradox is at once the central question of any reading of Spinoza, in that it poses all of the old questions of the relation between the infinite and the finite, the substance and the modes, or of what Negri calls the organization of the infinite; and also, at least in Negri's reading, the question of the very grounds of thought and practice. The paradox is the division between order and organization, between emanation, which proceeds from substance to the modes, and constitution, which proceeds from the modes to substance. The first foundation of the *Ethics*, which Negri locates in parts I and II, is not only the exposition of this paradox, but its partial and incomplete resolution through the mediating order of the attributes. The attributes, thought and extension, are what the intellect perceives as the essence of substance (Spinoza 1985: *E* I D3–4, 408). The first foundation tends towards emanation rather than constitution; emanation is not just a relation of priority or degradation between substance, mode, and attribute, but the harmony or linearity of this relation (Negri 1991b: 59). For Negri, another name for this first foundation, displaced to the political register, is 'Utopia', or the preexistent rationality of production and its ordering.[3]

The second foundation, or at least the problem of the second foundation, is developed at the point where the paradox of the mode–substance relation is brought to its extreme point, and thus to the destruction of any pregiven mediation. The second foundation is not simply a question of the resolution of a paradox, but also a refusal of any mediating ground of consciousness, any finalized or pregiven order of being. Negri locates the beginning of this foundation, which is also a destruction, a *pars destruens* of the last remnants of the idealism of emanation, in Spinoza's development of the relationship between power, *conatus*, and corporeality. This later part of the *Ethics*, which makes up parts III and IV, develops the double exigency of the *pars destruens–pars construens* relation. First, it constitutes the destruction of any ontology as static, concealed, and grounding in the strong sense. This destruction is necessary for any rigorous thought of constitutive power, which is to say, a thought of praxis that is anything other than an actualization of nature, the forms, the Idea, or some other presupposed ground or foundation. The disjunctive conjunction of *pars destruens and pars construens* is also a critical engagement with the priority of thought as primary, and prior to the body and its activity. These two demands converge in relation to the problem of the attributes, which install the primacy of thought in the order of being.[4] According to Negri, the veritable elimination of the attributes in Parts III and IV is part of a destructive and critical movement. *Pars destruens* is the destruction of ontology as a reification of the world as order, and the priority of thought as knowing over doing (Negri 1989: 160).

From the opening of the *Ethics* the exposition of power is aligned with a critical movement of *pars destruens*. Spinoza's exposition of power is both a political critique as well as an ontological transformation. In Part II of the *Ethics* Spinoza distinguishes between God's power as *potentia*, inseparable from its actuality, and the legislative power of *potestas*, which is predicated on the separation between will and intellect (Spinoza 1985: *E* II P3 S, 449). As Gilles Deleuze writes, Spinoza's development of the concept of power is immediately a political critique. A deconstruction of *potestas* as the analogy of divine and legislative power is interwoven throughout the appendices and scholia of the *Ethics*: 'One of the basic points of the *Ethics* consists in denying that God has any power (*potestas*) analogous to that of a tyrant, or even an enlightened prince' (Deleuze 1988a: 97). Spinoza's critique of the anthropocentric idea of God, God as the supreme legislator of the universe, undoes any argument for authority that would base its legitimacy on such an analogy.[5] There is no kingdom in heaven that would justify the authority of worldly kings. As Deleuze argues, Spinoza's scholia carry out an immediate political critique, rushing ahead of the general ontological argument to draw out the political consequences in a battle with the existing forces (Deleuze 1997: 146). For Negri, Spinoza's idea of power extends beyond its immediate political critique, the image of God, to any attempt to subordinate the productivity of being to a hierarchical order whatsoever, which in part accounts for its relevance. Spinoza is not just a critic of God, or the monarch in the image of God, but also of the state and the ideal of the market.

... [T]he idea of the market is close to the idea of the state. In these two cases the productive cooperation of subjects and their reciprocal vital association are mystified into an organization of value, of the norm, of command; and human association is thus subordinated to the capitalist function of exploitation ... (Negri 1997b: 230)[6]

Thus, this political critique has as a precondition the development of an immanent ontological organization that is directly opposed to transcendent order. As Negri writes;

Potentia as the dynamic and constitutive inherence of the single in the multiplicity, of mind in the body, of freedom in necessity—power against Power—where potestas is presented as the subordination of the multiplicity, of the mind, of freedom and of potentia. (Negri 1991b: 190)

The denial of any speculative priority to potestas (or power) opens the possibility of a new ground of ontology. It is this new ground which is developed in the 'second foundation' of the Ethics, in the material and practical horizon of the modes.

As Negri indicates, the transformation of the 'second foundation' is in the first instance a radical inversion or destruction of the metaphysics of emanation. It inverts the order of being by developing a 'physics' of the material relations of the modes. This inversion is made possible by the univocity of being, by Spinoza's refusal to maintain any hierarchy between thought and extension, or any teleology or finality to being. 'If God is all, all is God. The difference is important: on one side an idealistic horizon, on the other side a materialistic potentiality' (Negri 1991b: 64). Univocity and power (potentia) are the conditions for an affirmation of singularity and materiality as the only possible ground.[7] Being is only in its multiple and disjoined organizations. As ground, potentia constitutes an essentially different terrain from the ground of thought as emanation, or of an ontology of transcendence in the first foundation. It is rigorously materialist, in the sense that acting, the body, force, and organization are given priority over reflection, universality, and order. There is no original hierarchy of being, no ideal form or predetermined value, from which to judge the different singular expressions of power (potentia).

Central to the transformation from the first and second foundation is Spinoza's writing of the Theological–Political Treatise, a work that Negri argues was written in the midst of the Ethics as a response to the political and ideological conjuncture. The Theological–Political Treatise transforms the Ethics not simply through what it says, its critique of superstition and its interrogation of the force of the imagination, but also in the manner in which it turns Spinoza's attention to the materiality of history. The *Ethics* immediately dispenses with the 'anthropo-theological imaginary', the idea of God as man and man as a kind of God, as being founded on inadequate ideas of power, being, and causality, but the *Treatise* considers the effects this idea had in history. In the *Theological–Political Treatise* Spinoza interrogates scripture; however, he is not content simply to oppose reason to the imagination of the prophets. Rather, in examining scripture Spinoza finds that as much as prophecy must be considered to be false, since the mind cannot know the future, it is real in that it determines the actions of individuals, becomes the ground for obedience, and ultimately constructs the world. As Spinoza writes, 'the object of knowledge by revelation is nothing other than obedience' (Spinoza 1998: 7). There are of course elements of the rational and libertarian critique of religion in Spinoza's writing, but these become tools in the excavation of what Althusser calls 'the materiality of the existence of ideology' (Althusser 1997: 10). Spinoza is never content simply to critique what he calls superstition in a sterile opposition of truth to falsity, or reason to imagination; rather he finds in the imagination, in the language of prophecy and miracles, a force that affects and transforms human society. 'But what seems important here is that this is the first unfolded emergence of the constitutive power of human action' (Negri 1991b: 97). The obedience that is secured by revelation makes possible the formation of community itself, and, since nothing is more useful to man than man, this community, or society, is the precondition of the development of reason. 'Imaginative activity reaches the level of an ontological statute, certainly not to confirm the truth of prophecy but to consolidate the truth of the world and the positivity, the productivity, and the sociability of human action' (Negri 1991b: 98). The *Ethics* speculatively affirms that all power is *potentia*, immanent, actual, and self-organizing, and the *Theological–Political Treatise* confirms and radicalizes this by showing how the idea of *potestas*, of God the legislator, is itself a product of *potentia*, of the power of the human imagination, and that it is this power which effectively makes the world.

The *Theological–Political Treatise* cannot be separated from the *Ethics* as a work to be classified under the heading of politics, or philology. It transforms the *Ethics*. As Negri writes:

After the development of such a radical *pars destruens*, after the identification of a solid point of support by which the metaphysical perspective re-opens, the elaboration of the *pars construens* requires a practical moment. The ethics could not be constituted in a project, in the metaphysics of the mode and of reality, if it were not inserted into history, into politics, into the phenomenology of a single and collective life: if it were not to derive new nourishment from that engagement. (Negri 1991b: 84)

Pars destruens–pars construens must be opened to the difference between thought and its occasion. This difference, this exposure to historicity and the social, is what the affirmation of *potentia*, power in its practical constitutive moment, demands. This displacement, or shift, is not exterior to the relation *pars destruens–pars construens* as its application, nor is it entirely interior, as its speculative foundation, but it is the movement where the practice of thinking finds itself intersected with and transformed by its encounter with the materiality and history of the existing world. 'Politics is the metaphysics of the imagination, the metaphysics of the human constitution of reality, the world' (Negri 1991b: 97). Thus, as much as Negri's work on Spinoza provides the fundamental elements of an ontology, a constitutive ontology that affirms the sociality, collectivity, and productive nature of being, it also underscores the fundamental orientation for the production of such an ontology—it is an ontology which can only be produced through the displacement, and disjuncture, that exposes thought to its constitutive conditions in historical reality.

While the *Theological–Political Treatise* constitutes a fundamental displacement of the problems of the *Ethics*, from order as metaphysical problem to the historicity of the organization of human desires and beliefs, it does not complete this process. The *Theological–Political Treatise* does not supplant the *Ethics*. Negri argues that the *Treatise* does not follow through on its most radical insights. It begins with the materiality of the imagination, with the power of constitutive praxis, but it ultimately crashes upon the universals of 'natural right' and the 'natural light of religion', universals which undermine the constitutive process (Negri 1991b: 108). The contract subordinates the powers of society to a transcendent order and a preconstituted end, thereby limiting the constitutive process. However, the results of the *Treatise* are fundamentally ambiguous: as much as the contract is introduced as an ordering structure of society, it is modified by the idea of power. As Spinoza writes, 'Nature's right is co-extensive with her power' (Spinoza 1998: 179). This redefinition of right as power fundamentally undermines two of the constitutive dimensions of natural right that philosophy exemplified by the contract, 'the absolute conception of the individual foundation and the absolute conception of the contractual passage' (Negri 1991b: 109). In place of the absolutely individualistic foundation that paves the way for the absolute authority of the sovereign, Spinoza introduces a new theoretical object, the 'passions of the body social'. Right is coextensive with power, there is no natural state of power, nor a final goal, only the historicity of its various organizations. There is thus no transfer of power, no actual passage from *potentia* to *potestas*, there is just the organization of *potentia*, of the striving (*conatus*), desire (*cupiditas*), and affects of the multitude.[8] It is precisely this organization that is examined and developed in what Negri calls the 'second foundation' of the *Ethics*, Parts III and IV, which develop the logic and sociability of the passions. This second foundation not only develops the idea of *conatus* as the essence of each individual (Spinoza 1985: *E* IIIP7, 499), it also develops the logic of the affects as the determination of this desire. The affects begin with the most immediate and simple determinations: pain, pleasure, love and hate, and gradually unfold to encompass the constitutive conditions and constitutive power of subjectivity, which is not an autonomous starting point but is immersed in the power of affects. 'The nexus of composition, complexity, conflictiveness, and dynamism is a continual nexus of successive dislocations that are neither dialectical nor linear but, rather, discontinuous' (Negri 1991b: 151). Thus, as much as the *Theological–Political Treatise* disrupts the remnants of a metaphysical order through its provocation that the historicity of desire and affects are constitutive of the world, it demands a renewed ontological speculation. It is neither the *Theological–Political Treatise* nor the *Ethics* that makes up the foundational book of constitutive power, but rather the movement, the displacement, from the one to the other. In Negri's book on Spinoza this movement continues to a reading of the *Political Treatise*, thus passing from metaphysics (the *Ethics*) to politics (the *Theological–Political Treatise*) only to return to politics (the *Political Treatise*) which in turn informs a new metaphysics (the 'multitude' as a concept produced in the interstices of the *Ethics* and the *Political Treatise*), while at the same time stating that 'Spinoza's true politics is his metaphysics'. This statement should be read not as a choice, placing Spinoza's metaphysical works over his political writings, but as a slogan of displacement. Constitutive power as praxis is developed through a practice of philosophy as a continual displacement that moves from metaphysics to politics and back, and this movement continues beyond a reading of Spinoza.

At a crucial point in the *Grundrisse*, Marx insists on the difference, perhaps irreducible, between the appropriation of the world in thought and a practical material relation to that world (Marx 1973: 101). In Negri's reading this difference has as its consequence a continual shifting, or displacement, of the terrain of research, what Marx describes as the difference between research (*Forschung*) and presentation (*Darstellung*) (Marx 1976: 102). The shift of research is not simply a conceit of the intellectual, the continual rewriting and reorganizing of drafts and notes in order finally to perfect that great book, but is a recognition of the limit of thought. As Deleuze famously commented to Foucault, 'Practice is an ensemble of relays from one theoretical point to another, and theory is a relay from one practice to another. No theory can develop without encountering a wall, and practice is necessary in order to pierce the wall' (Deleuze and Foucault 1977: 206). Deleuze's almost canonical remarks on practice are in part based upon his reading of Spinoza. For Deleuze, the first two parts of the *Ethics* are speculative, articulating the common notions of substance and mode according to their specific logic, while the following two are practical, demonstrating how common notions can be constructed from the practices of a singular mode of life. For Negri the displacement from speculation to practice, metaphysics to politics, extends beyond the *Ethics*, encompassing Spinoza's political works. Spinoza's thought moves from ontological speculation to the practical reality of the theological–political imagination, back to an ontological examination of the power of the imagination and affects. The relays that pass from theoretical speculation to practical activity and back again produce the possibility for liberation.

The movement from ontology to politics is a movement that maintains the two in an intimate relation that is never quite identity, but never quite separation. The transition between ontology and politics is the movement from the difference between *potestas* and *potentia* as a difference of ontological ground, and the difference between *potestas* and *potentia* as they relate on the social–historical terrain of antagonism and constitution. This shift of terrain involves an apparent inversion of priority between *potestas* and *potentia*; while it is possible to reduce transcendent order to immanent organization on the terrain of ontological speculation, the social–historical political world seems to resist such a reduction and inversion. The texts of history, and our own daily existence, would continually remind us of the practical and material primacy of constituted or instituted power (*potestas*) over constitutive power (*potentia*) (Hardt 1991: xiv). Constitutive power seems blocked at every point by the deadweight of constituted, or instituted, power, by the ordered forces of the market and the state. Yet, as Spinoza's own encounter with the history of religion has demonstrated, *potestas*, even in its extreme form as God's law, must be seen as nothing other than an expression and an application of constitutive power, of *potentia*. The apparent priority of *potestas*, in its worldly form of the capitalist market, must be exposed as the workings of *potentia*, but this can only be done by deepening the ontological and sociopolitical determinations, by moving from ontology to politics and back again.

PART TWO: LIVING LABOR

Negri's idea of constitutive power is not developed exclusively through Spinoza; it encompasses several figures, most notably Machiavelli and Marx, making up a tradition that extends beyond Spinoza's texts. As Negri writes in the *Savage Anomaly*, 'In each case Machiavelli, Spinoza and Marx represent in the history of Western thought the irreducible alternative of every conception of the bourgeois mediation of development, of every subordination of productive forces to capitalist relations of production' (Negri 1991b: 141). This tradition and trajectory will take on more importance in Negri's later works, adding more depth and breadth, as the list of names is extended and the specific analyses are developed in such works as *Insurgencies* and *Empire* (coauthored with Michael Hardt). In this regard, Negri's work can be productively compared with the work of Deleuze and the later Althusser, both of whom sought to create a 'countertradition' of materialist and immanent philosophy, opposed to the dominant tradition of idealism and teleology. There are multiple ways to create a tradition, however, from the inquiry into influences and sources, which would track down 'who read what' with the scrupulous eye of a detective, to the invention of relations and connections (Negri 2004a: 61). As Jorge Luis Borges wrote with respect to Kafka, 'every writer *creates* his precursors. His work modifies our conception of the past, as it will modify our future' (Borges 1964: 201). Thus, every tradition is itself the production and object of a practice of philosophy and must be judged as such.

Negri's particular practice of philosophy is situated towards the second pole, the pole of the invention of a tradition through the development of intersections and connections of concepts. In developing the series 'Machiavelli–Spinoza–Marx', Negri is less interested in the extent to which the different philosophers read each other's works, and more interested in what this intersection makes possible (Negri 2004a: 61).[9] This is not to suggest that Negri completely overlooks these historical relations of influence. His retrieval of politics and historicity is based on finding the traces of Machiavelli in Spinoza, just as his retrieval of democracy in Marx owes much to Marx's reading of Spinoza. Negri goes beyond the actual connections, to develop the intersections that the respective thinkers themselves may have overlooked: intersections and points of contact made manifest by the changes of history. In *Insurgencies*, the lineage 'Machiavelli–Spinoza–Marx' is intersected and punctuated by the history of political revolutions, American, French, and Russian, and, in *Empire*, the same philosophical trajectory is intersected with the history of labor, sovereignty, and colonialism; these historical and political events deepen and extend the philosophical connections.

Within this series Marx occupies a fundamentally ambiguous position. First, as it has been argued above, for Negri, Spinoza's innovation—the innovation that makes him the 'savage anomaly'—is based on the manner in which he develops an ontology of the forces of production that are not subordinated to any order of the relations of production. Marx thus defines the general political and philosophical problem, the problem of the relationship between production and human liberation, through which the revolutionary potential of Spinoza's philosophy can come to light. If Negri's *practice of philosophy* can be at least provisionally described as a discontinuous series of relays between 'metaphysics' and 'politics', gradually unfolding and developing the idea of constitutive power through this continual displacement, it would seem at first glance that the engagement with Marx would fit entirely within the context of 'politics'. In the list of names that constitute the tradition of constitutive power, Marx would be the proper name of that engagement with the practical immersion in the existing historical and political realities of the development of capitalism. Marx provides the sociopolitical context for the interpretation of Spinoza, while Spinoza transforms this context, redefining production beyond a strictly economic definition to encompass the production of obedience, ideas, and affects. Far from being limited to the side of metaphysics in the transition from politics to metaphysics, Spinoza broadens and redefines the definition of the political. Thus, it is possible to argue that the practice of philosophy that Negri develops does not remain satisfied with static oppositions between politics and metaphysics but continually redefines politics and metaphysics in the passage from one to the other.[10]

Negri's engagement with Marx also encompasses a movement of dislocation from politics to metaphysics that defines and determines the fundamental idea of constituent power. This is especially true for Negri's recent works, the works written in the last decades of the previous century, which explicitly develop the idea of 'constitutive power' from decades of political struggle and theoretical research. The intersection of politics and metaphysics in Marx, the point where metaphysics and politics make contact only to be transformed, is living labor. As Negri writes:

> As long as we follow the political Marx, political revolution and social emancipation are two historical matrices that intersect on the same terrain—the constitutional terrain—but still in an external manner, without a metaphysical logic of this intersection being given ... This necessity resides at the core of Marx's theory of capital, where living labor

appears as the foundation, and the motor of all production, development, and innovation. This essential source also animates the center of our investigation. Living labor against dead labor, constituent power against constituted power: this single polarity runs through the whole schema of Marxist analysis and resolves it in an entirely original theoretical practical totality. (Negri 1999a: 33)

It is in Marx's critique of political economy in the mature works, often considered to be beyond philosophy, that Marx's idea of living labor is developed. Negri argues that this concept, or logic, of living labor has a metaphysical or ontological, rather than a simply economic or political, dimension, defining the productive capacity of human action. Moreover, as the quote above indicates, it is through this 'metaphysics of living labor', and not the various manifestos and pronouncements of the young Marx, that Marx's true politics are to be found. Thus, as with the reading of Spinoza, Negri's reading of Marx extends and develops a philosophy of praxis through a new practice of philosophy. It is a practice that cuts across the divisions that separate politics from economics, and politics from metaphysical speculation.

Negri's interpretation of Marx, like his reading of Spinoza, has a prehistory. In the case of Spinoza, this prehistory included the development of a materialist understanding of Spinoza by such philosophers as Althusser, Deleuze, Macherey, and Matheron. In the case of Marx this prehistory includes the political movements known as 'autonomist Marxism'.[11] While it would be too lengthy to go into this history here, it is at least necessary to pause over what has come to be known as the 'autonomist hypothesis' as it was formulated and developed by Mario Tronti. Tronti's important theoretical discovery was to invert the dominant interpretation of capitalism. Rather than analyze the structures and transformations of the capitalist mode of production, Tronti argued that it is necessary to examine the history and movement of the working class. 'We too have worked with a concept that puts capitalist development first, and workers second. This is a mistake. And now we have to turn the problem on its head, reverse the polarity, and start again from the beginning: and the beginning is the class struggle of the working class' (Tronti 1979: 1). What Tronti proposed is ultimately a 'Copernican revolution' of sorts, an investigation that takes as its starting point not capital but the working class in order to examine how capital adapts itself to and is transformed by working-class struggle. There is immediate similarity between the political and historical 'autonomist hypothesis' and Spinoza's metaphysics. Spinoza argued '*Deus sive Natura*', that God is nothing other than nature; in other words, that there is only *potentia*, the immanent power of self-organization. Furthermore, in the *Theological–Political Treatise* Spinoza demonstrated how the appearance of God's law, of the order of *potestas*, was nothing other than *potentia*, human practice, desires, and imagination struggling in the world. Just as Spinoza unmasks the appearance of divine authority, revealing *potestas* as *potentia*, the 'autonomist hypothesis' unmasks the power of capital, revealing it to be nothing other than an inversion of the power of the working class, of living labor.

As with the case of Spinoza, this critical *pars destruens* has an ontological, political, and interpretive dimension. The interpretive dimension is turned not towards scripture, but towards Marx's texts, texts that have been criticized as fixated on the workings of capital. These texts must be reinterpreted in order to reveal the power of living labor. Marx argued that the dual nature of the commodity, as exchange value and use value, necessitated that labor too have a dual nature. In order for commodities to be exchanged as values and quantities, the labor that makes them must be quantitatively interchangeable. The concrete labor of different individuals must be transformed into exchangeable units of concrete labor time; it must be made into abstract labor. As Marx writes, 'let us remember that commodities possess an objective character as values only in so far as they are all expressions of an identical social substance, human labor, that the objective character as values is therefore purely social' (Marx 1976: 139). This abstract labor is produced by all of the techniques, from machinery to surveillance on the factory floor, that make labor interchangeable. These two sides of labor are given in the opening pages of *Capital*, and from them it is possible to understand all of *Capital* (not to mention capitalism) as a struggle of capital's tendency to reduce labor to abstract, unskilled, and interchangeable units against the concrete materiality of laboring individuals. In the opposition between 'abstract' and 'concrete' labor, the worker confronts capital, with its tendency to reduce all labor to interchangeable cogs, as an individual, as a laboring body.

Living labor cuts across the duality of concrete and abstract labor. For the most part, Marx's use of living labor (*lebendig Arbeit*) plays a rhetorical role in his writing. Rhetorically it informs and underlies an entire metaphorics of life and death which presents the opposition between 'living labor' in the form of the working class, and 'dead labor' as capitalist wealth and machinery, as the opposition between 'life' and 'death'; or, more dramatically, life and the 'living-dead monstrosity of capital' (Marx 1976: 302). Beyond this rhetorical function, Negri argues that there is a concept, and a metaphysics, of living labor underlying Marx's writing. The concept of living labor crosses the division between concrete and abstract labor; it is their antagonistic articulation (Negri 1991a: 47). At the same time, it cuts across the division that places an individual worker against the collective force of capitalism. From abstract labor, living labor takes its flexibility and indifference—it is the capacity to do any work whatsoever; from concrete labor it gets its determination and its connection to need. As Marx argues in the *Grundrisse*, living labor can be defined by the fact that the fundamental condition of labor in capital, as poverty, freed from any determinate means of production, is at one and the same time poverty and power.

> This living labor, existing as an *abstraction* from these moments of its actual reality [raw material, instrument of labor, etc.] (also, not value); this complete denudation, purely subjective existence of labor, stripped of all objectivity. Labor as *absolute poverty*; poverty not as shortage, but as total exclusion of objective wealth … Labor not as an object, but as activity; not as itself value, but as the *living source of value* … .Thus, it is not at all contradictory, or, rather, the in-every-way mutually contradictory statements that labor is *absolute poverty as object*, on one side, and is, on the other side, the *general possibility* [*allgemeine Möglichkeit*] of wealth as subject and as activity, are reciprocally determined and follow from the essence of labor, such as it is *presupposed* by capital as its contradiction and as its contradictory being [*gegensätzliches Dasein*], and such as it, in turn, presupposes capital. (Marx 1973: 295–6)

Living labor is the possibility for the creation of any value whatsoever. Or, framed in more antagonistic terms, living labor is the situation that the capitalist mode of production is itself dependent on a powerful, flexible force of subjectivity that it has not created and cannot control.

As a concept, living labor does not appear beyond a few references in the *Grundrisse*. It is for this reason that Negri argued in the 1970s for the superiority of the *Grundrisse* over *Capital*: the *Grundrisse*, Negri argued, is a superior work fueled by the intense antagonistic force of subjectivity. However, in the years since the publication of *Marx Beyond Marx*, Negri has developed living labor as a perspective that extends beyond that privileged text to all of Marx's corpus and into all of social reality. The challenge in both cases is to unearth the productivity of living labor from the apparent productive power of capital. In capitalism it is not just the individual commodity that is fetishized, concealing the labor and social networks that give it value, but capital itself becomes the ultimate fetish. Wealth appears to generate wealth: the productive power of living labor is everywhere concealed.

For Negri, Marx's analysis of the productive power of living labor and its obscuring by capitalism comes to light in the chapters on 'cooperation' in

Capital. In the factory a large group of workers are assembled under one roof in order to work together, and this collective structure of work produces a surplus above and beyond the individual surplus value. As Marx writes,

> the special productive power of the combined working day is, under all circumstances, the social productive power of labor, or the productive power of social labor. This power arises from cooperation itself. When the worker co-operates in a planned way with others, he strips off the fetters of his individuality, and develops the capabilities of his species [*Gattungsvermögen*]. (Marx 1976: 447–9)

For Marx, 'cooperation' is a basic fact—people working together produce more than individuals working in isolation; however, it is how this fact shapes the historical development of capitalism and the logic of *Capital* which is of interest to Negri. The cooperative power determines the particular power relation of capitalism: as more workers are assembled it becomes more necessary to supervise such workers. 'That a capitalist should command in the field of production is now as indispensable as that a general should command on the field of battle' (Marx 1976: 448). At the same time the newly collective workforce also struggles against capital outside of the factory, shortening the working day, and in turn altering the structure of capitalism.[12] As Negri writes:

> The strong result of Marx's analyses of the struggles around the length of the working day and the Factory Acts consists thus in indicating a new constitutive process, not inside but outside the dialectic of capital and situated in the autonomy of cooperation, that is, in the subjectivity of the working class. (Negri 1999a: 262)

Cooperation is not just the fact that a group is more productive than an individual, it is the materiality and facticity of living labor. Cooperation makes possible the struggle over the working day which in turn forces a restructuring of the capitalist enterprise. If exploitation cannot be based upon the length of the working day, on absolute surplus value, it must be based upon the intensity of the labor performed, on the relative surplus value made possible by new technologies. 'Every constitution of a new structure is the constitution of antagonism' (Negri 1991a: 56). At each turn in the restructuring of capital, from the massive factories to high-technology production, one does not find the all-powerful force (*potestas*) of capital remaking the world in its own image, but the *potentia* of living labor. 'Living social labor takes the place of the capitalist *mise en forme* of the social totality. It becomes the absolute protagonist of history. A radical inversion takes place: all that constituted power codifies, constituent power frees' (Negri 1999a: 265). The power of living labor does not simply transform the accumulation of capital, it does so in a way that intensifies the cooperative dimension of living labor: the transition from absolute to relative surplus value is also a transition in which capital relies more and more on the cooperative associations of labor itself.[13]

From Negri's reading of 'cooperation' it is possible to grasp the full extent of the intersection of the strategy of the autonomist approach to Marx and what has been called Spinoza's strategy of the *sive*.[14] Spinoza wrote '*Deus sive Natura*', 'God, that is, nature', finding the materialist immanent causality of *potentia* beneath God's law. In Negri it is possible to produce the statement *capital, that is, living labor*. Of course, as with Spinoza, such a statement turns against the dominant ideology, and against common sense. During Spinoza's time it appeared that God was the sovereign author of the world, the ultimate justification for all that transpired in it, and in ours it appears that capital itself is productive, producing wealth. As Marx argued in a draft of the sixth chapter of *Capital*, titled 'The Results of the Immediate Process of Production', the more labor becomes 'socialized', distributed across society, and integrated with the technological conditions of capitalism, the more it appears that it is capital itself which is productive.[15] This is due in part to machinery and technology, which as fixed capital is nothing less than the objectification of capitalism itself. As Negri argues, this is also due to the fact that as living labor is distributed across society, as all of society comes under the rule of capital, labor paradoxically disappears as it is integrated into all of society. 'As capital develops, the force of associative productive labor increases at such a rate that it begins to become indistinguishable from social activity itself' (Negri 1999a: 260). Thus, Negri's reading of Marx could be at least provisionally identified as an application of Marx to our modern demagogues and prophets who (falsely) attribute the power of living labor to capital, a reading which adapts Spinoza's critical *pars destruens* to the illusions and mystifications of classical political economy, orthodox Marxism, and conventional wisdom, all of which see the power (*potestas*) of capital making the world and not the *potentia* of living labor. Moreover, in both Spinoza and Marx there is a similar passage from metaphysics to politics and back again. While it is possible to locate a formulation of living labor in the *Grundrisse*, and it is even possible to locate the precursor of this idea in the young Marx's use of the term 'species being' (*Gattungswesen*) to describe the metaphysics of human activity, the concept of living labor is sharpened and concretized through a historical examination of the struggle over the working day. The reading of Marx repeats and extends a dimension of the reading of Spinoza: a metaphysical concept requires a passage through the terrain of history in order to become determinate. As much as Negri's reading of Marx applies Spinoza's critique of the mystification of constituent power to labor, and the conflict of labor and capital, it does so in a way that the very problem is itself fundamentally transformed.[16] Marx's critique of political economy is expanded by Spinoza's analysis of the passions and desires of the body politic, just as Spinoza's ontology of *potentia* is developed and determined by the investigation of labor. Negri's reading of Marx continues a strategy of displacement from politics to metaphysics (and back again).

Negri does not limit his reading of living labor to Marx's critique of capital, to the 'mature works' of *Capital* and the *Grundrisse*. Negri's idea of living labor is developed by following a trajectory that cuts through all of Marx's works, from the early writings to the political and polemical pieces and, ultimately, to the critique of political economy. It can even be glimpsed in such early works as *The Contribution to the Critique of Hegel's Philosophy of Right:*

> Democracy is the essence of every political constitution, socialized man under the form of a particular constitution of the state. Its stands related to other constitutions as the genus to its species; only here the genus itself appears as existent, and therefore opposed as a particular species to those existents which do not conform to the essence ... Democracy is *human existence*, while in the other political forms man has only *legal* existence. That is the fundamental difference of democracy. (Marx 1970a: 30)

Marx's early understanding of democracy is indebted to Spinoza in that it posits democracy as the essence of every political form: all states are in fact democracies in that they all must rely on the power and imagination of the people, while at the same time situating it as the ideal of any and all revolution. It also develops the problem of constituent power in that it makes the fundamental problem of politics the problem of the 'alienation' of constituent power in some constituted structure or order. For Marx, the critique of politics takes its bearing from the critique of religion developed by Feuerbach. 'The immediate task of philosophy, which is in the service of history, is to unmask human self-alienation in its secular form now that it has been unmasked in its sacred form' (Marx 1970b: 132). The fundamental question of Marx's early works is how to complete the critique of religion. How is it possible to develop an understanding of constituent power, the power of human practice, that is not immediately alienated and betrayed in some structure or institution, in the state or in the market? Negri argues that the solution of this problem arrives somewhat belatedly in living labor, in the critique of political economy, but the force of this concept extends beyond political economy to encompass a new understanding of praxis as such. For Negri, Marx's later writings on political economy which develop the idea of living labor complete and answer the question of democracy and human liberation which preoccupied Marx in his youth. Thus, the cryptic and often cited formulation 'Human anatomy contains a key to the anatomy of the ape' can be understood as a way of making sense of Marx's writing (Marx 1973: 105).

In the later works Marx produces the concept of living labor, which is not just the foundation for a critical understanding for a history of capital, but also resolves and completes the questions posed by the young Marx. Living labor is constituent power that does not produce a constitution, a structure that would deprive it of its revolutionary power, but rather continually reinvents new orders and structures—it makes the world immanently from below. This is demonstrated, albeit obliquely, in *Capital* and the *Grundrisse*, where it is shown that it is the antagonistic force of living labor that restructures capitalism, pushing it to new levels that socialize and develop the power of labor. Thus, in Negri's reading, Marx's critique of political economy also completes his early demand for a critique of politics, paradoxically finding the solution to political problems in breaking down the distinction between politics and economy (the social).

> The abolition of the political as a separate category is nothing but the definitive hegemony of constituent power, of creative free labor. Constituent power does not eliminate the political but makes it live as a category of social interaction, in the entirety of human social relationships and in the density of cooperation. (Negri 1999a: 267)

In the *Theological–Political Treatise* Spinoza limited the force of constituent power, of *potentia,* by situating it within a contract, by limiting it to a determinate political structure. In order for constituent power to free itself from constituted power, from a state, structure, or constitution, it must be radically open to its process of transformation and self-transformation. The solution of this problem is to be found in overcoming the separation between the social, the power of affects, desires, and bodies, and the political, the structures that organize the body politic. Marx situates constituent power on an immanent and even quotidian horizon, on the day-to-day practices of living labor, the relations of cooperation and antagonism that make and remake the world.

Living labor is on the one hand entirely indebted to a Spinozist ontology and concept of politics, but it moves beyond these areas to include and transform the critique of political economy. 'Cooperative living labor produces a social ontology that is constitutive and innovative, a weaving of forms that touch the economic and the political; living labor produces an indistinct mixture of the political and economic that has a creative figure' (Negri 1999a: 33).

CONCLUSION: A NEW PRACTICE OF PHILOSOPHY

The movement that has been traced here, from Negri's encounter with Spinoza to Marx's idea of living labor, could be reversed. It is well known that the actual chronological itinerary of Negri's thought moves from Marx to Spinoza. Negri's interpretation of Spinoza and his anomalous position within philosophy is in part indebted to a Marxist interpretation of the historical conjuncture within which Spinoza wrote. It is equally possible to read Marx through Spinoza or Spinoza through Marx, and this is the direction in which Negri's thought seems to be moving with works such as *Insurgencies* and recent essays on the concept of the 'multitude'. Negri's return to Spinoza (in the essays collected in *Subversive Spinoza*) and to Marx (in *Insurgencies*) establish a relay that does not move in one direction, from Marx to Spinoza or Spinoza to Marx, but continually loops back on itself, expanding Marxist problems by way of Spinoza and Spinozist concepts through Marx. This looping effect is not limited to Spinoza and Marx, but expands to include other figures of Negri's tradition such as Machiavelli, Foucault, Deleuze and Guattari, etc. What is clear is that for Negri no figure of philosophy can be limited to a prescribed area within the history of philosophy, politics, metaphysics, economy, and that every addition to the series would further deepen and transform the idea of constituent power. That is not to suggest, however, that what Negri is proposing is some sort of eclecticism in which every possible theoretical and political perspective can be added together. No, what Negri is developing is a practice of philosophy that is adequate to the complexity of the real, in other words *materialism*.

Materialism has a paradoxical status as philosophy. There is no need to rehearse here all of the various charges leveled against this philosophical position. It is worth noting that one of the strongest statements of the paradoxes of materialism came from Marx himself. As Marx argued in the *Theses on Feuerbach*, most of what is called materialism, in that it begins with the idea of matter, is, despite itself, idealist. As Marx wrote:

> The chief defect of all hitherto existing materialism (that of Feuerbach included) is that the thing, reality, sensuousness, is conceived only in the form of the *object or of contemplation*, but not as *sensuous human activity*, *practice*, not subjectively. Hence in contradistinction to materialism, the *active* side was developed abstractly by idealism—which of course does not know real sensuous activity as such. (Marx 1970b: 121)

In order to avoid this problem, materialism must ground itself on the idea of sensuous human activity, as practice. However, this solution poses new problems in that 'practice' is said in multiple senses. There are multiple practices, political, economic, etc., each with its own particular levels of effectivity and materiality. These practices constituted the world and philosophy's place in the world, but philosophy is itself a practice, a practice that can only affect the world insofar as it sees itself determined by it. (Descartes, with his notion of radical doubt, is only the first of a long line of philosophers who, because of their fundamental belief in their transcendence from existing conditions, change nothing, and end up affirming the existing values.) 'Being in materialism means conceiving constituent power as determinate practices—both of destruction and of creation. It means confronting the determinate conditions and depths of the historical passages' (Negri 1999a: 266). The movement from metaphysics to politics and from political economy to politics that defines and determines the multiple names of constituent power, *potentia*, living labor, etc. is not simply the gesture of theoretical humility, but is the practice which determines and enriches the concept, demonstrating its efficacy and force in the world. It is only by practicing philosophy in its continual displacement and encounter that one can produce an idea of praxis that can change the world.

Finally, it is worth noting that Negri's particular tradition, like that of Deleuze and Althusser, is made up of fundamentally different figures than those of what is generally identified as the continental tradition, a tradition that Negri at times calls negative thought (Kant, Hegel, Nietzsche, Heidegger, etc.), a tradition that has identified the present as an 'end of philosophy'.[17] Thus, to risk hyperbole, it is possible to say that what is at stake in Negri's particular practice of philosophy is nothing less than a reinvention of philosophy, a reinvention of philosophy as a practice of liberation. Thus the challenge of Negri's recasting of the history of philosophy can be framed through a statement applied to Machiavelli, the third, and, in this case, overlooked major thinker in this tradition: 'To think the new in a total absence of its conditions' (Negri 1996: 54). The task is not to invent a countertradition of philosophy, but to make that tradition the tool for transforming and inventing a new future. As with Spinoza and Marx, this new tradition cannot simply be constructed through the history of philosophy alone; it must encounter the weight of history and the passions and desires of politics.

NOTES

1. William Haver has suggested that the conjunction of *pars destruens* and *pars construens*, or a doing that necessarily exceeds knowing, in the thought of Negri and Hardt should be understood as a practice of invention (see Haver 1997).

2. A note on the distinction between 'order' and 'organization': As Hardt indicates, order of being, truth, or society is a structure which is always above, prior to, and in part exterior to the material relations it organizes, while organization is the development of the accidental and immanent relations between various forces and relations (Hardt 1993: xv). However, these definitions are only meant to provide the starting point for investigations and developments of their relation between order and organization on the terrain of metaphysics, politics, etc.

3. Pierre Macherey has indicated that Negri makes the same mistake as Hegel in interpreting the attributes as the 'mediation' and 'degradation' of substance, and such a reading misses the force of Spinoza's concept of substance as 'self-caused' (Macherey 1992b: 249; see also p.12 in this volume). While Macherey's reading offers criticism which in some sense cannot be refused, any thorough response, and there is neither time nor space for one here, would have to return to what Negri means by 'crisis' as the starting point for his reading of Spinoza, and the manner in which this crisis is at once political, ontological, and epistemological. The intersection and overlap of the 'first foundation' and the ideology of utopia would already indicate the complexity of ontological and political questions that Negri's reading of Spinoza both presupposes and develops. This complexity, a complexity which is at times presented as a simple homology of attributes and the market, would mean that there are always more than interpretive questions at stake in Negri's reading and refusal of the attributes.

4. As Michael Hardt indicates, the attributes pose a problem for any materialist reading of Spinoza, in that they would seem to necessitate a priority of thought in their very definition, which makes perception, or thought, the site of the division between thought and extension. As Hardt indicates, Negri's resolution of this problem, which is based on a historical and thematic interruption between the two 'foundations' of the *Ethics*, is not without its difficulties (Hardt 1993).

5. Warren Montag notes that the object of Spinoza's critique is not simply any analogy between God and kings, but extends to the ideal of the free subject underlying various humanisms and liberalism. 'The God who lies beyond the (material) world and is free to direct it according to his unconditioned will is thus the mirror image of the man who transcends the physical world and governs his own body with absolute mastery, itself a mirror image of God: a vicious theological anthropological circle' (Montag 1999: 39).

6. For Negri, Spinoza's anomaly, his break with liberal thought, is not simply located in his refusal of the social contract, but more importantly in his refusal of the market. Negri follows C.B. Macpherson's *The Political Theory of Possessive Individualism* (Macpherson 1962) in finding the conflict and competition of the market society underlying the idea of a state of nature. From this perspective the sovereign is the necessary force to sustain market relations. As Negri argues, Hobbes is the Marx of the bourgeoisie. Against this ideal, which subordinates production to order, Spinoza traces the immanent organization of production: it is production, as a collective and social relation, which constitutes the world.

7. Negri traces a thread of singularity that begins with the opening definitions of part II of the *Ethics*. These two definitions begin to unfold an ontology of univocity where the 'thing' is defined as an expression of its singular power of acting (Spinoza 1985: E II D2, 447). From these definitions Negri locates a fugitive thread of singularity working through the *Ethics* (Negri 1991b: 60–3).

8. Etienne Balibar's essay 'Jus–Pactum–Lex: On the Constitution of the Subject in the *Theologico-Political Treatise*' (Balibar 1997) provides the strongest illustration of the overdetermined and hence singular nature of any contract, or any foundation of the state.

9. It is well documented that Spinoza was well acquainted with Machiavelli; Spinoza's treatises on politics bear the unmistakable mark of the latter's thought, a point to which Negri does return several times in *The Savage Anomaly*. With respect to the connection between Spinoza and Marx, see Maximilien Rubel, 'Marx à la rencontre de Spinoza', Alexandre Matheron, 'Le Traite Theologico-Politique vu par le jeune Marx',

and Albert Igoin, 'De l'ellipse de la theorie politique de Spinoza chez le jeune Marx' as well as Marx's hand-copied pages of the *Theological–Political Treatise* in *Cahiers Spinoza* 1 (Summer 1977).

10. Once again a useful point of intersection is to be found in Althusser, who defines his particular 'practice of philosophy' against the established divisions between 'politics' and 'metaphysics'. As Althusser writes, 'Of course this conception of philosophy as struggle—and, in the last instance, as class struggle in theory—implied a reversal of the traditional relation between philosophy and politics ... I claimed that it was necessary to get rid of the suspect division between philosophy and politics which at one and the same time treats the political figures as inferior—that is, as non-philosophers or Sunday afternoon philosophers—and also implies that the political positions of philosophers must be sought exclusively in the texts in which they talk about philosophy' (Althusser 1990b: 206).

11. Negri's writing on Marx covers a long history of polemics, arguments, and theoretical developments, a history which is intimately interwoven not only with other philosophical and theoretical works but with political struggles as well. A good introduction to this history can be found in Wright 2002.

12. For more on the relationship between 'cooperation' and the logic of capital, see my *The Micropolitics of Capital* (Read 2003).

13. Here I am briefly referring not only to certain theses advanced by Marx, but also to Negri's sociohistorical research, which trace the different forms and figures of living labor from the mass worker to the productive power of immaterial labor. See for example Negri 1988, Negri 1989, and the collective research project *Le Bassin de travail immateriel (BTI) dans la métropole parisienne* (Negri et al. 1996).

14. On the strategy of the *sive* see Tosel 1997: 155.

15. As Marx writes: 'This entire development of the productive forces of *socialized labor* (in contrast to the more or less isolated labor of individuals), and together with it the *uses of science* (the general product of social development), *in the immediate process of production*, takes the form [*stellt sich dar*] of the productive power of capital. It does not appear as the productive power of labor, or even of that part of it that is identical with capital. And least of all does it appear as the productive power either of the individual workers or of the workers joined together in the process of production' (Marx 1976: 1024/95).

16. In a footnote to a later article, Negri argues that the most productive intersection between Marx and Spinoza is not to be found in the latter's reformulation of the idea of forces of production, but rather in the application of Spinoza to the contemporary representation of capital. 'But if the forms of research trying to retrace in Spinozan materialism a germ of the critique of political economy are revealed to be apologetic and pointless, the Spinozan reading of the eminently sociopolitical organization of exploitation is, by contrast, undoubtedly relevant. In other words, in the postindustrial age the Spinozan critique of representation of capitalist power corresponds more to the truth than does the analysis of political economy' (Negri 1997b: 246).

17. The difference between these two traditions, which are also and at the same time practices of philosophy, can be traced through a recent discussion between Negri and Jacques Derrida. Commenting on Derrida's attempt to purge Marx of any ontological dimension in *Specters of Marx*, Negri writes: 'Today, exploitation, or, rather, capitalist relations of production, concern a laboring subject amassed in intellectually and cooperative force. A new paradigm; most definitely exploited, yet new—a different power, a new consistency of laboring energy, an accumulation of cooperative energy. This is a new—post-deconstructive—ontology' (Negri 1999b: 12). Derrida continues to refuse to use the term 'ontology' but recognizes that Negri's ontology, because it passes through history and politics, is perhaps something different than what is traditionally meant by that term. As Derrida writes, 'perhaps the two of us could, from now on, agree to regard the word "ontology" as a shibboleth, which only pretends to mean what the word "ontology" has always meant ... In philosophical company, we could act as if we were still speaking the language of metaphysics or ontology, knowing full well, between us, that this was not at all so' (Derrida 1999: 261).

3
Legality and Resistance:
Arendt and Negri on Constituent Power

Miguel Vatter

MACHIAVELLI AFTER MARX: RADICAL DEMOCRATIC THEORY TODAY

In contemporary political theory there exists an increasingly hegemonic tendency to join, as it were a priori, the two central features of a modern republic: the constituent power of the people (i.e. political freedom) and the rule of law (i.e. civil freedom). The tendency is to see power and law as stemming from the same source, which has paved the way for the juridification of freedoms.[1] Arendt and Negri represent two distinct efforts within democratic theory to break away from this tendency. Their work argues for the lack of synthesis between power and law. They think the identity of popular power and political freedom in order to show the tension of these with every form of rule of law. Yet this lack of synthesis between constituent power and rule of law does not entail their irrelatedness, but, on the contrary, is the key to understanding the kind of legitimacy that any rule of law, any constituted power, can aspire to. In this chapter I wish to show how these theoretical attempts to think the nonsynthetic, yet internal relation between power and law, between constituent and constituted powers, in Arendt and Negri form part of a 'return to Machiavelli', of a unique reconceptualization of the autonomy of the political, that situates itself 'beyond Marx', and that holds the most promising developments for future radical democratic theory.

A new radical democratic theory, having as some of its most important referents thinkers as diverse as Arendt, Lefort, the later Althusser, and Negri, takes much of its impetus from the reappropriation of Machiavelli, both with and against Marx. This return to Machiavelli betrays, first, a need to salvage the 'autonomy' or 'separateness' of the political from its reduction at the hands of Marxist economism and Weberian sociologism. In salvaging the autonomy of the political, this democratic theory sees itself as preserving the authentic space of freedom and power. Second, the autonomy of the political provides the basis from which democratic theory develops a new understanding of the complex relation that exists between state (constituted power) and revolution (constituent power) in late modernity. That the modern state must have a revolutionary origin if it is to be legitimate is a presupposition shared by liberalism and Marxism. But whereas liberal theory tends to internalize this origin into a discourse of constitutionalism that subjects political freedom to the requirements of rule of law, and Marxist theory tends to internalize the state into the revolutionary process, so that political freedom becomes mere ideology, radical democratic theory seeks political freedom in what I shall call the mutual resistance between state and revolution. My reading of Arendt and Negri is a contribution to the task of mapping out the conceptual terrain of this new radical democratic theory.

The association of the autonomy of the political with Machiavelli comes from the early decades of the last century, especially in the work of Meinecke and Croce. This feature of Machiavelli's discourse was quickly employed, by both liberal and Marxist thinkers, to account for the emergence of new forms of tyranny.[2] With Lefort's groundbreaking interpretation (Lefort 1972),[3] Machiavelli the republican theorist of political freedom comes together with Machiavelli the advisor of princes in order to address, and perhaps redress, what is perceived as the weak point in Marx: the conflation of political freedom with the state, and the consequent misunderstanding and rejection of political freedom as merely ideological. The democratic reactivation of Machiavelli as a thinker of nondomination permits a critique of the reduction of political freedom into 'negative liberty' that develops in nineteenth-century British and French liberal thought—the very development that had motivated Marx's strong rejection of political freedom to begin with.[4]

Beginning with *On the Jewish Question*, and never disavowed in his later writings, Marx contends that the republican ideal of freedom as nondomination cannot be realized exclusively at the political level, apart from its realization in society as a whole. Like Machiavelli before him, Marx perceives the tension between political freedom and political form as the essential feature of politics in modernity (see Abensour 1997). But, unlike Machiavelli, he attempts to overcome it. Marx is thereby led to posit a new kind of freedom, which he calls 'human freedom', whose main feature is the requirement that the political freedom of the citizen be realized in and through a revolution of social relations 'so that social force is no longer *separated* from him in the *form* of political force'.[5]

The return to Machiavelli 'beyond Marx' that distinguishes recent radical democratic theory turns on a revaluation of the very 'separation' of political power that Marx chastises. What emerges is a Machiavellian critique of Marx's critique of the autonomy of politics. Read from this post-Marxist perspective, Machiavelli offers a theory of political freedom as nondomination that understands the separation of the political from the social as the condition that keeps political freedom from finding its synthetic unity in the political form, thereby placing the state form in a situation of crisis which is constitutive of its possibility. In returning to Machiavelli, radical democratic theory rediscovers two fundamental theses: first, that freedom exists (only) in the separation (autonomy) of the political; second, that political freedom entails the rejection of a synthesis with political form.

The concept of constituent power is what allows one to think political freedom both in terms of its separation from the social and in terms of its rejection of synthesis with the political form. The power to constitute or begin *ex nihilo* a new state of affairs is grasped in its nonsynthetic character. The new cannot be caused by its social basis, but comes about through a separation or cutting-off from this basis, a loss of ground that bespeaks one sense in which political freedom is an abyss. While, at the same time, this constituent power does not stand in a synthetic relation to what is constituted by or through it: political freedom as the ungrounding ground of every constituted power.

Both Arendt and Negri interrogate the autonomy or separateness of the political through two interpretations of constituent power which emphasize opposite aspects of that complex relation between state and revolution, constituted and constituent powers, that lies at the heart of the modern political. Arendt analyzes constituent power in order to understand revolution as the origin of *the state*, so that revolution comes to mean the process of *constitutio libertatis*, the process of giving freedom a legal constitution such that the political remains separate from the activities that constitute the social dimension of the world. For Arendt, Marx's politicization of the social, as much as his socialization of the political, is tendentially totalitarian. Democracy requires the separation of the political. In particular, democracy comes to stand for a community of singulars in a situation of no-rule and without the operation of any division of labor whatsoever, since such a division is understood as coextensive with the social. Negri, for his part, analyzes constituent power in order to understand *revolution* as the origin of the state, so that revolution comes to mean the process of the permanent crisis of the state, of constituted power. For Negri, the political is also a power of separation, but one that breaks away from every constituted power, from institutionalized politics, in order to effect a return of constituent power back to the social, to the domain of living labor. Democracy here names the employment of constituent power in the project of emancipating labor from the domination imposed by its social division, and thereby produces both community and singularity in the movement Negri calls 'communism'.

Both recastings of the concept of constituent power make their case by way of Machiavelli. The Florentine appears both as the thinker of the constitution of political form, and as the thinker of the revolutionary constitution of political freedom. In this sense, Machiavelli's discourse exposes the true grammar of the term *constitutio*, which from its earliest inception in modern political thinking[6] contains inseparably a moment that is 'constituent' and one that is 'constituted', corresponding respectively to a formless subject of the political (designated as 'nation', 'people', or 'multitude') and to a subject of political form (designated as 'state'). Machiavelli explores the *internal relation* between these two moments of political constitution, without reducing one to the other. And it is precisely this nonreductivist understanding of constituent and constituted powers that permits a reading of revolution as the ungrounding ground of the state. From this follows an understanding of democracy in terms of what is foundational about the abyss (of freedom) and what is abyssal about the foundation (of freedom).

CONSTITUENT POWER AS REVOLUTIONARY GROUND OF LEGALITY—ARENDT

With *The Human Condition* (1958) and *On Revolution* (1963) Arendt sets out to recover the autonomy of politics from the oblivion into which it is cast during the nineteenth and early twentieth century, when politics becomes an object of the emergent social sciences and philosophies of history. *The Human Condition* defines political freedom as the capacity of radical spontaneity, of unconditionally beginning something genuinely new. But it does not consider such a concept of free action as a constituent power; it does not link it to the problem of its political foundation.[7] *On Revolution* explicitly identifies this concept of action with revolutionary politics. In modern revolutions 'the idea of freedom and the experience of a new beginning' coincide (Arendt 1963: 29). But Arendt adds that a revolution exists only when this freedom becomes constituent.[8] Or, put differently, the foundation of freedom entails 'the constitution of a republic', where the term 'republic' means the 'form of political organization in which the citizens lived together under conditions of no-rule, without a division between rulers and ruled' (Arendt 1963: 30). The republic is the constituted moment of political freedom as constituent power.

Even though the republic is called a 'form of political organization', Arendt emphasizes the fact that because it is nothing other than the realization of freedom as no-rule, a republic is in the end something other than a 'legal' or 'constitutional' government in which liberation (encoded by a system of natural rights) is safeguarded by the rule of law (Arendt 1963: 33).[9] The deeply ambivalent use of the distinction between freedom and liberation, which determines political freedom at one time as constitutional (in so far as freedom is supposed to be foundable in a given political form or legal order) and at another time as extraconstitutional (in so far as political constitutions merely safeguard liberation but do not assure freedom), is symptomatic of the difficulty Arendt has in articulating the grammar of foundation or constitution (*arché*) with that of freedom as no-rule (*anarché*). *On Revolution* is Arendt's epic effort to reinvent the meaning of the political as revolution: unlike both the liberal conception of revolution as the transition from a state of arbitrary rule to one of law-bound, limited rule, and the Marxist conception of revolution as the abolition of the state at the hands of an emancipated society, Arendt wants to understand revolution as the *state* of no-rule, as the *well-founded or authoritative* deployment of what is anarchic.

Arendt engages in such theoretical brinksmanship to show that freedom can be founded politically in the form of the state without resorting to violence, i.e. without negating itself. In so doing, she sees her project as a return to Machiavelli. Not only because '[f]reedom as inherent in action is perhaps best illustrated by Machiavelli's conception of *virtù*' (Arendt 1968: 153); not only because he 'was the first to think about the possibility of founding a permanent, lasting, enduring body politic' (Arendt 1963: 36); but principally because Machiavelli, before Robespierre and Marx, is the one who argues most effectively that these two things, freedom and foundation, cannot be united without violence.

> Machiavelli's insistence on violence ... was the direct consequence of the twofold perplexity in which he found himself theoretically and which later became the very practical perplexity besetting the men of revolutions. The perplexity consisted in the task of foundation, the setting of a new beginning, which as such seemed to demand violence and violation, the repetition, as it were, of the old legendary crime (Romulus slew Remus, Cain slew Abel) at the beginning of all history. This task of foundation, moreover, was coupled with the task of lawgiving, of devising and imposing upon men a new authority, which, however, had to be designed in such a way that it would fit and step into the shoes of the old absolute that derived from a God-given authority. (Arendt 1963: 38–9)

Arendt understands her own thinking about revolution as an alternative solution to Machiavelli's 'perplexity': the task is to show how a nonviolent foundation of freedom is possible, and how the realization of freedom in a legal framework does not require an appeal to a source of absolute authority.

Arendt claims that freedom can be given a foundation without violence as long as it is understood as freedom from domination, rather than from necessity or need. Freedom can be founded, can become constituent, only if it is *always already* separated from the domain of necessity. A central thesis of *On Revolution* is that those modern revolutions which turned to violence did so only because the priorities of the 'task of foundation' were changed around: those revolutions that require violence are involved in the task of freeing man from necessity rather than from domination.[10] Arendt's critique of violence in modernity (e.g. the terror of the 'social' revolutions of France and Russia, or the phenomenon of modern totalitarianism) is ultimately predicated on the belief that freedom from necessity requires making of man the 'absolute' means (totalitarianism would thus be the nightmarish realization of that ideal of freedom), whereas freedom from domination is the appropriate expression of the fact that man is an end in himself (republican *constitutio libertatis* would thus be the realization of this other ideal of freedom).[11]

The problem of theorizing *constitutio libertatis* is the following: how can freedom as 'the spontaneity of beginning something new' also be freedom as 'a stable, tangible reality' (Arendt 1978: 203)?[12] What is the nature of the internal relation between constituent and constituted powers? For Arendt, this question concerns the relation between power and law. When freedom becomes constituent it gives itself a constitution: this is the revolutionary act par excellence (Arendt 1963: 145). But to constitute freedom, as Arendt frequently states, does not mean to institute a government under the rule of law that safeguards negative liberties. Drawing from the thought of Montesquieu, Arendt defines the act of constitution of freedom as the act that creates power, rather than delimits it.

> The true objective of the American Constitution was not to limit power but to create more power … . This complicated and delicate system, deliberately designed to keep the power potential of the republic intact and prevent any of the multiple power sources from drying up in the event of further expansion … was entirely the child of revolution. The American Constitution finally consolidated the power of the Revolution, and since the aim of revolution was freedom, it indeed came to be what Bracton had called *Constitutio Libertatis*, the foundation of freedom. (Arendt 1963: 154)

Freedom and power are united in the constitution of freedom (Arendt 1963: 150–4).[13] Because of the internal relation that obtains between freedom and power, what she means by 'constitution of freedom' is not the same as what is meant by 'constitutional government'. The latter is defined in terms of the ability that a system of law has to exercise and check government rule; whereas the former entails the empowerment of those who are subject to government. Strictly speaking, for Arendt the constitution of freedom and power is an extraconstitutional affair; it cannot be comprised within the boundaries of the rule of law. But, concurrently, Arendt wants to endow her conception of positive freedom with those qualities that only constitutional government can provide, namely, the stability and formality provided by a system of law. The constitution of freedom also means the stabilization of freedom.

The constitution of freedom has therefore two essential aspects: freedom has to be simultaneously related to power (constituent power) and to law (constituted power). According to the first sense, the act of constitution creates power through the 'compact' of the people (Arendt 1963: 167ff.).

> The grammar of action: that action is the only human faculty that demands a plurality of men; and the syntax of power: that power is the only human attribute which applies solely to the worldly in-between space by which men are mutually related, combine in the act of foundation by virtue of the making and keeping of promises, which, in the realm of politics, may well be the highest human faculty. (Arendt 1963: 175)

The republican dimension of the foundation of freedom grants power to action (as capacity to begin something radically new) in binding the action of a plurality of human beings through promises or compacts.

Still, the problem of foundation is not resolved until the second sense of constitution, the one related to law and authority as opposed to power and freedom, is articulated. According to this sense, the source of law is to be found in the regulations of a constitution, understood as a written document of political principles, rather than in the 'will of the people' (Arendt 1963: 157). Only the internal relation of freedom and law, only the translation of popular power into a political form, can grant 'stability' to the affairs of men. For Arendt, it is the distinguishing characteristic of the American revolution, unlike the French revolution, that it did not ground law and authority upon the power of the people. Without this precaution, political freedom would not have found its stability and form. The reason is that popular power, based on promises made among equals in a moment of no-rule, is an evanescent phenomenon: it has no end outside of itself; it is not productive of order because it does not command or rule over things and over agents, and consequently it cannot provide stability to political freedom.[14]

Because the law cannot be founded on the basis of the power and freedom of the people, but, conversely, this freedom is supposed to find its stability and form in the law, there emerges in the act of political constitution a 'problem of law' which can be formulated in terms of 'Sièyes's vicious circle: those who get together to constitute a new government are themselves unconstitutional, that is, they have no authority to do what they set out to achieve' (Arendt 1963: 184). If not from the 'grammar of action' and the 'syntax of power', then from where is the constitution, understood as the 'fundamental law' that grants authority to all other positive laws, to receive its own authority?

That such a problem emerges at all is testimony to what I take to be Arendt's most disconcerting intuition: political freedom and political power carry no 'authority' and are, in a crucial sense, beyond legitimacy.[15] At the same time, every appeal to extrapolitical, metaphysically ascertained absolutes in order to found political freedom is self-defeating, since such a freedom (qua unconditioned spontaneity) entails the absence of heteronomy and domination, whereas for Arendt every 'absolute truth' is precisely a source of external constraint because it 'compels without argumentative demonstration or political persuasion' (Arendt 1963: 192). Neither legal authority nor philosophical truth can serve as foundations for political freedom, which therefore emerges, in Arendt, as truly abyssal.

In *On Revolution*, Arendt attempts to resolve the 'problem of the law' by arguing that this unfoundable political freedom as no-rule can itself serve as the ground of rule, that is, as the source of the authority for legal commands, for a political form, which in turn grants political freedom 'a space where this freedom could be exercised' (Arendt 1963: 235), grants freedom the desired 'stable, tangible reality'. Arendt's decisive claim is that the constitution, understood as fundamental law, derives its authority from the fact that the act of foundation is itself an absolute beginning. 'From this [possibility] it follows that it is futile to search for an absolute to break the vicious circle in which all beginning is inevitably caught, because this "absolute" lies in the very act of beginning itself' (Arendt 1963: 204). This solution, at first, just seems to confirm the radical separation of power from authority: the source of authority does not (cannot) come from the 'performative' aspect of power and freedom, but must come from *positing* such 'performance' *as an absolute (beginning)*. The novelty of Arendt's solution lies in the conceit that the *absoluteness* of beginning alone is called upon to effect the transition from constituent to constituted power, i.e. to constitute freedom as a state or form of government.

But in what sense does an absolute beginning have an internal relation to the possibility of authority, and, furthermore, how is the beginning posited as absolute? How can no-rule become a source for rule once it is posited absolutely? What is no-rule absolved from in the act of foundation? Arendt never provides a direct argument for why a beginning, once it is posited as an absolute, is 'in itself' authoritative. The demonstration proceeds in a regressive way, from the effects of authority to its purported origin. Comparing the 'devotion' of Americans to their constitution with the *pietas* of the Roman citizen, who is religiously 'bound back to the beginning of Roman history, the foundation of the eternal city', Arendt surmises that the 'stability and authority of any given body politic [must derive] from its beginning ... . *One is tempted to conclude that it was the authority which the act of foundation carried within itself ... that assured stability for the new republic'* (Arendt 1963: 198–9, emphasis mine). The internal relation between authority and act of foundation is surmised from the fact that a system of authority maintains that act 'present' through history by increasing its significance. *Auctoritas* in fact means 'to augment, to increase and enlarge, the foundations as they had been laid down by the ancestors. The uninterrupted continuity of this augmentation and its inherent authority could come about only through tradition' (Arendt 1963: 201). For Arendt, the system of authority augments the founding act only by allowing for a process of continuous constitution making, which is said to amount to the 'retrieval' or 'repetition' of the revolutionary beginning itself.

> The very concept of Roman authority suggests that the act of foundation inevitably develops its own stability and permanence, and authority in this context is nothing more or less than a kind of necessary 'augmentation' by virtue of which innovations and changes remain tied back to the foundation which, at the same time, they augment and increase. Thus the amendments to the Constitution augment and increase the original foundations of the American republic; needless to say, the very authority of the American Constitution resides in its inherent capacity to be amended and augmented. (Arendt 1963: 202)

Such a possibility of 'repeating' the revolutionary beginning in and through the system of authority, were it tenable, would support Arendt's contention that the synthesis of freedom and authority, of constituent and constituted powers, is attainable.

Arendt's bold thesis, then, amounts to this: constituent power founds itself as constituted power, as a system of legal authority, *because* this system can only exist as the *repetition* of the revolutionary beginning. At the heart of Arendt's solution to Sieyès' problem lies the conceptual figure of historical repetition, or, to use the formula employed by Machiavelli, of 'return to beginnings'.[16] And yet it is not to Machiavelli that Arendt goes in search of a theory of historical repetition. Once again, she steps out of the Machiavellian horizon and moves to the ancients, in this case to the Roman understanding of authority as a retrieval of origins. But in so doing Arendt loses the possibility of articulating a theory of repetition on its own terms. For the Romans offer a discourse on foundation for which repetition is secondary. Whereas it is only with Machiavelli, for whom the *return* to the ancients coincides with the formulation of 'new modes and orders', with the decision to open 'a path as yet untrodden by anyone' (Machiavelli 1996: bk. 1, preface, 5),[17] that one can speak about a radical coincidence of repetition and beginning, about a conception of originary repetition. In her formulation of the revolutionary ground of legal authority, Arendt misses the distinction between an internal (Machiavelli) and an external (Romans) relation between repetition and beginning.[18]

Indeed, in order for the repetition of the beginning to have *authoritative* effects, the relation between repetition and beginning must be an *external* one. In this case, the revolutionary beginning is said to function as a ground (of authority) because it causes or conditions the repetition of 'itself'. Arendt never considers whether the *repetition* itself begins anything radically new. For this to occur, an *internal* relation between beginning and repetition needs to obtain. That is why the repeated beginning, or what Arendt calls the 'augmentation' of the constitution, e.g. in the forms of amendments, is recognizable as falling under the same fundamental law, i.e. as being more of the same. When Arendt says that the repetition of the revolutionary beginning amounts to 'a *coincidence* of foundation and preservation by virtue of augmentation', the 'coincidence' refers to the homogeneity of the augmentation with respect to the original constitution (Arendt 1963: 202, emphasis mine).

One can now see what it means for the beginning to be an absolute. In a first sense, the process of augmentation absolves a beginning from being 'just another beginning' so that it can retroactively be posited as the 'first beginning'. In this way, 'other' beginnings come to be interpreted as instances of 'its' repetition, thereby reinforcing its primacy and granting it its authority. If augmentation is a process of 'continuous foundation', it is one whose very continuity disallows for new beginnings, for revolutionary ruptures.

The system of authority sketched by Arendt does not augment the occurrences of free beginnings, of republican events, of revolutionary discontinuities in the fabric of tradition. Quite the opposite: authority maintains the state in its capacity to rule 'freely' (as opposed to violently), but it does not allow for the advent of freedom from rule. The system of authority is, ironically, the permanent negation of the act of revolution itself (understood as the emergence of the radically new) since 'by virtue of *auctoritas*, permanence and change were tied together, whereby, for better or worse, throughout Roman history, change could only mean increase and enlargement of the old' (Arendt 1963: 201).

The desire for the uninterrupted presence of the revolutionary beginning reveals the second sense in which the system of authority constructs an absolute concept of beginning. Authority absolutizes a beginning by absolving it from its own advent, from its own event character. By keeping the beginning 'always present', the system of authority actually stifles the rebirth of the 'revolutionary spirit' because it is only the event character of the beginning that seals its finitude and discontinuity, thereby allowing for the dissemination of other beginnings.

Arendt claims that the act of foundation qua new beginning has 'inherently' a capacity to conserve itself, i.e. creates for itself its own authority. This thesis actually stands in contrast to another idea of beginning that is equally present in Arendt's text, namely, the idea that each beginning is *its own* principle: 'What saves the act of beginning from its own arbitrariness is that it carries its own principle with itself' (Arendt 1963: 212). This formula can be taken to mean that each beginning is a principle *only unto itself*, i.e. that it cannot rule over other beginnings. This self-limitation of the beginning as 'its own principle' is what 'frees' the possibility for other beginnings, and is responsible for giving the 'principle' of beginning its emancipatory and antiauthoritarian significance. To phrase my point differently: that each beginning is its own principle means that each beginning is always already a repetition, in the sense that each beginning is 'just another beginning', and in no sense can it be posited as unique or absolute. Such a claim means that *there is no beginning which is not already a return*, that the sphere of politics is characterized by the absence of originals to be imitated, examples to be followed. In short, that politics is the space of simulacra. This trait makes it impossible for there to be a principle that *rules* over the advent of any beginning. In this sense, beginnings are thoroughly *indiscriminate* (in every sense of the term) as a condition for their having the power to *discriminate* (cut, divide, interrupt) the continuum of time, and thus 'turn the times around' or 'return to beginnings'. Authority, in contrast, is intended to prohibit just this proliferation of beginnings: 'turning around' every action towards the foundation (in order to give action its religious sanction), authority maintains the continuity of the times and the consolidation of rule. The very maintenance of a beginning as foundation undoes the possibility of beginning again.

In effect, *On Revolution* is a text that does two irreconcilable things. On the one hand, it attempts to offer a theory of the internal relation between freedom and authority, revolution and state, constituent and constituted powers, that would justify the project of providing political freedom with a 'stable, tangible reality', the project of *constitutio libertatis*. On the other hand, this text also stages the aporetic nature of this project, the illusory character of such a solution, the irresolvable tension between political freedom as event and legal form: the former existing only as an originary repetition, as a return to beginnings, that as such cannot aspire to any absolute status and is thoroughly given over to the contingency of historical becoming; the latter existing only as an external repetition of the revolutionary beginning, that at once absolutizes it and, in and through rehearsing its 'spirit' in an authoritative rule of law, conjures away any possibility for this spirit to survive. This 'tragic' realization of the aporia of *constitutio libertatis* finds its figure, in Arendt as well as in Negri, in the question of the 'commune': the only true name of a republic. At the end of this chapter I return to discuss such a 'communist' understanding of political freedom in Arendt and Negri.

CONSTITUENT POWER AS REVOLUTIONARY DISSOLUTION OF LEGALITY—NEGRI

Since the early 1980s, Negri's work has come to prominence for reconstructing 'the historical materialism that develops a radical concept of democracy from Machiavelli to Spinoza to Marx' (Negri 1999a: 29). But in a fundamental sense, his theoretical aim has remained constant since the 1960s and 1970s: to dismantle the separation of politics and economics, of state and social movement, that characterizes the autonomy of the political and that Arendt defends.[19] The novelty of *Insurgencies: Constituent Power and the Modern State* consists in Negri's attempt to achieve this aim by putting to work, against the grain, the concept of constituent power, which is the linchpin for every theory of the separation of the political. Negri engages the debate concerning the autonomy or separation of the political by working through its groundbreaking articulation in Arendt. *Insurgencies* offers Negri's best account of how a return to Machiavelli is needed in order to think Marx beyond the crisis of Marxism.[20]

The result is both forceful and ambiguous. Negri's reconstruction of constituent power emphasizes the revolutionary and democratic senses of the concept, pointing out its radically extraconstitutional reality. In this sense, Negri is today the most forceful thinker of the political 'beyond' and 'outside' the state.[21] By the same token, the antistatist pathos of his thought repeatedly overwhelms its theoretical apparatus and casts its results into question. Negri roots constituent power in 'living labor', the fundamental element of his social ontology. As a consequence, the political is not only understood apart from the state, but is understood as a function of its capacity to turn back, to reduce, institutional politics to the social. This raises the first question: does the political ultimately get abolished in the emancipated social, or is it preserved in the social, the latter becoming immediately political or 'autonomous'? Second, and most problematic, Negri's relocation of the concept of constituent power in the social renders it inoperative when it comes to giving an account of the permanence of the state, which, as I shall argue, is precisely what recommends a return to Machiavelli in the first place. If I am right in holding that Negri's theory of constituent power cannot, in the end, account for the power (*potere*) of the constituted, then one would have to say, paradoxically, that his is a 'weak' theory of constituent power (*potenza*).[22]

Insurgencies displays the concept of constituent power on two distinct planes of analysis. On the political plane, constituent power is said to hold the true sense of democracy. On the social plane, constituent power is meant to account for the 'political' dimension of 'living labor'. Ultimately, Negri wishes to collapse these two planes into a single 'plane of immanence'. Whether he succeeds can be answered only after following his reconstruction of the concept of constituent power on both analytical planes.

Negri's first major thesis is that the constituent power of society is the true content of democracy. Both constituent power and democracy share the essential feature that they 'resist being constitutionalized' (Negri 1999a: 2). Democracy resists constitutionalization because 'it is in fact a theory of absolute government, while constitutionalism is a theory of limited government, and therefore a practice that limits democracy' (Negri 1999a: 2).[23] Analogously, constituent power as 'all-embracing power' and source 'of production of constitutional norms' is nothing other than 'the revolution itself'. Constituent power is a concept that works against both juridical thought and constitutionalism, whose defining task consists in 'bringing the revolution to a conclusion' by reducing constituent power to 'the norm of the production of law' and incorporating it into 'the established power' (Negri 1999a: 3). In sum, democracy and constituent power both name that in society which *resists* the constituted forms of political life.

Negri's extraconstitutional conception of democracy as constituent power radicalizes Arendt's intuitions regarding the abyss that obtains between a 'free republic' and 'constitutional government'. But with the second ground for the identification of constituent power and democracy, Negri markedly departs from Arendt. In fact, he holds that both constituent power and democracy share the character of being 'absolute'. This retrieval of 'absoluteness' in politics is the fundamental motivation behind Negri's historicopolitical genealogy of modernity, intended to reveal 'another tradition of modern metaphysics from Machiavelli and Spinoza to Marx [that] sees the development of the dynamic of constituent power as absolute, but here that absoluteness never becomes totalitarian' (Negri 1999a: 29). Constituent power and democracy both point to the political as an 'absolute'. They manage to escape the 'totalitarian' implications that Arendt reads into them because, for Negri, democracy and constituent power are also a 'resistance' to that other political reality, the sovereignty of the state and of constituted powers, whose absolutization is deemed to be the real manifestation of totalitarianism. In a formula: constituent power articulates the political as *absolute resistance*. I find this formula for the political to be essential to radical democratic theory. My remarks will therefore not seek to reject the formula, but instead to give it another reading, one that avoids the problems found in Negri's interpretation of it.

The absoluteness of constituent power excludes any *internalization* of constituent power into the workings of constituted power. For Negri most of the prevalent juridical and political theories of constituent power, from Jellinek and Kelsen to Rawls and Habermas, are flawed because they desire to impose external limits on what is absolute. So, for instance, he finds that in such theories, constituent power

> is juridically preformed, whereas it was claimed that it would generate the law; it is in fact absorbed in the notion of political representation, whereas it was supposed to legitimize this notion. Thus constituent power, as an element connected to representation (and incapable of expressing itself except through representation) becomes part of the great design of the social division of labor. This is how the juridical theory of constituent power solves the allegedly vicious circle of the reality of constituent power. But isn't closing constituent power within representation ... nothing but the negation of the reality of constituent power, its congealment in a static system, the restoration of traditional sovereignty against democratic innovation? (Negri 1999a: 29)

It is important to reject the claim that constituent power is always already *internal* to constituted power because such a claim covers up a necessary feature of the reality of constituent power, namely, its capacity to place the state in a congenital crisis of legitimation. Negri rightly insists that 'if in the history of democracy and democratic constitutions the dualism between constituent power and constituted power has never produced a synthesis, we must focus precisely on this negativity, on this lack of synthesis, in order to try to understand constituent power' (Negri 1999a: 12), that is, in order to understand its concept as that of 'crisis' (of the state).

But Negri's attempt to separate constituent power from constituted power goes too far and fails to establish an *internal relation* between constituent and constituted powers.[24] Negri's absolutization of constituent power tends to absolve it from any relation to constituted power. As a consequence, the concept can no longer explain the emergence and perdurability of the political form as such. It is as if for Negri the existence of an 'internal relation' between two terms necessarily entails that one of them has to be 'internalized' by the other. Undoubtedly, constituent power must be thought starting from its nonsynthetic relation to constituted power, and hence in terms of a resistance to legality. At the same time, and precisely because of the lack of synthesis with constituted power, one is left with the most difficult and pressing task of explaining how constituted power comes to be and lasts, how it is self-standing. *Insurgencies* never accounts for this *in political terms*, but solely *in economic terms*. In so doing, Negri falls back on the reassuring Marxist assumption that the state, the constituted power, is ultimately an illusion which, if only one could correctly grasp constituent power in its absoluteness, would whither away.

Negri's arguments rejecting the synthesis of constituent and constituted powers bear a detailed examination in order to identify where they depart and where they coincide so strikingly with Arendt's own formulations. The first claim, then, is that constituent power cannot be synthesized with constituted power. Negri offers three reasons for such a claim: first, constituent power is self-founding; second, it is unlimited in space and time because it is the power of 'innovative singularity', of a radical, unforeseeable beginning; third, constituent power is 'strength' (*potenza*), not institutionalized power (*potere*). Strength is defined against power, whose highest figure is sovereignty, as negative is defined against positive: absence, desire, refusal are on the side of strength; power, possession, domination are on the side of sovereignty (Negri 1999a: 13–14). As Negri acknowledges, these characteristics of constituent power match those assigned by Arendt to political freedom: freedom as foundation, as beginning, and as antisovereign power.[25]

But if Negri adopts the basic features of constituent power from Arendt, he also gives a Spinozist turn to the characters of constituent power by defining them as moments of an 'absolute process', where the 'absoluteness' of constituent power or freedom becomes 'process' in virtue of its 'expansiveness', 'unlimitedness', and 'unfinalized' essence (Negri 1999a: 18).[26] Although one may say that for Arendt 'the radical quality of the constituent principle is absolute [because] ... it comes from a void and constitutes everything' (Negri 1999a: 16), still what is of primary importance to Arendt is that the constituent principle serve as the foundation for the constituted political space, for law and authority, which alone provide political freedom with a 'stable reality'. *Constitutio libertatis*, the foundation of freedom, entails both that freedom is an absolute beginning and that it is a foundation for the rule of law. As I showed above, Arendt's idea of the foundation of political freedom is aporetic because political freedom ultimately cannot serve both as a beginning and as a foundation, and cannot do so precisely because it resists being inscribed with the character of absoluteness. Still, Arendt's theory of constituent power tries to give a figure to the *internal relation* between constituent and constituted power, between freedom and order, by turning the constituent power of beginning into an absolute that can legitimate laws and institutions. Negri, for his part, views any relation to the constituted moment as symptomatic of the refusal to absolutize 'the expansiveness of constituent power' (Negri 1999a: 18). This is why he rejects every attempt at figuring constituent power in a constituted form. This is also why he charges that Arendt's 'schema for the development of constituent power ... is linear and spontaneist as in the worst versions of sociological institutionalism', of which he takes Lefort and Castoriadis to be the exemplars (Negri 1999a: 18).[27]

The denial that there exists an internal relation between constituent and constituted powers is based on the assumption that 'constituent power ... is not even the institution of constituted power ... . No, the phrase "expression of strength" can never mean "institution of power". But at the very moment when strength gets instituted it ceases being strength' (Negri 1999a: 22). Political freedom cannot be the univocal source of legal authority and of the duty to comply with legal norms. This point is well taken and must be repeatedly attended to. But it should initiate, rather than terminate, reflection: for what then requires an explanation is the emergence of legal order and legal authority from political freedom *in such a way that their radical separation remains*. What must be accounted for is the relation between constituent and constituted powers in terms of their capacity for *mutual* resistance. This is the real task of any theory of constituent power, and it is here that a return to Machiavelli can deliver some of its most productive results.

Negri's construal of the 'ontological radicality' of the constituent principle as an 'absolute process' is hard pressed to provide an account of resistance as the content of the internal relation between constituent and constituted powers. The Spinozist construal of 'absolute process' remains ambiguous. If, as Negri says at one point, Spinoza's idea that finite modes are in the absolute process called 'God or Nature', because God is 'in' the modes, then the resistance that the constituted moment (the finite modes) effects against the constituent moment (absolute process, *Deus sive Natura*) is just as essential or constitutive as the resistance of the constituent against the constituted. But, on the other hand, if constituent power as absolute process should be understood as analogous to *natura naturans* that is constantly 'beyond' its products as *natura naturata*, then it is unavoidable that these products, i.e. the constituted powers, come to exist only as mere semblance, as unfounded appearance, and are therefore unable to offer any real resistance to constituent power. But would this not amount to repeating what Althusser calls the 'absolute limits' of Marx and Lenin, namely, their incapacity to understand the political not only as self-standing but also as capable of an active resistance and remolding of constituent power; their incapacity, to speak with Althusser, to think the priority of reproduction over production (Althusser 1978b)?[28]

There seems to be another, perhaps deeper reason for why Negri rejects the internal relation between constituent and constituted powers, rather than following Althusser's attempt to think the real character of this relation. For Negri, unlike for the later Althusser, the political features of constituent power are direct expressions of the social, and as a consequence the return to the social is an essential moment of the political.

Political liberation and economic emancipation are one and the same thing ... . Living labor against dead labor, constituent power against constituted power .... Cooperative living labor produces a social ontology that is constitutive and innovative, a weaving of forms that touch the economic and the political; living labor produces an indistinct mixture of the political and the economic that has a creative figure. (Negri 1999a: 33)

Constituent power can afford, so to speak, to be absolved from constituted power, from the problem of the self-institution of the political, because at bottom it is nothing but the internal movement of emancipating production from its own reification, of making living labor 'autonomous'.

At this point I am in a position to discuss the basic alternatives of the idea that constituent power is nothing other than the political as absolute resistance. For the political as absolute resistance can be articulated in at least two contrary ways. The political can express a process (or subject or substance) of resistance that is absolute in the sense of being absolved from every thing-like (mode-like) determination. This is Negri's 'Spinozist' understanding of constituent power, where the latter is radically delinked from any determination as constituted power. But the political can also be understood in a 'Nietzschean' way, if one takes it to express the absoluteness of resistance with respect to any process- or subject-like determination. In this second sense, resistance is found everywhere, in the constituted powers of the state as much as beyond it, in the constituent powers of revolution. That is, the absoluteness of resistance is just that relation between constituent and constituted powers as mutually resistant. For resistance to be everywhere, for everything to be resistant, conflict and struggle must be everywhere. But if every process or subject or substance comes to be in and through its conflictual relation to everything else, then there is no absolute process or subject or substance. The only 'absolute' is the radically contingent dimension of the event in which these elements emerge and pass away as a result of their conflictual encounter. Political is whatever happens in these encounters. In the terms of Foucault, 'politics is war pursued by other means' (Foucault 1980: 90; see also Foucault 1997).

The opposition between these conceptions of the political as absolute resistance can be formulated in terms of the question: is there, or is there not, an internal relation between revolution (constituent power) and state (constituted power)? Negri's idea of constituent power as absolute resistance allows him to define the political as whatever returns the state back to, and dissolves it into, the revolution or constituent power as absolute process. But is this move thinkable? In the absence of a strong theory of the state (constituted power) is it possible to have an effective theory of revolution (constituent power)? Two answers are possible here: yes, if there is no internal relation between them, as Negri has it. No, if such a relation obtains, as I shall argue below.

For Negri the political exists only in the limiting sense of being the agent for the reduction of instituted politics to the social, the agent of the dissolution of constituted powers. Constituent power both emerges and vanishes at the limits of politics: either it emerges into politics from 'pure' living labor in order to seek its emancipation,[29] or it returns to living labor under a political form, which Negri calls 'democracy as absolute government', that seeks to dissolve the state and every political form in its separateness, in order to realize the emancipation of living labor (analogous to the Marxist concept of the dictatorship of the proletariat). The lack of an internal relation between constituent power and constituted power does not allow Negri to answer the question that both Arendt and Althusser pose: from where does the state make its beginning *ex nihilo*? How can the state be understood as self-standing, as having the power to separate itself from and resist the constituent power that begins it?

In fact, such questions do not pose themselves for Negri, because only revolution, the moment of dissolution of constituted power, as opposed to the moment of its constitution, has an internal relation to constituent power. 'Neither constituent power nor revolution has ever come to an end when they have been internally connected', that is, when constituent power has been understood as 'an ontological notion of the formative capacity of historical movement' (Negri 1999a: 23). Constituent power is not simply the capacity to make history in and through revolutionary changes of circumstances: it is the *unlimited* power to effect such changes. 'The process started by constituent power never stops. The question is not to limit constituent power, but to make it unlimited. The only possible concept of constitution is that of revolution: precisely, constituent power as absolute and unlimited procedure' (Negri 1999a: 24). Revolution becomes necessary, 'as necessary as the human need to be moral, to constitute oneself ethically, to free body and mind from slavery, and constituent power is the means toward this end' (Negri 1999a: 24). It is symptomatic that at this point of his argument, the talk about 'laws of history' reappears, and Negri approvingly cites Condorcet's idea of a 'revolutionary law ... that starts, accelerates, and rules the course of the revolution' (Condorcet, cited in Negri 1999a: 24). Negri thinks of the revolution as an infinite, ongoing process that is simply not recognized as such by the power (*potere*) that ideology and the state have to occlude this basic ontological reality. But does not the revolutionary event, as source of law here, undergo a subreption into the form of the law that destroys the capacity of revolution to be a truly 'fundamental act of innovation'? Can a theory of permanent revolution account for the events of radical historical change? And, conversely, does the idea of permanent revolution make sense of the duration and suspension of political forms, or does it simply bypass these phenomena, assuming that the duration of political form is illusory?

These are the fundamental questions raised by Negri's theory of constituent power. No radical democratic theory can afford to ignore them. They reflect the three basic theoretical nodes that characterize a thinking that wishes to go 'beyond Marx'. First node: is the character of political freedom as constituent power *ontological* or *eventual*? If the former, then the relation between revolution and state can conceivably be subsumed under a necessary law of history; if the latter, if the character of their relation is that of the event of their mutual resistance, then such laws are in principle impossible. Second node: is the state an illusory reflection of a blocked constituent process, or a self-standing, 'autonomous' power that actively resists its constituent beginning? Third node: can constituent power, in its difference from every constituted power, take the form of a revolutionary government, or does it express a resistance to every instance of government (whether revolutionary or legal) as such? Negri develops his answers through an engagement with Machiavelli, and it is on the terrain of Machiavelli's discourse that I shall engage Negri.

The basic ontological elements of Machiavelli's theory of political freedom consist in the situatedness of human action in historical conditions that change (the dimension of *fortuna*), and in the possibility for human action to change these conditions (the dimension of *virtù*).[30] Negri acknowledges the reality of these elements, while at the same time identifiying a limit and a drawback in Machiavelli's understanding of their relation:

> That remarkable strength [*virtù*], capable of overdetermining strength and of producing new ontological reality, always runs into an obstacle [*fortuna*]. Who creates the obstacle we do not know. Machiavelli does not pose the problem; for him it is enough to have shown that formidable radical power invests the world and builds it again, as if out of nothing. (Negri 1999a: 53)

As if Machiavelli's belief that *virtù* is finite, that it always encounters constituted power or *fortuna* as an obstacle, as a resistance, betrays an unwillingness or inability to fully ontologize and absolutize constituent power, to think the possibility of permanent revolution, which would be unarrestable by *fortuna*.

Yet Machiavelli's theory of *virtù* and *fortuna* can be given an alternative reading that does not see it as an unfortunate foreclosing of the concept of 'absolute' constituent power. The play of resistance (*virtù*) and counterresistance (*fortuna*), in fact, is a consequence of their eventual, rather than ontological, character: these elements exist only as a function of their conflictual encounter or match (*riscontro*), and do not preexist it.[31] The resistance of *fortuna* is indicative of what I call the *essential* character that the situation has in relation to the action which finds itself in it. For Machiavelli there cannot be a radical change of situation (*virtù* as constituent power) unless the situation (*fortuna* as constituted power) is essential, radically nonaccidental. It is part of the essence, of the grammar, of a situation that it can be changed. Therefore, the more one grasps the situation in its essence, and not as a mere illusion or contingency, the more one grasps the possibility of its radical change. But the more one grasps the situation as essential, the more does its radical change depend on the radically situated character of the action that changes it. Essentiality of the situation and radicality of its change stand in a relation of mutual resistance because they exist only as a function of the event of their conflictual encounter or match, which is neither predetermined nor determining of future encounters, but is the event of originary discontinuity.

Machiavelli's theory of the match (*riscontro*) between constituent and constituted powers shows that a radical change of situation is possible only if the encounter between constituent power and situation (constituted power) is itself situational, i.e. eventual. If this constituent power acquires the character of a subject or substance, if it is absolute process as Negri holds, then no discontinuity, no rupture is truly possible, and hence also no revolution as event of innovation. Either the revolution is finite, an eventuality, rather than a permanent process, or it never comes to pass.

Mutatis mutandis, the same goes for the question of form: if change is permanent, then no form is at all possible in its reality. Whereas if radical change is eventual, then form is possible as the reification of such eventuality, as what Althusser calls the 'accomplishment' of the fact whose result is the 'accomplished fact'.[32] Both Arendt and Althusser follow Machiavelli in their belief that political change is eventual, not ontological; the change of situation is itself situational, an event, and not a structure or a law. The reason for this is simple and fundamental: if the situation, any situation, is rooted in a substance-like process, in an eternal becoming or an absolute process, then it becomes impossible to encounter it in view of changing it, and changing it in an encounter. It is only when a situation no longer hangs on an a priori ontological structure, when it is no longer the instance of some law, the diachronic instantiation of a synchronic structure, that it is possible to think its radical change. But its radical change will be at once also radically situational, not an ontological state or process.

By ontologizing *virtù* or constituent power, as Negri does, one is forced to conceive the emergence of *fortuna* or constituted power as a *politically passive* process of accumulation.

> The constituent principle and strength are in fact absolute, but any actualization opposes them, wants to deny their absoluteness. If the absolute overflows or is dislocated, it finds itself confronted by the rigidity and irrationality of the constituted. This is the problem of constituent power, and this is the problem of the new prince. *Every time virtue is realized, it discovers that it is working to accumulate something that, once it becomes strong, is opposed to it* ... . The capability of acting on time from inside time, to constitute it as much as overdetermine it, must be armed: virtue becomes constituent power in this moment because it is on the relationship with arms that virtue forms the social orders. But not even this is enough: the themes of the exercise of power, of government are foregrounded, but here once again is verified the inconclusiveness of the principle, its crisis, and its always unresolved and often perverse dialectic. (Negri 1999a: 61, emphasis mine)

Here the cause of the resistance posed by *fortuna* and constituted power to *virtù* and constituent power is ultimately located in the economic substructure, in the process of 'accumulation' of living labor as dead labor (capital). But the reference back to economics actually explains nothing. What need to be conceived are the *political* conditions of possibility of 'primitive' accumulation in the first place. Constituted power needs to be understood autonomously, from a political perspective, primarily, and not as mere ideological superstructure of a capitalist economic system.[33] What is missing in Negri is a *political* analysis of the resistance of *fortuna* to *virtù*.

This analysis has a name in Machiavelli's discourse: it is the theory of the new prince (*The Prince* (Machiavelli 1998), chs 8–9 and 15–18; *Discourses on Livy* (Machiavelli 1996) book 1, chs 16–18) who founds the state by getting 'arms of its own', that is, by arming the 'people'. But for Negri, Machiavelli's theory of the new prince only figures an insufficiently elaborated concept of constituent power that is constantly being disarmed by an external process of accumulation of *fortuna*. On the contrary, I suggest that the new prince also figures the passage to constituted power by giving a *political foundation* to the process of accumulation of *fortuna*. Machiavelli calls a 'civil principality' that constituted state in which the accumulation of *fortuna* (capital) is politically founded. In Machiavelli, the new prince is ultimately nothing other than the *civil prince*, who is so called precisely because he or she founds the state by securing its separation from the radicality of the social conflict through the institution of a *civil society*. Civil society here means a state that actively promotes institutions through which the people's desire for no-rule is reinterpreted into the appetite for negative liberty, with the security of possessions that follows from it. Only on the basis of this new appetite and of this new security can 'primitive' accumulation take place and unfold.

Constituted power, therefore, founds itself, becomes the 'accomplishment' of constituent power, by making possible a civil society. A society becomes 'civil' by pacifying the social conflict that is constitutive of it: 'In every city these two diverse humors are found, which arises from this: that the people desire neither to be commanded nor oppressed by the great, and the great desire to command and oppress the people' (Machiavelli 1998: ch. 9, 39).[34] Between the desire to dominate and the desire for nondomination there is asymmetry: no political form whatsoever, no instance of political unity, can possibly synthesize their opposition. More precisely, the permanence of social conflict, of the social division, is due to the desire for nondomination found in the 'people'. Nondomination, or no-rule, cannot be synthesized in any form of rule because it is, by definition, in-different to and disinterested in every form of rule. Because no form of rule can bring into a unity the desire of the people, social division perdures, and every attempt at establishing political order must position itself *with respect to its conflict*.

The state of the new prince builds its foundation, that is, erects constituted power, through an interpretation or self-positioning with respect to the people's indifference to rule. The institutional expression of this princely interpretation of the people's desire for no-rule is civil society: a formal equality of all members before the law, based on the security of each member's negative liberty (i.e. of its possessions). The state of the new prince is nothing other than the active corruption of the desire for nondomination into negative liberty, the secured pursuit of which defines the space of a civil society.

The elision of the figure of the civil prince in his interpretation of Machiavelli accounts for Negri's inability to see in Machiavelli's text the answer to his own question: 'for whom are the arms? For the prince or for the people? How can "one's own arms" not be democratic arms?' (Negri 1999a: 53). In fact, for Machiavelli there is no univocal answer: the people's arms are both for the state and for the people. The series that constitutes the state is revolutionary, as revolutionary as the revolution that suspends it. In the former case, constituent power is employed by the civil prince on the people so as to make them serve as foundation of constituted power, by arming them and securing them at the same time, and by captivating their desire for no-rule in the form of the secure pursuit of negative liberty.

It is important to note that for Machiavelli there is no 'necessity' for constituent power to accomplish itself as constituted power founded on a civil society. This accomplishment is only a contingent, but effective, political interpretation given by the new prince to the indifference of the people to every form of rule. In the *Discourses on Livy* Machiavelli also outlines the contrary scenario that unfolds once the indifference to rule of the 'people' becomes constituent, and the legal domination of a civil society is resisted in the revolutionary emergence of a republic.

This republican moment of Machiavelli's discourse is both identified and miscontrued by Negri's reading of the *Discourses on Livy* as a

> celebration of the republican prince. The absoluteness of the political, invented in *The Prince*, is made to live in the republic: only the republic, only democracy, is absolute government ... . Machiavelli puts the principle [constituent power] at the service of democratic government. (Negri 1999a: 62)

Negri's synthesis of *The Prince* and *Discourses on Livy* in the idea that the republic is the prince, or democracy is the principle of constituent power, is overly hasty. In one sense it is correct, because 'the *Discourses* will be nothing but the demonstration that the only content of the constituent form is the people, that the only constitution of the Prince is democracy. A research toward the "*institutio populi*"' (Negri 1999a: 66). In fact, Machiavelli does think the people as constituent power, as political agency. But Negri's outright identification of the sense of this agency with that of the new prince misses the point that the people cannot become constituent power in the same way as the new prince: their agency is not directed to the foundation of a form of government at all, but to the contestation of, and resistance to, every instance of government as such. The *institutio populi* is intentionally aporetic: it achieves itself only in the practice of the critique and revolution of every 'institution', of every form of government.

For Negri, conversely, a 'republican synthesis' between 'people' and government is eminently possible: 'the virtue of the Roman consul and his youth are called to exalt the force of the plebs in the construction of the republican synthesis ... vindication of the legitimacy of the government of the multitude—thus of democracy as the best form of government' (Negri 1999a: 69). But such a synthesis requires belief in the reassuring *topos* of the productivity of social conflict: 'only when disunion has become the key of institutional relations absolute government can be formed: as democratic government that does not hide differences, but asks the citizens to always reconstruct unity out of differences' (Negri 1999a: 80). Social conflict and difference become the means towards an institutional end: the resistance to and revolution of constituted government is for the sake of *revolutionary government*, of 'the prince [as] democracy ... . Machiavelli's problem will never be that of closing down the revolution: the constitution for him is always the opening of the revolutionary process of the multitude' (Negri 1999a: 81). Here it is clear that the revolution is kept open-ended, unlimited, not by itself but only through the repeated intervention of a revolutionary *government*, of a princely democracy which employs its constituent power to found a paradoxical form of government: the government that counters every constituted, civil government, what Negri also calls revolutionary government as 'counter-power'. In the reading of Machiavelli that I am suggesting, instead, the social conflict between rule and no-rule is irresolvable in any political form of government, whether revolutionary or civil, and is the ungrounding ground of the political as constituent power of separation from the social. The 'people' emerge as constituent power precisely to reduce the political form to its conflictual origin, to reinscribe in every future political form the insurpassable difference between governing and resisting government.

At stake in these divergent readings is the meaning of Machiavelli's theory of 'return to beginnings' which crowns his idea of revolutionary action.

Because I am speaking of mixed bodies, such as republics and sects, I say that those alterations are for safety that lead them back toward their beginnings. So those are better ordered and have longer life that by means of their orders can often be renewed or indeed that through some accident outside the said order come to the said renewal. And it is a thing clearer than light that these bodies do not last if they do not renew themselves. (Machiavelli 1996: bk 3, ch. 1, 209)

Negri's interpretation of Machiavelli is significant also because he identifies the connection between Machiavelli's idea of the conflictual relation of *virtù* (constituent power) and *fortuna* (constituted power) and his theory of return to beginnings. Where Negri errs, in my opinion, is in understanding the theory of the return to beginnings as a *resolution* of the conflictual relation between constituent and constituted powers, rather than as describing the character of its historical happening.

For Negri, the lack of synthesis between constituent and constituted powers (i.e. the conflictuality between *virtù* and *fortuna*) can be *turned back* into a force for achieving synthesis *in the social and as the social*. It is only in the *returning* of constituent power *back to its beginning*, i.e. back to social production, that a revolution takes place.

> Constituent power is the capacity to return to reality, organize a dynamic structure, and construct a forming form that, through compromises, balances of force, different orders and equilibria, always recuperates the rationality of the principles, that is, the material adequacy of the political with respect to the social and its indefinite movement. (Negri 1999a: 305)

Negri employs the negativity of the political (its absence of synthesis with constituted powers) towards a synthesis at the level of society, of labor. And it is such a return of the political into the social that he calls the 'reform of the Renaissance', a reform that is carried forth by that 'other tradition of modern metaphysics from Machiavelli and Spinoza to Marx'.

> What is the Renaissance? It was the rediscovery of freedom and with it of the virtue of constructing, of inventing: at the same time it was the discovery of the possibility and the capacity of accumulating. Yet through accumulation fortune was built, and fortune so established opposed virtue .... The only possibility of resisting the perversion of the development of virtue and its dialectic is the foundation of a collective subject that opposes this process, who tries to fix the accumulation not of fortune but of virtue .... Only in the forms of democracy and of the government of the multitude will this project be conceivable. (Negri 1999a: 76)

For Negri, Machiavelli's idea of the political in its autonomy from the 'economic' shows itself first and foremost as a synthesis of labor that fixes 'the accumulation not of *fortuna* but of virtue'. The final goal of every constituent 'return to beginning' is 'inserting the production of the political into the creation of the social' (Negri 1999a: 307).

REVOLUTION AND REPETITION:
THE COMMUNE AND MACHIAVELLIAN DEMOCRACY

The reduction of the political into the social in Negri, although it seeks to abolish all constituted power, does nonetheless preserve a separation between the political and the social. Negri's description of constituent power as what achieves the emancipation of living labor does have a distinguishable political character, exemplified by the Paris Commune of 1871. In the commune, constituent power takes the shape of 'a working men's government', 'a government of the people by the people',[35] a democracy as 'absolute government' in which 'the critique of [constituted] power is combined with the emancipation of labor', i.e. in which constituent power is assigned the task of abolishing the state ('critique of power') and assumes, for once, a political form, but only, again citing Marx, 'the political form at last discovered under which to work out the economical emancipation of labor' (Marx, cited in Negri 1999a: 32). Absolute democracy of this kind, constituent power of this kind, is what Negri calls the 'subject that allows us to sustain adequately the concept of constitution as absolute procedure' (Negri 1999a: 30).

And yet an ambiguity remains: can this revolutionary 'subject' still be called 'citizen'? If the commune is that form of revolutionary government in which, as Marx puts it, 'real, individual man resumes the abstract citizen into himself ... . [and has] recognized and organized his *forces propres* as social forces so that social force is no longer separated from him in the form of political force', does there remain a space for political life? After all, will the commune, conceived as the form of government that leads to communism, not perish once its end, the emancipation of living labor, is achieved? In what sense can one say that communist cooperation, this final goal of the reduction of politics into the social, of the socialization of the political, is still 'political' or requires the 'politicization' of anyone?

Significantly, Arendt's *On Revolution*, in spite of its massive critique of Marx, ends up precisely in the same place where Negri identifies a 'Marx beyond Marx': in the theory of the commune. That this should be the case is not surprising, for by the last chapter of her text Arendt recognizes that her 'solution' to the problem of founding political freedom in a constitutional state is no such thing.

The failure of post-revolutionary thought to remember the revolutionary spirit ... was preceded by the failure of the revolution to provide it with a lasting institution ... . In this republic, as it presently turned out, there was no space reserved, no room left for the exercise of precisely those qualities which had been instrumental in building it .... The perplexity was very simple and, stated in logical terms, it seemed unsolvable: if foundation was the aim and the end of revolution, then the revolutionary spirit was not merely the spirit of beginning something new but of starting something permanent and enduring; a lasting institution, embodying this spirit and encouraging it to new achievements, would be self-defeating. (Arendt 1963: 232)

Arendt repeatedly speaks of the 'tragedy' represented by the American Revolution (Arendt 1963: 231–5). In giving itself a constitution, the revolution, far from preserving the 'spaces of freedom' where the 'people' could act as citizens, where they could exercise 'the right "to be a participator in government"' (Arendt 1963: 218), was directly responsible for the withering away of the revolutionary spirit, and 'eventually cheated them of their proudest possession' (Arendt 1963: 239).

For Arendt, the American Revolution, and along with it the entire modern revolutionary tradition, repeatedly betrays that 'entirely new form of government, with a new public space for freedom which was constituted and organized during the course of the revolution itself': the communes, the councils, the *Räte*, the *soviets* (Arendt 1963: 249). It is only in the communal council system, perhaps best represented for Arendt by Jefferson's proposed 'republic of wards', that all the elements of the social are *politicized*, not in a separated, constituted form of government, but *amidst the social itself.*

If the ultimate end of revolution was freedom and the constitution of a public space where freedom could appear ... then *the elementary republics of wards, the only tangible place where everyone could be free*, actually were the end of the great republic whose chief purpose in domestic affairs should have been to provide the people with such places of freedom and to protect them. (Arendt 1963: 255, emphasis mine)

In Arendt, as in Negri, the revolution is a return of the political, of constituent power, back to the social, but here, unlike in Negri, the task is the politicization of the social, down to its most 'elementary' constituents: 'the basic assumption of the ward system [is that] ... no one could be called either happy or free without participating, and having a share, in public power' (Arendt 1963: 255). The commune, for Arendt, is the name for the only *revolutionary form of government*, whereas for Negri the revolution has as its task the socialization of the political, giving rise to a *form of revolutionary government* that does not work toward the universalizing of participation in government, but rather toward the goal of cooperative production.

At this point, the question poses itself: is the 'tragedy' of the modern revolutionary tradition simply the fact that all revolutions repeatedly missed the chance to establish the only truly revolutionary form of government, as Arendt has it? Or does the 'tragedy' not reveal something more radical still, something expressed in the very *repetition* of revolutionary experiences throughout modernity: the inevitable aporia of institutionalizing, in any political form of government, the experience of political freedom? In this case, the repetition itself would not signal, as such, a failure of revolutions, but rather their most proper character: that political freedom as constituent power can only exist in the essentially iterable dimension of the event, rather than of form.

The last chapter of *On Revolution* lets itself be read as a meditation on the radical historicity of political freedom, on the sense in which the 'revolutionary spirit' manifests itself only through the repetition of political events from which emerge extraconstitutional 'spaces of freedom'. The accent falls here on the repetition of these events, more than on the possible 'form' or 'structure' of these spaces. What strikes Arendt is that 'the mere enumeration of these dates suggests a continuity that in fact never existed. It is precisely the absence of continuity, tradition, and organized influence that makes the sameness of the phenomenon striking' (Arendt 1963: 262). The phenomenon that calls for thinking is the emergence of republican events (communes) in which the 'revolutionary spirit' survives and gives rise to a paradoxical continuity between what is radically discontinuous, a paradoxical tradition of events that in themselves destroy tradition, a paradoxical inheritance coming from events which have nothing to offer, which are not constituent in any *positive* sense.

Although Arendt still mentions that the actors of revolutions always 'intended' to found the republic (as political form), at this point her attention is focused on why such intention is completely empty, why all 'foundations' fail, as it were a priori, to achieve this end (Arendt 1963: 264). By the end of *On Revolution*, Arendt no longer believes in the project of *constitutio libertatis*, in the coincidence of beginning and authority, of political freedom and state. Instead something quite different comes into the field of vision. First, the coincidence of beginning with what I have been calling the eventual. Second, the impossibility of thinking the eventual and the beginning otherwise than as an originary repetition, as a matter of inheritance (of coming, always already, 'after' what is, for ever, lost). Arendt intuits, without ever articulating it explicitly, that the republican event is a beginning only to the extent that it loses, for ever, its foundational or absolute instance: that is why this beginning, this event, is immediately also an originary repetition, and has the structure of inheritance. The last chapter is entitled 'The Revolutionary Tradition and Its Lost Treasure', and carries an epigraph by René Char: 'Notre héritage n'est précédé d'aucun testament'. Read in the light of all the foregoing, these texts now seem to say that the 'revolutionary spirit' survives if, and only if, there is an assumption of the fact that the 'treasure' (the mythical coincidence of freedom and foundation which every revolution seeks) is always already lost. The 'revolutionary spirit' emerges wherever the desire for a republic, the desire for freedom as absence of rule, understands itself as an event, that is, as a pure inheritance ('pure' in the sense that there is nothing to be inherited). One always inherits the lostness of a 'treasure'. This is the intrinsic 'poverty' of freedom, the inheritance of which, as Char says, cannot be preceded by any testament.

I will close by returning to Machiavelli's formula for revolution: the 'return to beginnings'. What is interesting in this formula is that it does not refer to a reduction of the political into the social, whether this reduction is for the sake of socializing the political, as in Negri, or for the sake of politicizing the social, as in Arendt. Whenever the 'people', the bearers of the desire for no-rule, become constituent power, what returns is the originary sense of the separation of the political: what returns is the irreducible difference between ruling and no-rule, the absoluteness of the facticity of resistance. Above all, what returns is the expression of this difference, the originary sense of the separation of the political, which is nothing short of the separation between beginning and founding. In Machiavelli, the 'people' become constituent power by returning to the beginning in its sovereign indifference to the project of founding any form of government whatsoever. The return to beginnings does not disclose the possibility of founding a form of revolutionary government, as Negri claims, nor does it disclose the possibility of founding a new, revolutionary form of government, as Arendt claims, but something quite different: the anti-foundational uncoupling of revolution from foundation, or, to put it in other terms, the *dissemination of beginnings*, which only as disseminated can be revolutionary. Such an understanding of Machiavellian democracy calls for two theoretical tasks: reformulating a theory of democracy as commune/ist, as the expression of a sovereign resistance to rule, which is the sole content of the constituent power of the people; and the formulation of a political theory of originary repetition as matrix of radical innovation, for the uncoupling of revolution and foundation requires that the event of political freedom be thought in terms of the coincidence of difference and repetition, of singularity and iterability. These are the unfinished tasks for radical democratic thinking today.

NOTES

1. The exemplary cases of such juridification of freedom in liberal–democratic discourse remain John Rawls and Jürgen Habermas.
2. In the 1920s and 1930s, Schmitt and Gramsci are among those who try to think about dictatorship (of the proletariat and otherwise) through the connection of Marx and Machiavelli. After the war, Cassirer, Aron, Strauss, and Arendt are among those who see this connection as tendentially totalitarian.
3. There are some important precedents to Lefort's project. See, for instance, the reading of Machiavelli with Marx offered by Maurice Merleau-Ponty in his 1949 text, 'A Note on Machiavelli' (Merleau-Ponty 1949: 211–23). In Italy, see the reading of Machiavelli proposed by Gennaro Sasso in the late 1950s. The appropriation of Machiavelli to the so-called 'republican revival' occurs later, beginning with Pocock's work and pursued, in different directions, by Skinner and, lately, Viroli and Pettit. In the American context, see the work of Michelman and Sunstein.
4. On the history and idea of freedom as nondomination, see Skinner 1998 and Pettit 1997.
5. Emphasis mine. The full citation runs as follows: 'Only when real, individual man resumes the abstract citizen into himself and as an individual man has become a species-being in his empirical life, his individual work and his individual relationships, only when man has recognized and organized his *forces propres* as *social forces* so that social force is no longer separated from him in the form of *political* force, only then will human emancipation be completed' (Marx 1975: 234). On the later critique of republicanism and on its social realization, see Karl Marx, *The Eighteenth Brumaire of Louis Bonaparte* and *The Civil War in France* in Marx 1996.
6. See the crucial essay by Pasquale Pasquino, 'The constitutional republicanism of Emmanuel Sieyès' (Pasquino 1994: 107–17).
7. The 'space of appearance' which is coeval with political freedom 'predates … all formal constitution of the public realm and various forms of government, that is, the various forms in which the public realm can be organized' (Arendt 1958: 199). For sure, Arendt does problematize the potential for this space of appearance, considered on its own terms, to last in time. In this context she elaborates a complex theory of promising. But one thing is to promise freedom, quite another is to give freedom a foundation, to secure it in a way that sidesteps the well-known adage that 'promises are only promises'. If promising may well have an essential relation to free action, foundation does not; or, at the very least, this relation is far from evident.
8. Only 'where the liberation from oppression aims at least at the constitution of freedom can we speak of revolution' (Arendt 1963: 35).
9. See Arendt's clear distinction between a 'free republic' and 'limited government' or 'civilized government' or 'civil rights': 'For political freedom, generally speaking, means the right "to be a participator in government", or it means nothing' (Arendt 1963: 218).
10. 'The direction of the American Revolution remained committed to the foundation of freedom and the establishment of lasting institutions, and to those who acted in this direction nothing was permitted that would have been outside the range of civil law. The direction of the French Revolution was deflected almost from its beginning from this course of foundation through the immediacy of suffering; it was determined by the exigencies of liberation not from tyranny but from necessity, and it was actuated by the limitless immensity of both the people's misery and the pity this misery inspired. The lawlessness of the "all is permitted" sprang here still from the sentiments of the heart whose very boundlessness helped in the unleashing of a stream of boundless violence' (Arendt 1963: 92).
11. The belief that one cannot free oneself from necessity without becoming enslaved is fundamental to Arendt. Here she departs from Machiavelli and the moderns and joins the ancients, for whom the distinction between what is necessary and what is contingent is determined by nature. Since every form of activity that is done 'from

necessity', such as taking care of one's basic needs, seems to be, by definition, an unfree or enslaving form of activity; and given that the cause of such slavery, i.e. what is necessary, is determined by nature, it follows that the domain of necessity calls for a 'natural' slavery, or a 'natural' and 'prepolitical' form of domination. For Arendt, the activity of labor, along with its division, and, in general, the whole realm of the social, is essentially linked to the domain of necessity and need, with its engendering of quasi-natural relations of enslavement.

12. In *On Revolution*, Arendt offers the following formulation: 'To the extent that the greatest event in every revolution is the act of foundation, the spirit of revolution contains two elements which to us seem irreconcilable and even contradictory. The act of founding the new body politic, of devising the new form of government, involves the grave concern with the stability and durability of the new structure; the experience, on the other hand, which those who are engaged in this grave business are bound to have is the exhilarating awareness of the human capacity of beginning, the high spirits which have always attended the birth of something new on earth' (Arendt 1963: 223).

13. The key point here is that for Arendt the 'separation of powers' amounts to the creation of powers. Here one sees the positive character of constituent power as the power of 'separation'.

14. For the definition of power as an 'end in itself', see Arendt 1972: 150–1.

15. Elsewhere Arendt does say that power 'needs legitimacy', but she immediately adds that 'legitimacy, when challenged, bases itself on an appeal to the *past*' (Arendt 1972: 151, emphasis mine). But if 'power springs up *whenever* people get together and act in concert' (Arendt 1972: 151, emphasis mine), then there is obviously a tension between power (which belongs to any possible present) and legitimacy (which belongs to a given past).

16. On this connection between Arendt and Machiavelli, see Honig 1993: ch. 4, passim.

17. For a detailed and argued exposition of my interpretation of Machiavelli suggested in this essay, I take the liberty to refer the interested reader to my *Between Form and Event: Machiavelli's Theory of Political Freedom* (Vatter 2000).

18. Theories of the internal relation between repetition and beginning, or originary repetition, are found in Derrida 1967 and Deleuze 1968a.

19. For the early texts, see Negri 1988.

20. On the theme of moving 'beyond Marx' one recalls Negri 1979 and Negri 1981. In *Insurgencies* the formula reappears: to theorize how 'constituent power constitutes society and identifies the social and the political in an ontological nexus' would be to go 'beyond Marx' (Negri 1999a: 328).

21. As can be seen from what is becoming his best known work, *Empire* (Hardt and Negri 2000).

22. In my opinion, but this would require another essay to demonstrate, the lack of a theory of constituted power is resolved in neither of Negri's early collaborative works with Michael Hardt: *Labor of Dionysus: A Critique of the State-Form* (Hardt and Negri 1994) and *Empire* (Hardt and Negri 2000). Since both turn around the idea of constituent power, they find their theoretical reservoir in the text of *Insurgencies*, on which my comments will focus.

23. Negri speaks of the 'mortal struggle between democracy and constitutionalism' (Negri 1999a: 11).

24. Or, as Negri puts it, between 'the right to resistance', with which he correctly sees constituent power linked from the beginning of its history, and the 'mechanism of representation' that is essential to every political form, both modern and ancient (Negri 1999a: 3). On the principle of representation, see Manin 1997.

25. 'Arendt well understood this truth about constituent power' (Negri 1999a: 15).

26. Negri refers to 'an absolute process—all-powerful and expansive, unlimited and unfinalized' (Negri 1999a: 14).

27. Negri does not treat Lefort or Castoriadis at any length: in two footnotes (Negri 1999a: 340) he simply dispatches their thought as a psychoanalytically inspired, 'neoliberal' dispersal of Arendt's central intuition concerning the absolute character of constituent power.

28. The posthumous writings of Althusser are crucial for the development of Negri's recent thought, but he does not seem to have recognized Althusser's point that, if there is no production without reproduction, then there is no constituent power without constituted power—a point that puts into question the very attribution of 'absoluteness' to constituent power. In this sense, Althusser is closer to Lefort's critique of Marx's idea of ideology in Lefort 1986: 200ff. There Lefort argues that ideology is part of the 'imaginary' of the social and emerges directly from it, as its attempt to occlude its own division and historicity. On Negri's relation to Althusser, see Negri 1996.

29. 'The praxis of constituent power has been the door through which the multitude's democratic will (and consequently the social question) has entered the political system—destroying constitutionalism or in any case significantly weakening it' (Negri 1999a: 10).

30. 'Machiavelli's chief theoretical operation thus consists of reading mutation as a global structure, traversed throughout by human action' (Negri 1999a: 40).

31. For a detailed analysis of Machiavelli's theory of *virtù* and *fortuna* along these lines, I refer to my essay 'Chapitre XXV du *Prince*: l'histoire comme effet de l'action libre' (Vatter 2001).

32. 'The world can be said to be *accomplished fact* [*le fait accompli*], in which, once the fact is accomplished, the reign of Reason, of Sense, of Necessity and of Purpose is established. But this *accomplishment of the fact* [*accomplissement du fait*] is nothing but the pure effect of contingency, because it is suspended to the aleatoric encounter of atoms due to the swerve of the *clinamen*. Before the accomplishment of the fact, before the world, there is nothing but the non-accomplishment of the fact, the non-world which is nothing other than the unreal existence of atoms' (Althusser 1982a: 542).

33. For another example of Negri's tendentially economistic interpretation of the corruption of *virtù*: 'Why does virtue, in its development, bypass freedom and congeal into fortune as wealth, power, destiny? Why is democracy always open to corruption? The analysis of power cannot, at this point [in Harrington], become what it should become: the anatomy of political economy of rising capitalism. Indeed, only at that level could it have been understood why virtue let itself be crushed by fortune ... . Even though the economic critique is missing, we witness nonetheless the founding of a new political science which also penetrates, and not by mere chance, into a reserved territory, until now untouchable, such as that of property, into the analysis of appropriation, and into the critique of appropriative classes' (Negri 1999a: 109–10).

34. See also *Discourses on Livy*, I, 5: 'if one considers the end of the nobles and of the ignobles, one will see great desire to dominate in the former, and in the latter only desire not to be dominated; and, in consequence, a greater will to live free' (Machiavelli 1996: 18).

35. Negri cites Karl Marx, *The Civil War in France*, in Marx 1996: 191–2.

Part II

Intensive Encounters

4
Antonio Negri, French Nietzschean? From the Will to Power to the Ontology of Power[1]

Judith Revel

Translated by Timothy S. Murphy

What Antonio Negri's thought owes to Machiavelli, Spinoza, or Marx can certainly be taken as the object of scholarly discussions; but the obviousness of this line of descent—and the explicit claim to this triple lineage, made many times by Negri himself—limits the possibilities of debate to questions of interpretation of one or another aspect of those authors's thought *within* an indisputable assumption of their centrality. The link between Antonio Negri's work and Nietzschean thought, on the other hand, poses quite different problems. The first problem immediately appears in the form of a stumbling block as soon as one turns one's attention to contemporary readings of Nietzsche. On the one hand, the majority of these readings— and the way in which their historical context has overdetermined their contents—require an extremely precise periodization which cannot be made without reconstituting a space of thought which corresponds to them.[2] On the other hand, the most complex of these contemporary readings— complex not only because of the number of agents engaged with them but also because of the wealth and variety of materials that they have produced—clearly seem to be linked to what some people have called 'the thought of '68 [*la pensée 68*]', which in fact today, nearly 40 years later, still possesses a great polemical charge. In both cases, it is obviously difficult to do entirely without what Foucault called a 'history of systems of thought' or, more banally, a history of the contemporary reception of Nietzsche, in order to pinpoint what we might characterize as a 'generational element' operating not only in Negri but also, in parallel fashion, in Deleuze and Guattari, in Lyotard, in Granier, to a certain extent in Derrida, and even in Foucault himself. In short, to pose the problem of the relationship between Negri's thought and Nietzsche's work is to pose the problem of identifying a philosophical 'generation', membership of which immediately reflects a determination that is simultaneously philosophical and political; but to pose this problem is also to see where these contemporary readings have conformed to different logics, uses, and necessities.

Then there is the second problem. Among the philosophers whom we have mentioned as illustrations of 'the thought of '68', neither the name nor the contents of which goes without saying since we find so many heterogeneous elements therein, there are no representatives of Italian thought. In fact, here we are actually referring more to French poststructuralism than to some generic 'thought of '68', and it is French poststructuralism that is generally charged with manifesting a Nietzscheanism that, in an extremely debatable amalgamation to which we will return, included a reaction to the dominant French Hegelianism of the early postwar years, a radical critique of the models of positivist historiography (as if Nietzsche suddenly crossed paths with Annales School historiography), and a more literary and 'Romantically' rebellious reading in the wake of '68 for which Nietzsche would become— along with Artaud, Klossowski, Bataille, or Blanchot—the tutelary figure of a vast questioning of bourgeois values and the very foundations of Western metaphysics. In short, Nietzsche was used simultaneously in anti-Kojévean, para-Braudelian, transgressive and relativist ways.

But Nietzsche was not being read only in France. In Italy, the reading of Nietzsche—and the intellectual ferment to which it gave rise—was just as intense from the start of the 1960s onward. Yet the French and Italian readings, which at the beginning were not without points of contact, gave rise to forms of thought that were radically different not only in their relationships to Nietzsche in the strict sense, but also in the philosophical, ethical, and political consequences in which they rapidly became engaged. Hence an obvious difficulty: why—and how—did Antonio Negri, trained in the heterodox Italian Marxism of *Quaderni Rossi* before 1968, professor of 'state doctrine' at the University of Padua, end up being a reader of Nietzsche who is infinitely closer to a Gilles Deleuze—who emerged not from Marxism but from the history of philosophy—than to a Giorgio Colli or a Mazzino Montinari, or even—and the difference is becoming blatant—to a Gianni Vattimo or a Massimo Cacciari? In short, how can we speak of Negri's 'French Nietzscheanism', even if we understand this geographical determination more as a genuine hermeneutical and political choice than as a 'national' qualification? And on the basis of what strategic stakes are the true divisions between French-style Nietzscheanism and Italian Nietzscheanism really articulated?

In a special issue of *Magazine littéraire* dedicated to Nietzsche and published in 1992 (*Magazine littéraire* 1992),[3] Negri contributed a short text on the relationship of Marxists to the author of *Zarathustra* (Negri 1992). In the same issue, Gianni Vattimo was given the task of discussing what he calls 'the Italian renaissance' of Nietzscheanism (Vattimo 1992). The difference between the two interventions is blatant, and not only because unlike Vattimo, whose double link to Nietzsche and Heidegger has been the object of explicit analyses and gives direction to his entire philosophical itinerary, Negri has never been claimed as a Nietzschean and has practically never written on Nietzsche. For Negri, it is first of all a matter of retracing the genealogy of a Marxism that sees in Nietzsche an astonishing precursor with an astonishing anticipatory power [*puissance*] on at least two essential terrains—on the one hand, the definition of materialism, and on the other, the judgment passed on modernity—which together comprise the two principal aspects of the critique of the bourgeois world. But it is also quite obvious that Negri actually considers himself to be separate from this genealogy that he reconstitutes, and that the idea of a Nietzsche who can be used as the keystone to a new materialism does not efface Nietzsche the simultaneously liberal and fascist 'enemy', the Nietzsche to whom Lukács refers, for example.

Thus he begins with Lukács's violent anti-Nietzschean charges. Citing *The Destruction of Reason* several times, Negri actually demonstrates how Lukács, taking up the Nazi interpretation of Nietzsche (particularly that of Alfred Bäumler, the official introducer of Nietzsche's works during the 1930s), is really directing his critique of Nietzsche much more broadly against both bourgeois irrationalism and Zhdanovist materialism at the same time. Nietzsche thus becomes a weapon against bourgeois decadence because he is the most flagrant example of it,[4] but at the same time he is also the terrain on which two opposed Marxist tendencies confront one another:

> Lukács's attack on Nietzsche, considered as the sublime representative of irrationalism, appears here in its true light: it is an attack directed against all the currents of socialism that do not assume modernization as the practical contents of utopia, which is to say—according to Lukács—the rational transformation of society according to the rules of progress, the all-out development of liberty, equality and peace. (Negri 1992: 82)

But if Negri understands quite well that which, in Lukács, was reacting to Zhdanovist populism and to that kind of cynical voluntarism in political matters, if he insists on the fact that 'the anti-Nietzschean Lukács is the anti-Stalinist Lukács', the fact remains that Lukács's reading merely throws down the gauntlet of a challenge—of progress, or of an Enlightenment spirit reinvested in the workers's movement—that was addressed first of all to the bourgeoisie, and that he paradoxically forgets to note that the first to diagnose the fate of the bourgeoisie as decadence and its essence as nihilism was precisely Nietzsche himself.

Thus we are invited, under rather strange circumstances, to the reconstruction of a debate within European Marxism—a reconstruction which, precisely because it sets in opposition not only two readings of Nietzsche but two interpretations of Marxism, actually allows Negri to situate himself in a third place, in an elsewhere that is based simultaneously on a different reading of Nietzsche and a different reading of Marx. Bizarrely, this third reading is not directly opposed to the two earlier ones, but is preceded by a final historical excursus on the way in which Nietzsche has been read instead as a materialist author—as if Negri had to pass by way of this rehabilitation in order to be able finally to speak of his own Nietzscheanism. The 'materialist Nietzsche' to which he thereafter refers corresponds to an entire literature that circulated during the 1950s but actually goes back to the 1930s, a literature that was bound up precisely with efforts to demolish the image of a Nazi Nietzsche. Because they were all adversaries of Nazism, Karl Löwith, Karl Jaspers, Edgar Salin, Erich Podach, and Heinrich Mann could credibly attempt to construct a different image of Nietzsche, and on the basis of that image, a new actuality of Nietzsche became possible 20 years later. This 'innocent' Nietzsche is no longer responsible for Nazism:

> and furthermore, he never ceased to denounce nationalism and declare culture and the State his antagonists. He was always on the side of the oppressed and conceived liberation as production—new production, free and young production. The Dionysiac theme is a materialist and productive theme: 'We are all workers'. (Negri 1992: 83)

But if we find this theme of new production 20 years later, in Deleuze as in Negri, in the form of a philosophy of power [*puissance*], as if it were a matter of passing Nietzsche through the riddle of Spinoza—but we will soon return to this essential point—Negri himself is the first to recognize that this bowdlerization of 'Nietzsche without Zarathustra', reduced to a sort of post-Enlightenment critique, is just as wholly artificial as the Nazi and/or irrationalist Nietzsche because it is truncated, not only denuded of an entire portion of the reflection that was precisely supposed to be restored to the reading, but also crystallized around the elements that are always the same ones, the dissolution of values and/or the definition of a materialism within a modernity that we never have done with reproducing.

At the end of his text, Negri finally arrives at his own relationship to Nietzsche, that is, at the Nietzscheanism of 1960s critical Marxism, but in a paragraph and a half he can only rapidly state three points that distinguish it from the Marxist readings that have preceded it. First: the fundamental turn actually corresponded to the introduction of a kind of interpretation that emphasized in Nietzsche 'the singular, progressive opening up of his anti-modernism' (Negri 1992: 83). This turn was first inferred by Mazzino Montinari, in the wake of the approach that Luporini and Timpanaro had applied to the works of Giacomo Leopardi, which could be considered in many ways as anticipating those of Nietzsche. '*De te fabula narratur*: the possibility of going beyond the oppressive stranglehold of socialism, rationality and modernity', Negri comments (Negri 1992: 83). Second: it was necessary to read Nietzsche no longer from within a modernity for which he would serve as the signifier of profound crisis, decadence or alternately even the horizon of redemption, but instead in an *antimodern* manner. This function of antimodernity had no intention of promoting a return to the premodern, or playing the minstrel of Rousseauesque nostalgia for a lost Garden of Eden, but dared to affirm—and this was its novelty—the necessity of overcoming modernity, or even the idea that a different model of modernity was possible, a model which in no way corresponded to that which had been realized in history. This alone is what made possible a use of Nietzsche that, for Negri, would join the lineage begun by Machiavelli and Spinoza—and of course via a reading of Marx that insists on 'the urgency of the critical need to go beyond capitalist modernity in order to construct socialism' (Negri 1992: 83) and refuses to allow itself to be trapped by the contingent (and in those days dramatic) necessities of 'real socialism', in either its Lukácsian or it Zhdanovist versions. Third: it involves displacing the epicenter of Nietzsche's work away from the idea of the transmutation of values (on which Lukács's anti-Nietzschean critique was essentially based) or away from the figure of the overman interpreted in a Bolshevik manner as the proletarian (in the Stalinist version of dialectical materialism) and toward the will to power [*puissance*] as the subjective power of creation and inauguration and the construction of a model of historicity that functions as a critique of scientific positivism and of the Hegelian dialectic at the same time. The extraordinary editorial work of Giorgio Colli and Mazzino Montinari, at the beginning of the 1960s, had made accessible what was in reality a true first edition of certain Nietzschean texts, including *The Will to Power*, *Ecce Homo* and the *Letters*. And the intersection of the reading of *Untimely Meditations* with attempts to redefine the regime of historicity of forms of knowledge [*savoirs*] and representation at the heart of European historiography permitted in parallel fashion a 'creative reopening of the historicity that critical Marxism called communism' (Negri 1992: 83). In short, critical Marxism found in Nietzsche a reformulation of the link between subjectivity and production from the viewpoint of creation, a violent polemic against a dialectical understanding of history, and a radical critique of real socialism in all its varieties, all at the same time.

We can see, then, where this triple perspective was able to intersect with the work of Gilles Deleuze or Michel Foucault. But if Negri, at the very end of his text, makes a fleeting allusion to this, he does not linger over this encounter. Before returning to the way that Italian critical Marxism was able to traverse—and in its turn be traversed by—French poststructuralist thought by means of a common motif which was precisely the emergence of this new reading of Nietzsche on the basis of a polemical will and a common critique, let's linger for a moment over another great Nietzschean current that appeared during the same period in Italy.

We have made several allusions to the very important editorial work of Colli and Montinari, published from 1964 onward by the Italian publisher Adelphi. This new critical edition which, as we mentioned, presented certain Nietzschean texts for the first time, would become the basis for all the other critical editions published in the following years in languages other than Italian (including the French standard edition, by Gallimard, and the German edition itself).[5] To understand the climate of that era, we must recall that the Einaudi publishing house, which was then the bastion of leftist culture on the Italian peninsula, had declined the project after intense internal discussions over the opportunity to publish a philosopher whose thought had been compromised by the uses to which Nazism had put it. This decision drove some Einaudi editors to resign in order to found a new publishing house, Adelphi,[6] the image of which would rapidly become associated not only with Nietzsche's works but also with Heidegger's, which Adelphi would soon publish.

Thus Colli and Montinari had the great merit of permitting readers to gain direct access to the texts and providing them with a significant critical apparatus, but they did not really leave much of a mark on the reading of Nietzsche from a theoretical point of view. Each of them of course published a certain number of essays,[7] but while Montinari concentrated largely on the philological aspects—which he considered essential tools for combating the antidemocratic, Nazi image of Nietzsche—Colli focused mainly on the early Nietzsche and on the more literary and Schopenhauerian aspects of his thought. Thus he saw *The Birth of Tragedy* as 'Nietzsche's most mystical work, in the sense that it necessitates an initiation ... Thus *The Birth of Tragedy* is also Nietzsche's most difficult work' (Colli 1996: 13). The Dionysiac aspects were evaluated by means of a sort of extreme aestheticization of the world that sometimes, unfortunately, bore a greater resemblance to a Romantic—perhaps even Nervalian—reading of Nietzsche than to a careful analysis of his arguments: 'A wave of the hand, and the world around us, with its leaden sky and its grating hours, is now only a nightmare, and the true life is dream, intoxication' (Colli 1996: 20).[8] The precedence granted to the Nietzsche–Schopenhauer or Nietzsche–Wagner connection is central to the economy of the work, which thereby privileges the tragic aspects while erasing everything that, in Nietzsche, involves the virulent critique of his own time. Very little is actually said about the complexity of Nietzsche's philosophical project, its successive modifications and different aspects; even less attention is given to the history of this thought, a thought that has so persistently been deprived of its determinate historical, social, and political context. This even leads to the paradox of commenting on Nietzsche's thinking about history—his violent charge against 'monumental history' is well known—not merely in an ahistorical manner but in an antihistoricizing one: thus Colli can say, apropos of the second *Untimely Meditation*, that it is a 'model of antihistoricity'. And Colli concludes,

> this consideration, more than any other, deserves to remain exempt from historical critique. To attempt to understand how Nietzsche arrived at the point of writing this text according to the development of his personality or the history of his time, according to whatever conditions and designs governed it, would be methodological impertinence. (Colli 1996: 37)

In short, for Colli it was not a matter of emptying out a certain model of historical intelligibility—built on teleological readings of history—but rather of rendering the philosophy impermeable to all history.

On the basis of this interpretation it will be possible to construct two great Nietzschean lines of descent that mirror one another. The first, more hermeneutic and internal to the work itself, will once again take up the centrality of tragedy, combining this with a reflection on nihilism and producing a kind of negative thought that will in reality owe everything to Heidegger's *Nietzsche*, published in two volumes in 1961. The second will claim to 'use' certain aspects of Nietzsche's thought rather than to offer a genuine effort of interpretation in the strict sense, and will insist primarily on two points that we have already mentioned: power [*puissance*] as subjective capacity for inauguration, and a new modeling of history that is simultaneously nonlinear, noncontinuous and nonteleological, which would also allow for the emergence of a new type of historiographical inquiry, the formulation of a philosophy of discontinuity, and the construction of a series of political models based on the radical opening up of time-to-come [*temps à venir*] that run counter to all the old dialectical models. In Italy, since the 1960s, Gianni Vattimo, Sergio Givone, and Massimo Cacciari—to cite only the best-known representatives of what would soon be called 'weak thought [*il pensiero debole*]'—have been the principal representatives of the first current; in the same era, mainly in France, where Heidegger's influence was weaker and historiographical reflection was extremely active,[9] philosophers such as Michel Foucault and Gilles Deleuze headed up the second current. And quite obviously, for a whole series of reasons to which we will soon return, Negri's thought belongs to the second current.

In the special issue of *Magazine littéraire* that we have already cited, Gianni Vattimo reflects on the way this Heideggerian Nietzscheanism, of which he has been one of the principal figures, was constructed. Having first recalled the fundamental importance of Colli and Montinari's work—and its limits (since Colli and Montinari 'launched a polemic against contemporary philosophy and the excessive updatings of Nietzsche's thought' (Vattimo 1992: 84))—Vattimo then emphasizes the renewal of the interpretation of Nietzsche that was inspired by Heidegger's *Nietzsche*. The Heideggerian perspective, besides privileging the mature Nietzsche instead of the young one, encouraged readings focused on two themes that are every bit as Heideggerian as (if not more so than) they are genuinely Nietzschean: the critique of metaphysics, and the relationship between nihilism and modern technics. In this way Nietzsche becomes 'the herald of a post-metaphysical thought that is based above all on nihilism as the dissolution of being that had been identified with presence, objectivity, and manipulation' (Vattimo 1992: 86). But, for Vattimo, the move to extend the Heideggerian inter-pretation involves identifying this dissolution with class conflict: 'What Heidegger calls metaphysics, and what Nietzsche helps us to overcome, is what we call in Marx's terminology the alienation connected to the division of labor' (Vattimo 1992: 86). We can understand, then, how this interpre-tation managed to dismay the adherents of critical Marxism, for whom Marx's analysis, applied to a reality of exploitation and suffering whose violence they observed daily at the factory gates and in the proletarian suburbs of northern Italy, had an entirely different content. Moreover, it is not certain that Heidegger would have recognized this as the consequence of his own thought—which, paradoxically, makes Vattimo's analysis infinitely more sympathetic than if it were limited to simple hagiographi-cal commentary.

Be that as it may, on the basis of these presuppositions Vattimo, along with a whole group of young philosophers, made up his mind to construct a thought for which

> the idea of an 'active nihilism', as Nietzsche calls it, would have to go all the way, since only on the basis of the weakening of the strong structures

of being could one hope that a new relationship between being and humanity, one that was no longer metaphysical, such as the one that Heidegger strives to think, would arise. This interpretation (which gave rise in Italy to what has been called 'weak thought') is heavily dependent on Heidegger, but one of its characteristics is that it 'doesn't take seriously' what Heidegger says about Nietzsche when he considers the latter to be merely the last thinker of metaphysics; on the other hand, it involves being faithful to Heidegger beyond the letter of his writings, by recognizing that in order truly to overcome metaphysics (being that has been reduced to presence, objectivity, etc.) one must follow Nietzsche along the path of nihilism. (Vattimo 1992: 87)

This long citation clearly demonstrates how, on the basis of the reversal of the Heideggerian image of Nietzsche as 'the height of western techno-scientific rationality' (Vattimo 1992: 86) but also—and paradoxically—on the basis of the reprise of Heidegger's theme of the critique of metaphysics, it becomes possible to make nihilism the 'constructive' moment of a new philosophy. This construction, therefore, permits it to overcome the pure negativity of the critique and make that negativity, understood here in the extreme form of nihilism, the constitutive moment of a postmetaphysical philosophy. Moreover, it is in relation to this constitutive dimension that the readings of Cacciari and Vattimo seem to diverge, the latter accusing the former of having reduced Nietzsche to the status of an instrument of deconstruction without making him the motive force of a new reality, that is, of having read Nietzsche in a disenchanted and masochistic manner: 'in Cacciari's reading [Nietzsche] is not the herald of any liberation or emancipation, but merely the adherent of an extreme and disenchanted "realism"', notes Vattimo (1992: 86), a realism whose willingness to consider nihilism as a productive matrix has instead thereby admitted that it will end up becoming the central motif of a reflection on the new forms of politics in the age of globalization.[10] It is not for us to judge the accuracy of the critiques addressed to Cacciari; even if certain passages of what remains one of Cacciari's most successful books sometimes support Vattimo's claims,[11] this is not enough to make the alternative formulated by the latter a fully convincing hypothesis.

We come now to the other great current, that of French Nietzscheanism. It is obvious that its insistence on other aspects of Nietzsche is explained by a history of the reception of German thought that is quite different, and more generally by an intellectual history that gives rise to what we have identified as the 'specificity' of French thought, particularly in the period following the Second World War. Without going into the fine details of this complex genealogy,[12] let us nevertheless emphasize the fact that the French intellectual climate has always been characterized by an ambiguous fascination with German thought: fascination insofar as it seemed to embody a tradition of the concept that was envied, perceived as excellent and to be encouraged in France; ambiguity insofar as German thought has always been submitted to an effort of reading, reinterpretation, and 'Frenchification', beyond the difficulty that the French have often had in speaking and reading the language of Goethe, that in one blow made philological care and the search for hermeneutic fidelity much less central than they had been in Italy. This is true of Kojève's and Hyppolite's Hegelianism; it is also true of all French sociology inspired by Dilthey and Weber in the wake of Raymond Aron's efforts; it is true as well for the reading of Jaspers and Husserl at the heart of what would become French existentialism; it is true, lastly, for the majority of French Heideggerian currents of the past half-century. Let us be clear: this relative indifference to philology does not in any way call into question the seriousness of the enterprises of reading that we have just mentioned; it is simply a matter of reading in order to forge tools that are useful for a thought whose necessities are themselves quite French and can be connected, on a case-by-case basis, to the contingency of the historical situation in which we find ourselves at such and such a moment, to intellectual debates that are taking place at the same moment within and outside the academic world, to phenomena of reaction in relation to intellectual tendencies that are perceived as hegemonic, etc.

All this is what Foucault is referring to when he looks back on his relationship to Nietzsche at the end of the 1970s, attempting to explain the strategic—and polemical—value of such a reference. It is undoubtedly significant that Foucault himself has indicated the pivot point of the only genuine intellectual rupture that he recognized in his reading of Nietzsche, in 1953.[13] Foucault's Nietzscheanism is actually in the first place seeking to refuse certain discourses that dominated the French philosophical scene immediately after the war, that is, the denunciation of Hegelianism on the one hand (let us not forget that Foucault was a student of Hyppolite) and a 'French-style' phenomenological discourse embodied in Sartre or Merleau-Ponty on the other. In the first case, as Foucault himself explained,

[i]t was a Hegelianism deeply penetrated by phenomenology and existentialism, which hinged on the theme of the 'unhappy consciousness'.
And essentially, that was the best the French university could offer; it was
the widest form of understanding possible for the contemporary world
which had just emerged from the tragedy of World War Two.

And he adds,

[t]he very experience of the war had shown us the necessity and the urgency of creating a society radically different from the one in which we had lived; a society that had accepted Nazism ... It's clear, then, that the Hegelianism ... which was proposed as an answer for us at the university, with its model of 'continuous' intelligibility, wasn't capable of responding to our needs. (Foucault 1991: 44–5, 47, 48)

Perhaps this is where, for Foucault, the junction with the other side of his critique opens up, that is, the side that calls into question the trans-historical or metahistorical status of the phenomenological subject. This critique is actually given a double objective: on the one hand, to attack the 'philosophies of the subject', and on the other, to attack the 'philosophies of history'. In the first case, it is a matter of refusing to settle for a preestablished theory of the subject that leads to posing the problem of such and such form of knowledge [*connaissance*] only on the basis of that theoretical self-justification [*auto-donation*]. The attack consists therefore in a critique of the subject itself, in the sense that all the solipsist philosophies descended from the Cartesian cogito give it; for Foucault, as we have already emphasized, it will be necessary to try to think the subject not as an independent, isolated, preconstituted entity which would enter into relations with the external world only on the basis of the solipsism that self-constitutes it—the vast myth of an interiority or a depth of consciousness which Nietzsche said was the invention of the philosophers—but as a decomposed self that has made 'a thousand now lost events proliferate in the sites and places of its empty synthesis' (Foucault 1977: 145–6, translation modified), a heterogeneous and diverse figure.

Furthermore, it is on the foundation of his reading of *The Genealogy of Morals, Untimely Meditations,* or *Human All Too Human* that Foucault builds his critique of the suprahistorical point of view, the notion of a history that would be a closed and reassuring unity that ultimately confines the infinite profusion of time and allows us to recognize ourselves everywhere, since consciousness is identical to itself at every point. Nietzschean discontinuity is thus also and above all the register in which the singularity of events is affirmed against the monumentality of History, against the reign of ideal significations and indefinite teleologies: it consists of tales of accidents, deviations and bifurcations, reversals, chance, and errors, which 'maintain passing events in their proper dispersion' (Foucault 1977: 146). The Nietzsche who interests Foucault is first and foremost the one who criticizes the project of a history that would function to 'compose the finally reduced diversity of time into a totality fully closed upon itself' (Foucault 1977: 152), the history that works to nullify the multiple figures of the disparate and the gap, the leap and the transformation—in a word, the figures of becoming or broken linearity. To return to the singular risk of the event, on the other hand, as Nietzsche reminds us in *Daybreak*, is to shake 'the dice-box of chance' (Nietzsche 1982: section 130) against the mystification of that unity which carries 'antiquarian history' along; and it is this dice-box that fascinates Foucault.

But what is interesting is the fact that it is not necessary to await the beginning of the 1970s and the explicit passage to the concept of genealogy in order to hear the echo of this Nietzschean influence. Before being 'genealogical', Foucault's thought is already discontinuous—or more precisely, it is in search of a model of discontinuity that will make the assumption of the genealogical dimension inevitable: if history, genealogically oriented, 'seeks to make visible all of those discontinuities that cross us' (Foucault 1977: 162), it is already present in Foucault during the 1960s in the form of a careful attention to events, i.e. temporal fissures, that manifest themselves in the form of isolated facts or through the emergence of general epistemic convergences that always present themselves against a backdrop of rupture—think of the analyses of *Madness and Civilization* (the event that represents the emergence of the reason/unreason binary of the classical age) and *The Order of Things* (the emergence of a discursive network that characterizes the human sciences), or later those of *I, Pierre Rivière* (the emergence of a case of absolute singularity) or *Le Désordre des familles* (the emergence of traces of singular existences).

Consequently, the genealogy he borrowed from Nietzsche offered Foucault a quadruple advantage: first, the possibility of thinking interruption, rupture, the leap otherwise than against a backdrop of continuity—which continued in fact to make up the notion of periodization and posed real problems of historical legitimation—or, in other words, the possibility of thinking the emergence of events without having to pose the problem of their origin; second, the possibility of stepping up the slow work of dissolving the figure of the subject that he had already begun to set in motion by means of an inverse mechanism of proliferation and dissemination of subjectivity; third, the possibility of bringing together the dimension of the episteme (concretely speaking, a medium or long duration) and that of events, and of giving an account of them simultaneously as the point of crystallization of the emergence of a discontinuity and as traces of existence; and fourth, the possibility that genealogical history is also—and above all—a problematization of our own actuality, or what Foucault will much later call a 'critical ontology of ourselves'.

Understood in this way, genealogical history is at last inscribed perfectly, even though it may appear strange, in the line of that history of the sciences of which we have already spoken, which sought to formulate the project of a history of rationality that would pose the problem of its own rationality, that is, the regime of truth upon which it was founded; and instead of seeking this truth at the foundation of every scientific endeavor, the common hypothesis held truth to be the result of discursive procedures and of relations that a certain state of knowledge [savoir] entertained with itself. Here Foucault could recognize exactly those new elements that his reading of Nietzsche had provided, namely the idea of a historicity of truth games and a determination, itself historical, of the figure of the subject as a shattered form always doomed to become other. Foucault would later write,

> This is a very important consideration in Canguilhem who, I believe, recognizes in himself a certain affinity with Nietzsche. That is why we find around the figure of Nietzsche, in spite of the paradox, a certain affinity, a certain nexus of movement and communication between the discourse about the dissolution of the subject in 'limit-experiences' ... where it was a matter of the subject transforming itself, and the discourse on the transformation of the subject itself through the elaboration of a knowledge [savoir]. (Foucault 1991: 68–9, translation modified)

That is, the attempt to retrace this history of the reciprocal constitution of objects of knowledge [savoir] and knowing subjects [sujets connaissants] will still be, in its own way, an experience 'in the style of Nietzsche'—an experience of the historicity of truth-telling and the productions of subjectivity that will be merely the point of departure for a true 'historical ontology of ourselves'.

In short, genealogy progressively constitutes itself in Foucault from within archaeology. It is a historical inquiry that is opposed to the 'metahistorical deployment of ideal significations and indefinite teleologies', opposed to the unicity of historical narrative and the search for origins, and which instead seeks the 'singularity of events outside of any monotonous finality' (Foucault 1977: 140, 139). Genealogy operates, therefore, on the basis of disparity and dispersion, chance beginnings and accidents: in no case does it claim to reassemble time in order to reestablish the continuity of history, but rather it seeks to restore their singularity to events. Do not be fooled—the genealogical approach is nevertheless not a simple empiricism, some sort of reduction to the disorder of facts made necessary by the renunciation of every perspective of linear continuity; and as Foucault specifies, this is no longer positivism in the ordinary sense of the term: in fact it is a matter of putting local, discontinuous, disqualified, illegitimate knowledges [*savoirs*] into play against the unitary theoretical instance that would claim to filter them, hierarchize them, order them in the name of one true knowledge [*connaissance*] ... Therefore genealogies are not positivist recourses to a form of science that is more attentive or more exact; genealogies are precisely *anti-sciences*. (Foucault 1994: 166)

The genealogical method is in reality an attempt to desubjectify historical knowledges [*savoirs*], that is, to render them as well capable of opposition and struggle against the 'order of discourse' that is also an order of knowledge [*savoir*].

Thus this reflection derived from Nietzsche can be summarized in the following terms: the historicization of truth, the definition of a nonteleological and discontinuous history that demands an attentive inquiry into the event, the emergence of the figure of subjectivity as simultaneously production and resistance, the transformation of the archaeological approach into a genealogical problematization, that is, into an interrogation of our own present and the discontinuity that we could establish within that present in light of a history from which we must measure our distance.

Foucault's work overlaps that of Gilles Deleuze, among others, particularly at the time of the French version of Colli and Montinari's critical edition published by Gallimard (Foucault and Deleuze 1994). Deleuze, who is more clearly situated 'within' Nietzsche's work than Foucault, is to that extent less connected to French historiography and Canguilhem's epistemology, but he in turn brings together Nietzsche and Spinoza (specifically around a concept which will subsequently be equally essential for Nietzsche, power [*puissance*]). Thus it is not surprising that their respective uses of Nietzsche would really be quite different. Of course, the joint enterprise of editing the fifth volume of the *Oeuvres philosophiques complètes* in 1967 gave rise to some shared positions. But if we compare Foucault's essay 'Nietzsche, Freud, Marx' (Foucault 1990) with any Deleuze text of the same period, we can readily grasp the major difference in approach that characterizes the two men.[14] Whereas Foucault limits himself in the last analysis to a rather punctual and restrained use of Nietzsche—broadly speaking, the Nietzsche of the *Untimely Meditations*—Deleuze is interested in something much vaster, which he often sums up in the figure of the eternal return.

Let us take for example the text that Deleuze writes for the closing session of the colloquium dedicated to Nietzsche that he organized in July 1964, 'Conclusions on the Will to Power and the Eternal Return'. It is striking to note the fact that Deleuze's whole discourse actually depends on the idea that

> the death of God, the dead God, deprives the Self of its only guarantee of identity, its substantial basis of unity: with God dead, the self dissolves or evaporates, but in a certain way, opens itself up to all the other selves, roles and characters which must be run through in a series like so many fortuitous events. (Deleuze 1967a: 118)

Heavily influenced by Klossowski's reading,[15] which he cites by name several times, Deleuze thus insists from the outset on that which for him represents the central element of Nietzsche's thought, namely the disappearance of the categories connected to identity and unity in favor of those of difference and multiplicity. This point is all the more essential for him because it allows him to execute a triple operation: in the first place, to redefine the will to power [*puissance*] at the heart of Nietzsche's *Nachlass*; next, to distinguish Nietzsche's eternal return from the formulations that were given to the notion in ancient philosophy; and lastly, to link the two figures together and relate them to what, for Deleuze, must be the task of philosophy today: to produce a new thought, which would be precisely the thought of difference and the multiple. Without entering into the details of the analyses that Deleuze develops, we must emphasize this close attention to 'Nietzsche's pluralism' (Deleuze 1967a: 118) insofar as it totally determines his reading of the texts, whatever angle of attack is chosen.[16]

In this context, Foucault's discourse is itself then bent to this reading when Deleuze, despite the fact that he does draw attention to 'Nietzsche, Freud, Marx', to which he actually only dedicates a few quick lines, goes on to reread certain passages from *The Order of Things* regarding that 'Nietzscheanism of difference and the dissolution of identity' that is his own version par excellence. Examples of these overlaps of reading—Deleuze as reader of Foucault *through Nietzsche*—are numerous. Thus Deleuze writes apropos of Nietzsche,

> Misfortune, sickness, madness, even the approach of death have two aspects: in one sense, *they separate me from my power*; in another sense, *they endow me with a strange power*, as though I possessed a dangerous means of exploration, which is also a terrifying realm to explore. (Deleuze 1967a: 125, my emphasis)

Certain passages of the book review that Deleuze wrote on the occasion of the publication of *The Order of Things* resound here in a strange yet identical manner. Apropos of the analytic of finitude that occupies the last part of the book, Deleuze notes the following:

At the same time, humanity [*l'homme*] discovers itself in two different ways: *on the one hand*, as dominated by labor, life, and language; henceforth as an object of new positive sciences, which will model themselves on biology or political economy or philology; *on the other hand*, humanity sees itself as founding this new positivity on the category of its own finitude: the metaphysics of the infinite will be replaced by an analytic of the finite ... Humanity thus comes to have a double being. What has collapsed is the sovereignty of identity in representation. (Deleuze 1966: 91)

The slippage from what Foucault said in his own 'Nietzscheanization' is plain: the split within humanity is simultaneously what separates it from power [*puissance*] and what endows it with a new power [*puissance*]; finitude, once it has been accepted, is actually the condition of possibility of positive knowledge [*connaissance*]; Deleuze reads Foucault's death of man [*l'homme*] and Nietzsche's death of God on the basis of the same interpretive matrix.

This last point, moreover, is totally explicit in Deleuze, for he never fails to place both on the same plane: thought must nevertheless be reinvented on the basis of the acknowledgement that neither humanity nor God is a term of a necessary alternative. In short, whereas Foucault limited himself to signaling the possibility of an effacement of this figure of man that we had believed was eternal—that is, outside of history—as a result of which he was content to remind us that every episteme, because it is historical and has a date of birth, also necessarily has a horizon of disappearance, Deleuze skips a step and presents an interpretation of Foucault's text that is a version of his own reading of Nietzsche:

For a long time philosophy offered you a particular alternative: God or man—or in philosophical jargon: infinite substance or the finite subject. None of that is very important anymore: the death of God, the possibility of replacing God with humanity, all the God–Human permutations, etc. It's like Foucault said, we are no more human than God, the one dies with the other. (Deleuze 1968b: 137)

This, then, explains Deleuze's insistence on the second motif that characterizes his reading of Foucault in the mid 1960s, that of a 'new thought'. This bias in reading 'a new image of thought' (Deleuze 1966: 93) into *The Order of Things*, for example—that is, discerning a second project just beneath the surface of the archaeological project of a history of our system of thought, a second project that would be the problematization of our own belonging to this system and its critique at the same time—this bias, then, is nothing more than the transposition into Foucault of the Nietzschean discourse on the 'creative selection' of the eternal return, that is, the way the eternal return, far from being the return of the identical, is on the contrary the movement that selects creative new forces and abandons the 'half-powers [*demi-puissances*]' of being. When, in reference to the 1966 book, Deleuze evokes 'a poisonous foundation [of the human sciences], an archaeology that smashes idols' (Deleuze 1966: 91); when, speaking of Nietzsche in a text that is nearly contemporaneous with the review we have been citing, he chooses to recall a passage from *The Gay Science* that says 'Suppress your venerations, or else suppress yourselves!' (Deleuze 1967a: 120);[17] furthermore, when questioned about contemporary philosophy, he assigns it the task of 'creat[ing] worlds of thought, a whole new conception of thought, of "what it means to think", [that] must be adequate to what is happening around us' (Deleuze 1968b: 138),[18] and he writes a few other very similar phrases apropos of the difference that exists in Nietzsche between 'established values' and 'new values',[19] we can only note the extraordinary convergence that he chooses to see between the two authors. Thus we do not find ourselves faced with two contemporary philosophers—Foucault and Deleuze—who draw their references from the same source—Nietzsche—but rather with a reading—Deleuze's—that is wholly centered on the double theme of difference as a creative matrix and the critique of the hegemony of identity on the one hand, and the project of a new thought on the other: a reading that is consequently applied to Nietzsche as well as to Foucault, or more precisely to Foucault *on the basis of Nietzsche*.

This is the context in which Negri's relationship to Nietzsche takes place. Undoubtedly Negri's 'French' Nietzscheanism stems above all from purely biographical considerations: we know, since he has explained himself with great clarity, that the French intellectual climate was familiar to him from very early on since he spent the 1954–55 academic year at the École Normale in rue d'Ulm, and at that time he followed the courses of Hyppolite, Alquié, Bachelard, and Gurvitch. The year before, as a responsible youth member of Catholic Action in Padua, he had chosen to spend a year on a Mapam kibbutz in Israel,[20] and there became a communist. By the middle of the 1950s, therefore, he was a communist—but one who had not arrived via Marxism and was not connected to the Italian Communist Party; he was raised on French culture and moreover was a great reader of Merleau-Ponty, who had himself just broken with Sartre and was attempting to elaborate a political philosophy that seems in many ways to anticipate the Italian Marxist critique in which Negri would play a part a decade later;[21] and finally, he had just begun to work on the themes that would undoubtedly determine a large part of his relationship to Nietzsche.

His first research thesis, in 1955–56, is actually dedicated to 'German Historicism from Wilhelm Dilthey to Max Weber'[22] and, in the years that follow, he returns in the wake of his reading of Dilthey to the young Hegel, whose philosophy of right he studies (Negri 1958)—work that will quite rapidly earn him a post at the University of Padua, even though he is not yet 30. These two points are important not only because they permit us to understand the relative 'immunization' against Husserlian phenomenology and Heideggerian thought that Negri displays, but also because they similarly explain what Negri will look for in Nietzsche. The 'internal' relationship—which is simultaneously passionate and critical—to German historicism as well as Hegelianism is expressed in an extraordinary sensitivity to new forms of contemporary historicism, particularly those connected with French historiography: everything happens as if, even though German historicism was still linked to a kind of Platonism whose weight Meinecke himself recognized, a certain kind of French historiography—and more generally a new historicization of the history of ideas, mindsets and representations—would permit the total rethinking of the political, economic and social determinations of an era. One sees, then, how work like that of Foucault or Canguilhem could have fascinated Negri, but this implied a relationship to history that demanded it be redefined as coherence and discontinuity at the same time, that is, as Foucault clearly explained in the passages we cited above, redefined in a perfectly Nietzschean manner.

Furthermore, his assiduous reading—and translation (Hegel 1962)—of the young Hegel gives Negri an intimate familiarity with dialectical thought; but the antidialectical use of Nietzsche, which is to say the violent critique of every perspective of *Aufhebung* or synthesis, does not imply—unlike what we saw in Massimo Cacciari—the ineluctability of the tragic; and it is in no way restricted to a perspective whose only imaginable horizon would be that of nihilism, even a nihilism that has been made constructive, as in Vattimo's case. The critique of the Hegelian dialectic in Negri immediately intersects with a reflection on power [*puissance*] as creative opening, as ontological production, as process of subjectivation, which is clearly understood to arise at the intersection of Spinozist *potentia* and Nietzschean will to power. And in this Negri is extremely close to Deleuze.

On the basis of this double lineage—a 'French-style' historicism of which Foucault will become the most striking figure, and a Spinozism of power [*puissance*] that owes so much to Deleuze—we can understand Negri's Nietzscheanism; but these two axes similarly allow us to grasp the stakes of his critical reading of Marx as well—a Marx stripped of the rags of dialectical materialism and given back that which, according to Negri, actually constitutes his grandeur: the double dimension, inextricably interconnected, of subjectivation and revolt, singularity and production of the common, historical critique and the creation of new being, politics and ontology.

'Nietzsche's "yes" is opposed to the dialectical "no"; affirmation to dialectical negation; difference to dialectical contradiction; joy, enjoyment, to dialectical labour; lightness, dance, to dialectical responsibilities', Deleuze writes in 1962 (Deleuze 1983: 9). To reinsert this joy not only into conflict and the relations of power [*pouvoir*] but also into the folds of subjectivation and ontological production is to make Nietzsche both Spinozist and Marxist—it is to make the search for untimeliness not a flight ahead of its own history but rather a passion that is simultaneously historical, political and joyful, a matrix of events, an instance of creation. So let us listen to Negri:

> Everything that serves power [*potere*] is dissolved little by little. The development of subjective power [*potenza*] gathers together all that has accumulated in being, all that being has produced, historically, by means of and against the mystification, toward a greater human sociability, and reappropriates it, redefines it, in the process of the destruction of the theological illusion. This process, however, does not come to an end until power can fully insist on itself, on its own absolute autonomy and productivity. (Negri 1991b: 227, translation modified)

Far from being a tragic, negative or weak thought, Negri's thought lies at the intersection of a thought of affirmation, joyful passion, the will to power and the production of subjectivity—a different way of making Nietzsche's noncontemporaneity into a thought of revolution as disutopia.

NOTES

1. Translator's note: Revel's subtitle depends upon the distinction between the two French words for 'power' that is difficult to reproduce in English: the phrase 'will to power' contains the word *pouvoir*, equivalent to the Italian *potere*, which is generally used to refer to fixed, institutionalized or 'constituted' forms, while the phrase 'ontology of power' contains the word *puissance*, equivalent to the Italian *potenza*, which is generally used to refer to fluid, excessive or 'constituent' forms. On the importance of this distinction, see Michael Hardt's foreword to his translation of Negri's *Savage Anomaly* (Hardt 1991).
2. From this perspective, we could refer for example to the work of Louis Pinto, *Les neveux de Zarathoustra: La réception de Nietzsche en France* (Pinto 1995). This book, which limits itself to a specifically French horizon, clearly shows the need to situate and periodize the readings and contemporary uses of German philosophy in an extremely precise manner in order to understand their effects and function in philosophical discourse and the field of ideas more generally.
3. This issue was republished in 2001 as 'Hors série' 3: *Nietzsche*; all citations refer to the later reissue.
4. Negri reconstructs Lukács's reading of Nietzsche in the following terms: 'In his work, Nietzsche proposes a vigorous interpretation of decadence as a fundamental

phenomenon of bourgeois evolution in his day and wants it to be seen as such in order to overcome it. The real "social mission" of Nietzsche's philosophy consists precisely in this—he aspires to be able to redeem the bourgeois intelligentsia that has been overwhelmed by the loss of the universal meaning of its proper function. Concealing the egoistic character of his motivations behind the pathetico-aggressive form of his style, Nietzsche proposes a "revolution" that would preserve all the privileges of the bourgeoisie and vigorously defend the privileged and parasitic position of the imperialist intelligentsia, a revolution directed against the masses' (Negri 1992: 81–2).

5.   Translator's note: An English translation of the Colli–Montinari edition of Nietzsche has recently begun to appear from Stanford University Press.

6.   From the moment of its founding, Adelphi would in turn be clearly marked as a leftist publishing house: Montinari was at that time a member of the Italian Communist Party, and his militancy probably helped him to gain access to the Nietzsche-Archiv in Weimar, which was then in the Democratic Republic of Germany (i.e. East Germany).

7.   See for example Colli 1980, which was also translated into French (Colli 1996), and Montinari 1975 and Montinari 1982.

8.   He goes on: 'Thereafter Nietzsche will no longer succeed in offering such a hope. Even *Thus Spake Zarathustra* is a projection toward the future that does not display a present experience, which could be touched, and the enjoyment [*jouissance*] it offers is not for everyone' (Colli 1996: 21). Everything thus proceeds as if we had no choice between an aestheticization of the dream as access to the present and a kind of philosophy reserved for aristocrats. On these questions and the political aspects they may conceal, see the remarkable work of Domenico Losurdo, *Nietzsche, il ribelle aristocratico* (Losurdo 2002).

9.   On the way that, in France, a Nietzschean reading of history intersected with a new historiography emerging from the Annales School, a discontinuist model for reading the history of the sciences under the influence of Georges Canguilhem, a certain number of literary experiments organized around the writing of the fragment, and ultimately a lasting anti-Hegelianism common to a whole generation of young intellectuals beginning in the 1950s, allow me to refer to my book *Michel Foucault: Expériences de la pensée* (Revel 2005).

10.   See for example Vattimo 2004.

11.   See Cacciari's *Krisis* (Cacciari 1976). On the basis of presuppositions that could just as well be those of Vattimo or even those of Negri himself (let us recall in passing that Cacciari was very close to Negri and *Quaderni Rossi*, and later to the group *Potere Operaio*, before choosing to rejoin the Communist Party around 1969), that is on the basis of a violent critique of the Hegelian dialectic, Cacciari does not manage to escape from the tragic mode that such a perspective implies. Apropos of the new orders that the critique of every synthetic perspective makes possible, he thus notes: 'But the *essential thing* is not such "new orders" in themselves, but rather the insoluble, constitutive contradiction between them and the persistence of the crisis, the impossibility of resolving synthetically the crisis of the classical dialectical system. This complex of relations, which constitutes to my mind the irrepressible tragic instance of *negatives Denken*, speaks in its most comprehensible, most formally organized language through the multiplicity of "dialects" of the series *Viennese Apocalypse*—and not through the *Logoi* of the epigones of the various "vanguards"' (Cacciari 1976: 8). To escape from the dialectic is thus to condemn oneself to the tragic.

12.   Let us recall the excellent analyses in Descombes 1980 and Dosse 1997.

13.   In this regard see Eribon 1991: 52: 'Maurice Pinguet described Foucault's discovery of Nietzsche on the beaches in Italy, during summer vacation in 1953: ... "I can still see Michel Foucault, reading his *Untimely Meditations* in the sun, on the beach at Civitavecchia"'.

14.   The difference is clearly perceptible if one reads the two books that Deleuze wrote on Nietzsche, *Nietzsche and Philosophy* (Deleuze 1983) and *Nietzsche* (Deleuze 2001).

For Deleuze, the encounter with Foucault takes place in a period of intense work on Nietzsche's thought. Thereafter, the friendship between the two philosophers transformed itself into a project on Nietzsche, the editorial work of 1967. It is equally interesting to read what Deleuze says about Nietzsche *at that very moment*, within that new collaboration. We might refer for example to three interventions that are particularly significant since they all date from 1967–68, at the moment the fifth volume of Nietzsche's *Oeuvres philosophiques complètes* was published and three years after the Royaumont colloquium organized by Deleuze around Nietzsche's thought, where Foucault presented 'Nietzsche, Freud, Marx'; 'Conclusions on the Will to Power and the Eternal Return' (Deleuze 1967a); 'Nietzsche's Burst of Laughter' (Deleuze 1967b); and 'On Nietzsche and the Image of Thought' (Deleuze 1968). The first of these texts is particularly interesting to the extent that it is built entirely around the articulation of the eternal return–will to power nexus and, unlike the other two texts cited, it contains only a very few allusions to the notions that Foucault utilizes in his own reading of the philosopher, in particular the notions of 'interpretation' and 'untimeliness'.

15. Klossowski's influence is equally obvious on Foucault during the same years, but for him it involves more the 'literary' Klossowski, who is taken as a 'case study' in the series of transgressors of the all-powerful order of language, than Klossowski the translator of Nietzsche.

16. Thus, apropos of the will to power: 'Ultimately, there is nothing except the will to power, which is the power to metamorphose, to shape masks ... ' (Deleuze 1967a: 119). And further: 'It is in this sense that Mr Klossowski wanted to show us a world of intense fluctuations in the Will to power, where identities are lost, and where each one cannot want itself without wanting all the other possibilities, without becoming innumerable "others", without apprehending itself as a fortuitous moment, whose very chance implies the necessity of the whole series' (Deleuze 1967a: 122). Apropos of the eternal return: 'In short, the world of the eternal return is a world of differences, an intensive world, which presupposes neither the One nor the Same, but whose edifice is built both on the tomb of the one God and on the ruins of the identical self' (Deleuze 1967a: 123); 'Essentially, the unequal, the different, is the true rationale for the eternal return. It is because nothing is equal, or the same, that "it" comes back. In other words, the eternal return is predicated only of becoming and the multiple. It is the law of a world without being, without unity, without identity. Far from *presupposing* the One or the Same, the eternal return constitutes the only unity of the multiple as such, the only identity of what differs ... ' (Deleuze 1967a: 124). Apropos of sense (and the use that Foucault makes of the theme of interpretation, specifically on the basis of Nietzsche): 'A thing never has only one sense. Each thing has several senses that express the forces and the becoming of forces at work in it. Still more to the point, there is no "thing", but only interpretation and the plurality of senses' (Deleuze 1967a: 118, translation modified).

17. The citation is drawn from *The Gay Science*, bk. 5, 346.

18. Three pages later in the same text, the allusion to Foucault (whose name is nevertheless not mentioned) becomes transparent in the aside on the work of 'collage', a term that Foucault's detractors sometimes used to reproach him for his method of juxtaposing the disciplinary fields he examined in *The Order of Things*: 'So, in philosophy, we're all experiencing this problem of formal renewal. It's certainly possible. It begins with little things. For example, using the history of philosophy as a "collage" (already an old technique in painting) would not in the least diminish the great philosophers of the past—making a collage at the heart of a properly philosophical picture. That would be better than "selections", but it would require particular techniques. You would need some Max Ernsts in philosophy' (Deleuze 1968: 141). Except for the fact that the resemblance between Foucault and Max Ernst would doubtless not have seduced Foucault himself, and the work of historical analysis that subtends the project of an archaeology of the human sciences is quite different from the image of the great 'properly philosophical picture' of which Deleuze speaks.

19. 'We already saw it in the will to power: there exists a difference in nature between "attributing current values to oneself" and "creating new values". This difference between them is the very difference of the eternal return, that which constitutes the essence of the eternal return: that is, "new" values are precisely those superior forms of everything that is. Some values, then, are born current and appear only by soliciting an order of recognition, even if they must await favorable historical conditions to be effectively recognized. On the other hand, some values are eternally new, forever untimely, always contemporary with their creation ... Such values alone are transhistorical, supra-historical, and bear witness to a congenial chaos, a creative disorder that is irreducible to any order whatsoever' (Deleuze 1967a: 126, translation modified). If the first part of this citation can almost be applied just as well and without great difficulty to Foucault's work—since Deleuze sees in it the creation of a new thought—the second part is on the contrary much more problematic: what sense can the idea of 'transhistorical, supra-historical' values that are 'always contemporary with their creation' have for the Foucault of *The Order of Things*? Even when Foucault makes reference to Nietzschean untimeliness, even when he formulates the idea of a discontinuous history, despite all this he remains wholly within the horizon of the historicity of systems of thought: for him there is no outside of history. Foucault's position is that of an epistemological critique of the continuist and linear model of history; Deleuze's position is the philosophical attempt to break with history by means of a kind of absolute 'creationism' that would be the real mark of eternity. And even when, almost 20 years later, Foucault will decide to broach directly the themes of creation and actuality—for example in the successive commentaries on Kant's 'What is Enlightenment?'—he will never abandon the presupposition that one never escapes one's own historical determinations: one can at most bend them to a will to rupture (knowing what our own determinations are in order to try to institute a difference between 'today' and 'yesterday'), or hollow them out by making them the terrain for a production of subjectivity that is effectively 'new', but never make them wholly into abstractions.

20. Translator's note: Mapam was an Israeli Marxist–Zionist political party active from the 1940s to the 1990s.

21. In light of this it would be interesting to compare, on the one hand, Merleau-Ponty's work, as well as the genesis of the work of Claude Lefort and Cornelius Castoriadis at the heart of *Socialisme ou Barbarie*, and, on the other, the analyses of the *Quaderni Rossi* group (aside from Negri, this included Romano Alquati, Raniero Panzieri, Alberto Asor Rosa, Mario Tronti, and others). In both cases, the attempt to renew the reading of Marx independent of and polemically against the 'party line' is patently clear.

22. Part of this thesis would be published three years later under the title *Saggi sullo storicismo tedesco: Dilthey e Meinecke* (Negri 1959).

5
Always Already Only Now: Negri and the Biopolitical

Alberto Toscano

QUESTIONS OF METHOD

The last few years have witnessed the constitution of a veritable biopolitical field in the domain of radical thought. I say field and not camp, not simply because of the loaded echoes of the latter term, but because the appropriations of the notion of biopolitics (and related terms such as biopower, or, more recently bioeconomics) have been numerous and disparate, even antagonistic. What is Negri's position within this field? How has the concept of biopolitics affected his intellectual trajectory, and how, vice versa, has the concept been inflected, transformed by its inclusion within Negri's philosophical machinery? So as to answer these questions, in order hopefully to generate some new (and rather less pedantic) ones out of them, I'd like to begin by tackling the most obvious 'genealogical' issue, that of Negri's indebtedness to Foucault.

Foucault is at the fulcrum of the current debate on biopolitics. Despite the fact that he did not coin the term—which had appeared in various guises ever since it was introduced in 1911 by the Swedish political scientist Rudolph Kjellen (Esposito 2004: 3–16)—it is Foucault's formulation of biopolitics in the first volume of the *History of Sexuality*, and his subsequent elaborations of it in the late 1970s (particularly in the recently published Collège de France lectures of 1976 to 1979), which serves as the touchstone for the contemporary debate. Though it exceeds the remit of this chapter to establish this point, I think it may be suggested that the vibrancy as well as the frequent vagueness and imprecision of the current use of the concept of biopolitics derive from some crucial features of Foucault's method. The dominant tendency among those with a predilection for this concept, Negri included, is to treat biopolitics as a kind of 'epochal' category, such that we may speak of an age of biopolitics, a biopolitical condition, biopolitical capitalism, and so on. Of course, though he subtracts historical and discursive periodization from any kind of cunning of reason, consigning them to the impersonal conjunctions of archive and event, Foucault's own introduction of the term is not devoid of an 'epochalising' impulse, in line with the epistemic dislocations traced in *The Order of Things* and *Discipline and Punish*.

And yet Foucault's methodology, especially as it concerns biopolitics, is also polemically positioned against the totalizing and universalizing approaches that he registers as common to both traditional political theory and Marxism. As he announces, at the very outset of his series of lectures on the 'birth of biopolitics' (which will actually turn out to concern mainly the excavation of neoliberal discourse):

> choosing to speak of, or to start from, governmental practice, is also an entirely explicit way of putting aside—as a first, primitive, pre-constituted object—a whole set of notions such as, for example, the sovereign, sovereignty, the people, subjects, the State, civil society: all those universals which sociological analysis, as well as historical analysis and the analysis of political philosophy, utilise effectively to account for governmental practice. (Foucault 2004: 4)

Foucault continues by distinguishing his method from that of historicism:

> Historicism starts from the universal and passes it, as it were, through the grater of history. My problem is precisely the inverse one. I start from the decision, both theoretical and methodological, which consists in saying: let us suppose that universals do not exist. And I pose at that point the question to history and historians: how can you write history if you do not assume a priori that something like the State, society, the sovereign, or subjects exist? ... So, not to interrogate universals by utilising history as a critical method, but, starting from the decision of the inexistence of universals, to ask what history one can make. (Foucault 2004: 5)

Such pronouncements have prompted Ian Hacking to write that 'Foucault's dynamic nominalism is a historicized nominalism' (Hacking 2002: 49; see also Balibar 1992). How is this methodological nominalism reflected in the introduction of the theory of biopolitics? In the first place, we can see it at work in the manner in which Foucault poses the problem of biopolitics, to wit, how did a domain of 'social life' come to be constituted as an object for knowledge and as a correlate of certain regulatory practices of power? How did an entity both epistemic and material, such as the 'population'—possibly the pivotal category of biopolitics—emerge at the intersection of statistical knowledge and epidemiological power? Note that Foucault's nominalism precludes him from positing the preexistence of the population, just as it makes him sensitive enough to its material constitution to forsake mere ideological critique of the term's misuses and instrumentalizations. Furthermore, biopolitics is approached through the discontinuous genealogy of discourses around the 'art of governing', and is thus envisaged through the lenses of political rationality.

What Foucault called 'the biopolitics of the population', which, together with the 'anatomo-politics' of discipline, makes up the protean 'bipolar technology' (Rabinow and Rose 2003: 2) of 'biopower', is thus included within the problematic of 'government', understood as that which 'enables a problem to be addressed and offers certain strategies for solving/handling the problem [and] also structures specific forms of *intervention*' (Lemke 2001: 191). Given the plurality of mechanisms (or *dispositifs*), agents, and points of application of this biopolitics, we may be said to encounter here a 'strategic logic of heterogeneity' whereby Foucault 'substitutes the proliferation of devices that constitute substantial unities, as much as degrees of unities contingent in each instance, for the totalising principle of the economy or the political'. Despite its capacity to delineate a major shift in the practices of power, the biopolitics of the population, which envisages 'the management of power as a management of multiplicity' (Lazzarato 2005), thereby appears as a category with a localized operation, aimed at describing a specific rationality, with all of its proper technologies and sui generis material effects, but *not* as a new universal to replace notions like the state or civil society. On the contrary, biopolitics is configured by Foucault as an 'anti-universal' concept.

MEDIATION IS DEAD, LONG LIVE BIOPOLITICS

Now, even a cursory glance at Negri's more recent writings will reveal that his employment of the term biopolitics is anything but an analytically restricted one. Indeed, not only does the notion of the biopolitical permit Negri to give a common framework to theoretical affirmations of an ontological, political, social, economic and historical character, it often appears, building on his distinctive use of the Marxian concept of 'real subsumption', as the master term to identify a situation of full social and productive immanence. Or rather, according to Hardt and Negri, Foucault, along with authors such as Deleuze and Guattari, 'has prepared the terrain ... for an investigation of the material functioning of imperial rule' (Hardt and Negri 2000: 23), inasmuch as his conceptualization of power and social reproduction allows us to wrest the notion of a real subsumption of society under capital away from 'the linear and totalitarian figure of capitalist development' (Hardt and Negri 2000: 25), infusing it with notions such as multiplicity, singularity, the event. Once the 'Foucauldian' elements have been properly integrated, biopower 'is another name for the real subsumption of society under capital, and both are synonymous with the globalized productive order' (Hardt and

Negri 2000: 365). As we shall see, Negri's approach to biopolitics as a Janus-faced notion—both a mark of the most endemic control and a sign of a new insurgent subjectivity—is closely tied to the historicopolitical paradox of real subsumption, which can be said to dominate all of his recent work. For it is within real subsumption that power at once 'unifies and envelops within itself every element of social life', thereby undoing the bases of mediation proper, but 'at that very moment reveals a new context, a new milieu of maximum plurality and uncontainable singularization—a milieu of the event' (Hardt and Negri 2000: 25). Over and over again, biopower and 'biopolitical production' thus appear not just in terms of a Marxian theory of socialization, but as bywords for the fusion of domains hitherto considered functionally separate into a single field of production and antagonism, without transcendent measure and without an outside.

Hardt and Negri can thus write that the 'powers of production are in fact today entirely biopolitical; in other words, they run throughout and constitute directly not only production but also the entire realm of reproduction' (Hardt and Negri 2000: 364); or—in the more recent attempt in *Multitude* to encompass even the latest round of military interventions and occupations under a biopolitical aegis—that 'in a sort of concert of convergence of the various forms of power, war, politics, economics and culture in Empire become finally a mode of producing social life in its entirety and hence a form of biopower' (Hardt and Negri 2004: 334). This idea of a biopolitical convergence of hitherto distinct domains of human activity also affects the political universals which Foucault sought to meth-odologically undermine with his study of political reason (Barry, Osborne, and Rose 1996), so that civil society, for instance, is said to be 'absorbed in the state, but the consequence of this is an explosion of the elements that were previously coordinated and mediated in civil society' (Hardt and Negri 2000: 25). It is within this unmediated or immeasurable explosion that Negri discerns the traits that prefigure—within what he daringly dubs a 'materialist teleology'—a social and political ontology of the 'common': the 'destruction of the separation between public and private', the 'nomadism and the flexibility of labour-power, the new configuration of the social as the structure of the common (in all its biopolitical dimensions), the emergence of mass intellectuality' (Negri 2003a: 223). The whole of (Hardt and) Negri's recent thought is thus characterized by a tension between the vision of a biopower that 'regulates social life from its interior, following it, interpreting, absorbing it, and rearticulating it' (Hardt and Negri 2000: 23), and that of a biopolitics from below, as it were, which, 'through the cohesion of a network of singularities' (Negri 2003a: 188), and the powers of 'love' and 'poverty', produces a new common world against biopower.

I will return below, via Foucault, to this dichotomization between biopower and biopolitics. At this juncture, it is important to note that, whichever sign they take, whether positive or negative, these categories are aimed at affirming the termination of any mediation and any dialectic (between public and private, state and civil society, and so on). In an earlier text, appended to his *The Politics of Subversion*, Negri, following the thesis that under conditions of real subsumption capitalist power increasingly manifests itself as sheer command and terroristic crisis, declared: 'Mediation is dead. The production of goods takes place through domination. The relationships between production and reproduction, between domination/ profit and resistance/wages cannot be harmonized' (Negri 1989: 183; see also Toscano 2003). This quasi-Manichean disharmony remains at the heart of the theory of the multitude. Perversely making use of an *über* dialectical category, Hardt and Negri configure it in terms of the opposition between two *totalities*: on the one hand, 'the totality of right and the State, the tendency toward the affirmation of an imperial right and a new sovereignty that extends over the global set of social, economic, juridical and political relations of our planet' and, on the other hand, 'at the same time, in the same logical space, there is the insurgency against this right and against this new imperial authority'. In other words, we have the confrontation between two unmediated totalities, one involving Empire's new biopolitical sovereignty, and the other for which 'the total object is not power but rather what Spinoza called "the democratic absolute"'. This second totality, then, the concern of a 'dogmatic science of desire', is antidialectical, antiteleological and antitranscendental (Hardt and Negri 2002: 196).

But if power 'is always domination with the common, that is, within the biopolitical common', and 'in the biopolitical, the name of politics understood as command is dispelled' (Negri 2003a: 256, 214), how are we to understand the unmediated antagonism which is supposed to mark our biopolitical age? Surely, a (bio)power that regulates life from the inside— i.e. that 'takes care' of it, micromanaging the individual and collective capacities and infirmities of its population—cannot be simply relegated to the status of transcendent command? Despite Hardt and Negri's attempt to depict capitalist imperial power as parasitic on the constituent 'love' of the multitude, it is not clear that the supposed fusion of distinct domains into a biopolitical continuum can really permit us to isolate, within the operations of the production and reproduction of life, a collective communist subject that wouldn't be shot through, incited and restricted by innumerable dispositifs of biopolitical control. If Negri's philosophy can be best understood as the shifting, unstable attempt to dedialecticize class struggle and immerse proletarian subjectivity into a plane of immanence, it is not certain that: (1) it can withstand the nonmediated micropolitics of biopower, with its dissolution of clearly distinguishable class subjects; (2) it can proceed on the basis of the spectral thesis of two totalities, which are 'not only opposed but also *asymmetrical*, not only asymmetrical but also *atopic*—that is, they constitute different places' (Hardt and Negri 2002: 197). Supposing that the law and the state are increasingly employing biopolitical instruments, and thus governing life 'from within', in what sense can the life of the multitude ever *separate* itself from the insidious control of forms of power that eschew classical mediation? It is not impertinent to ask, for example, if the destruction of the public–private barrier, lauded by Negri, is not actually in the first instance a repressive and exploitative tool, rather than an augur of red dawns to come.

Should we then follow Rabinow and Rose's advice and disregard Hardt and Negri's use of biopower as 'encompassing, totalising', 'a superficial description of certain aspects of our present, framed within the kind of towering worldview that other theorists of postmodernity have proclaimed a thing of the past' (Rabinow and Rose 2003: 5, 6)? The authors of *Empire* are hardly apologetic about their penchant for grand ontological narratives. Where Rabinow and Rose wish further to refine the analytical purchase of biopolitics on the present via notions such as 'risk politics' and 'molecular politics' (Rose 2001: 1) and the study of the modes of subjectivation that accompany the new genetic medicine (Rabinow and Rose 2003), Hardt and Negri emphatically declare that the context of any analysis 'has to be the very unfolding of life itself, the process of the constitution of the world, of history' (Hardt and Negri 2000: 30). Is this to say that their use of terms like 'biopower' and 'biopolitics' is merely an illegitimate hypostasis of Foucault's nominalist methodology?

At this point, it is worthwhile delineating the steps leading to Hardt and Negri's appropriation of Foucault's concept, their 'totalization' of biopolitics, together with the theoretical and methodological resistances that Foucault's work might present to such a totalization. The key moves in the appropriation–transformation of Foucault's concept of biopolitics appear to be the following:

- biopolitics is subjectivized and linked to the Marxian notion of 'living labor';
- biopolitics is viewed no longer as an internal articulation of the governmental practices and rationalities of biopower, but as its antagonist;
- the periodization of biopolitics is transformed.

The problem with criticisms such as Rabinow and Rose's is in effect that they ignore Hardt and Negri's explicit treatments of this shift, which are revealing both of their own project and of the distance they take from Foucault.

THE BIOPOLITICAL SUBJECT OF LIVING LABOR

In *Il potere costituente* (translated into English as *Insurgencies*) and *Time for Revolution*, among many other texts, Negri has affirmed the centrality of the Marxian notion of living labor to his whole enterprise. Rather than a simple *capacity*, or the sum of all physical and intellectual attitudes existent in corporeality, disciplined for and dominated by the imperatives of capital, for Negri living labor is a veritable ontological principle of production, which can autonomize itself from capital, engaging in constant processes of self-valorization. As he writes:

> The theme proposed by Marx is the omniexpansive creativity of living labour. Living labour constructs the world, creatively modelling, *ex novo*, the materials it touches. … Its projection onto the world is ontological, its prostheses are ontological, its constructions are constructions of new being: the first result of this indefinite process is the construction of the subject. (Negri 2002c: 403)

In this regard, Negri, consistently with his previous work, wishes to move beyond the strict confines of philosophical anthropology and think, within and beyond Marx, a humanism which incorporates the lessons of antihumanism (Hardt and Negri 2000: 91). This is why he opts for a maximal interpretation, as it were, of Marx's famous statement on living labor: 'Labour is the living, form-giving fire; it is the transitoriness of things, their temporality, as their formation by living time' (Marx 1973: 361). Incidentally, this means giving short thrift to Marx's argument, also in the *Grundrisse*, whereby the productivity of living labor only exists as incited and disciplined by capital:

> The use value which the worker has to offer the capitalist, which he has to offer to others in general, is not materialized in a product, does not exist apart from him at all, thus exists not really, but only in potentiality, as his capacity. … As soon as it has obtained motion from capital, this use value exists as the worker's specific, productive activity; it is his *vitality* itself, directed toward a specific purpose and hence expressing itself in a specific form. (Marx 1973: 267, my emphasis; see also Assoun 1999)

The worker's 'own' vitality here appears as a result of the capital relation imposed upon him, not as a preexistent productive drive merely 'captured' by capital.

Now, what is the role of living labor when Hardt and Negri come to their treatment of Foucault?[1] Despite Foucault's seminal contribution to a theory of social reproduction under conditions of empire, Hardt and Negri chastise him for a 'structuralist epistemology' that sacrifices the 'dynamic of the system' and 'the ontological substance of cultural and social reproduction' (Hardt and Negri 2000: 28). Beneath the rather slapdash use of the epithet 'structuralist' lies the idea that Foucault, despite or because of his attention to biopolitical 'modes of subjectification' (Rabinow and Rose 2003: 4), is incapable of postulating a productive ontological subject beneath historical transformations. Of course, the point is that this is not a passing peccadillo in Foucault's case, but rather, as was indicated above, a methodological and theoretical decision. When Hardt and Negri complain that, were we to ask Foucault 'who or what drives the system, or rather, who is the *bios*, his response would be ineffable, or nothing at all' (Hardt and Negri 2000: 28), they ignore the fact that Foucault's methodology rejects in principle the very question they wish to pose to it, especially since the idea of 'the system', for better or for worse, is precisely one of the universals that his genealogy and analytics of political reason is seeking to suspend.

Moreover, when Hardt and Negri seek to infuse the fire of living labor into Foucault's biopolitics, they bypass the issue of Foucault's own relationship to this very concept. Notwithstanding Foucault's explicit, if unexplored, link between biopolitics and capitalism, cited by Hardt and Negri (Hardt and Negri 2000: 27), his stance towards labor was profoundly dismissive. Already in *The Order of Things*, the Marxist analysis of labor had been depicted as introducing 'no real discontinuity' vis-à-vis the work of Ricardo, a conjunction of 'the historicity of economics', 'the finitude of human existence' and 'the fulfilment of an end to History', which bore all the limits of that episteme. Foucault's verdict was harsh: 'Marxism exists in nineteenth-century thought like a fish in water: that is, it is unable to breathe anywhere else' (Foucault 1989: 285). Only Nietzsche, for Foucault, truly broke with this nineteenth-century paradigm.

Even when—buoyed by a certain sympathy for Marxist (or more precisely, Maoist) politics which was more a product of his engagement with the aftereffects of May '68 than an immanent theoretical development—Foucault sought to make his methodology complementary rather than antagonistic to that of Marxism, the concept of labor was still portrayed as an obstacle. Lecturing in Brazil in 1974, Foucault argued that Marxism's traditional concern with the exploitation and alienation of labor, viewed as the concrete essence of man, must be put aside if we are to recognize the artificiality of labour itself, and the fact that 'the capitalist system penetrates far more deeply into our existence' than Marxists are willing to countenance. This is because 'for there to be surplus-profit, there must be subpower', a 'capillary, microscopic political power ... fixing men to the apparatus of production .... The link between man and work is synthetic, political; it is a connection operated by power', subpower, not the 'State apparatus, nor the class in power, but the ensemble of small powers, small institutions situated at the lowest level. What I have tried to do is the analysis of sub-power as the condition of possibility of surplus-profit' (Foucault 2001: 1490).[2] Though Negri has certainly tried to incorporate the 'death of man' into his reinvention of revolutionary humanism (hence the turn to authors such as Deleuze and Guattari, and his own conceptualization of the 'man–machine'), and is attracted by the concept of biopolitics primarily in order to offset the penetration (real subsumption) of society by capital, he does not seem to be able to appropriate Foucault without positing, via an ontologized notion of living labor, a class subject, the multitude. What is more, even when it comes to biopolitics, Negri, unlike the Deleuze of the societies of control, or even his erstwhile collaborator Lazzarato (Lazzarato 2005), does not wish to follow Foucault in bypassing sovereignty and the state altogether and focusing his analytical attention on the proliferation of biopolitical microinstitutions. For this, as I have alluded above, would seem to clash with the thesis, crucial to Negri's work for quite some time, that the capitalist function has become parasitical, and therefore appears as pure crisis and command, in other words as *war* (Negri 2003b: 72).[3]

FROM BIOPOLITICS TO CLASS STRUGGLE AND BACK AGAIN

Now, Negri is perfectly aware that the bulk of Foucault's work on biopolitics approaches it as a technology of power dealing with a population, 'an ensemble of living beings who present particular onto/biological traits and whose life is susceptible to being controlled with the purpose of insuring, together with a better management of labour-power, an orderly growth of society' (Negri 2003b: 79). However, he discerns within the work of Foucault a tension between the delineation of biopolitics as a science and rationality of the police (*Polizeiwissenschaft*) and the attempt to generate 'a political economy of life in general'; between the treatment and maintenance of populations and the notion of a general ontological fabric that straddles the division between state and society. The question is: 'Must we think politics as an ensemble of biopowers deriving from the activity of governing or, on the contrary, to the degree that power has invested life, does life too become a power?' (Negri 2003b: 80). Negri thus evidently wishes to bracket, as cumbersome 'structuralist' remnants, Foucault's nominalist or antiuniversalist propedeutic, lending the analytic of biopolitics the full ontological weight which he accords to living labor.

Biopolitics is therefore to be recast as 'a power that expresses itself from life, not only in work and language, but in bodies, affects, desires, sexuality' and this powerful 'life' as 'a counter-power, a force, a production of subjectivity that presents itself as a moment of de-subjection' (Negri 2003b: 81). Like Lazzarato (Lazzarato 1997, 2002), Negri also wishes to generate a new distinction between biopolitics and biopower at a remove from Foucault's own (whereby, as noted above, biopolitics is the populational component of an overall biopower). This realignment of the terms means that biopower is on the side of subjection and control, while biopolitics is rethought in terms of subjectivity and freedom. However, unlike Lazzarato, Negri's gamble is that, via the ontologized concept of living labor, this conceptual shift can take place without sundering a commitment to revolutionary Marxism. Against the 'soft' biopolitics of risk, or, even worse, the use of Foucauldian discourse as a machine against welfare policies, Negri's gambit is that, via the infusion of living labor, we can realize that 'biopolitics is an extension of class struggle' (Negri 2003b: 83). This idea of biopolitics as an extension or even (following Negri's reading of real subsumption) an intensification and culmination of class struggle requires that Foucault's concept be presented as one that may be complemented (rather than displaced or abolished) by a Marxian analysis of class and its composition. Thus, Hardt and Negri write that when Foucault 'discusses biopower he sees it only from above … as the prerogative of sovereign power', but that 'when we look at the situation from the perspective of labour involved in biopolitical production, on the other hand, we can begin to recognize biopower from below' (Hardt and Negri 2002: 197; Hardt and Negri 2004: 94–5). Now, though there are certainly profound and stimulating ambiguities in the relationship between sovereignty on the one hand and both biopower and biopolitics on the other (Esposito 2004: 38), it is bizarre to argue that Foucauldian biopower is the 'prerogative of sovereign power' since, as we noted, Foucault's methodological starting point for the study of governmental practices was based on questions such as 'What if the sovereign didn't exist?' Moreover, Hardt and Negri's confidence in the autonomy of this biopolitical subject or 'biopower from below' seems unwarranted if we consider that the existence of capillary, micropolitical forms linking subpower to surplus profit constantly puts such autonomy in doubt. If labor under capitalism is the result of political *syntheses* that demand a plurality of institutions—not all (or most) of them encompassed by the sovereign or the state—and if, following Foucault, even a resistant biopower from below would engender its own insidious mechanisms of self-management and self-control, can we really be so confident that the new, biopolitical class struggle can simply be formulated as yet another righteous battle between immanence and transcendence? And what of Foucault's provocative suggestion that the concept of class *struggle* is not unrelated to the polemical and biopolitical history of racism (Foucault 2003: 83, 261)?

But what does it mean to say that biopolitics is an 'extension' of class struggle? On the one hand, it suggests that biopower, 'the tendency for sovereignty to become power over life itself' (Hardt and Negri 2004: 334), is, in line with Negri's workerist allegiance to the anteriority of constituent power and the 'primacy of proletarian subjectivity' (Callinicos 2006: 139; see also Toscano 2003), a consequence of the potent struggles whereby insurgent multitudes have forced an increasingly polyvalent and microphysical response by capitalist power. But, on the other hand, the very emergence of a biopolitical regime, the regime of the real subsumption of *life* (and not just society) under capital, means that 'biopolitical' class struggle bears little resemblance to its traditional forms. In effect, it is no longer the struggle between classes per se, but the struggle of a class with a seemingly limitless and protean 'composition' against dispositifs of power which are not straightforwardly located at the heart of the bourgeoisie, or even of a transnational capitalist class. The struggle seems to take the guise of a direct fight against the 'classification' of living labor by biopower, where the former is driven by a surplus of immanence that no power can ever really exhaust or tame:

> Our innovative and creative capacities are always greater than our productive labour—productive, that is, of capital. At this point we can recognize that biopolitical production is on the one hand *immeasurable*, because it cannot be quantified in fixed units of time, and, on the other hand, always *excessive* with respect to the value that capital can extract from it because capital can never capture all of life. (Hardt and Negri 2004: 146)

If living labor and biopolitics are synthesized in the concept of biopolitical production, then this concept is endowed with formidable ontological import: 'Biopolitical production is a matter of ontology in that it constantly creates new social being, a new human nature' (Hardt and Negri 2004: 348). But is the mere invocation of the excess of living labor sufficient? Can a new narrative of class struggle rest on the incessant reference to the struggle of immanence against transcendence, of creativity against capture?

The problem is once again that this dichotomization of biopower (either into two variants, one oppressive and one insurgent, or into biopower versus biopolitics) papers over, without really subjecting them to sustained critique, some of the key tenets of Foucault's account—to begin with, the idea that biopolitical rationality can eschew the dimension of sovereignty or state power, and work at a microinstitutional and infrasubjective level. If that is the case, then what 'side' are these institutions and biopolitical operators on? What gives them their class marking? How are the biopolitical strategies from above and from below concretely distinguished? More starkly, if production is increasingly becoming the production of social life, who is doing the producing? Simply to argue, as Hardt and Negri sometimes seem to do, that all the creativity is on the side of living labor is implausible on their own terms—after all, don't they themselves write that 'the various forms of power, war, politics, economics and culture in Empire become finally a mode of producing social life in its entirety' (Hardt and Negri 2004: 334)? And that 'biopolitical' corporations 'produce producers' (Hardt and Negri 2000: 32)? If power is productive, as our Foucault 101 course would have it, then this surely counts, regardless of the protocol that may help us tell them apart, *both* for biopower from below and biopower from above, through all their strategic confrontations. A purely parasitic biopower is a contradiction in terms. Moreover, the very technologies of biopower, and even more of the 'societies of control' (two distinct paradigms that Hardt and Negri tend to blur), cannot by any means be regarded as forms of transcendental measure which merely reduce the immeasurable excess of the multitude. On the contrary, one might even think that it is the excess of biopower itself, of the myriad mechanisms of regulation and securitization, which defies measure. If biopolitical rationalities are best understood in terms of multiplicities 'conducting the conduct' of other multiplicities,[4] then it is difficult to see how we could stop biopower from above from constantly bleeding into biopower from below, in an intricate topology that makes the retention of a Marxist conception of antagonism tenuous at best. Thus, if the term 'biopolitical' indicates 'that the traditional distinctions between the economic, the political, the social, and the cultural become increasingly blurred' (Hardt and Negri 2004: 109), how can we affirm the clarity of the line separating the two opposing sides within a global class struggle, a struggle which would seem to take the guise of a global civil war?

PERIODIZATION AND PRODUCTION

Foucault's relationship with history is notoriously complex. We have already cited his antihistoricist methodological provisos. We could add that, in terms of biopolitics and biopower, it is possible to discern in his work a shift from a more 'epochal' treatment of the term—namely in the first volume of *History of Sexuality*, where biopower seems to signal a shift away from sovereignty and representation—to a far more localized and methodologically cautious one, such as we find, for instance, in the treatment of the link between neoliberal rationality and the biopolitical. Negri's injection of the concepts of living labor and class struggle into the concept of biopolitics, and its articulation with the Marxian notion of real subsumption (perhaps the touchstone of Negri's entire project), also has significant consequences for the historicity of the biopolitical. On one level, when Negri enlists Foucault to think the new mechanisms of social reproduction, biopower emerges to qualify the novelty of an imperial power which, devoid of simple localization and detached from a purely national context, works through the social from within. Biopower would thus characterize a shift in the dominant paradigm of power.[5] On another level, however, in particular when Hardt and Negri refer to 'biopolitical production', a far more momentous point is being put forward—to wit, that *only now*, in a situation of fully-fledged real subsumption, have the biopolitical traits that *always already* determined living labor come to the fore, only now have they been fully invested by an insurgent political subjectivity.

Thus, the very perspicacious argument according to which the inherently and transhistorically biopolitical character of capitalism as such trumps Hardt and Negri's impressionistic and voluntaristic thesis of a 'biopolitical stage of capitalism' (Holdren, forthcoming) appears short-circuited: yes, capital has always involved a 'biopolitical' social relation, but only now, when the economic is a concentrated version of the political (Negri 1989: 215), is this relation capable of being subjectively assumed in full. In this regard, Paolo Virno has produced a remarkable theory, beginning from the reduction of biopolitics to labor power qua capacity, of this insertion of metahistory into the present. According to Virno, it is only today that labor power manifests its full pertinence as a social and political concept, inasmuch as the regime of immaterial labor, by directly investing the linguistic capacities of the worker qua commodity, reveals the real paradox of labor power—which is that it is precisely when it is 'transcendental' possibility which is being sold that the *bios* of the empirical body of the laborer, the ineliminable substrate of the purchased *dynamis*, becomes crucial (Virno 2002). Labor power is thus a 'not-now subject to supply and demand' (Virno 1999: 121), and the body is controlled and manipulated as its simulacrum or bearer. What's more, to the very extent that the object of capitalism is pure capacity, the body becomes the site of strategies of measurement: 'to obtain the only good that he desires, power [*potenza*], the capitalist offers a remuneration that corresponds to the maintenance of that which instead has no value, life' (Virno 1999: 127). What is the historical meaning of this predicament? According to Virno—much of whose absorbing recent work is devoted to this very problem—prior to the onset of immaterial or post-Fordist capital, our capacities, which is to say our 'biological invariant' (our 'non-specialization, neoteny, lack of a univocal environment' (Virno 2003: 167)) only came to the fore in the midst of catastrophic anomalies, social states of exception, that is, when the immunizing and compensatory pseudoenvironments furnished by culture faltered or collapsed. The destruction of these pseudoenvironments by the icy calculation of advanced capitalism brings our indefinite species being, our generic essence, ever more to the fore: 'amorphous potentiality, i.e. the chronic persistence of infantile characteristics, does not threateningly emerge in the midst of a crisis, but pervades every aspect of the most trite *routine*' (Virno 2003: 170). And it is precisely in this situation, where there is a premium on 'flexible' capacities, that norms (or controls) proliferate and become ever more plastic, as well as more insidious (Virno 2003: 173). There is a clear isomorphy here with the argument made by Marx in the *Grundrisse* regarding both labor and money, of which Marx writes:

> this very simple category ... makes a historic appearance in its full intensity only in the most developed conditions of society ... when it is economically conceived in this simplicity, 'labour' is as modern a category as are the relations which create this simple abstraction. (Marx 1973: 103)

But, as we have already noted, Negri's focus on living labor, rather than on labor power per se, is based on the desire to move beyond a 'naturalist' discourse of capacities and towards a veritable ontology of production. This, incidentally, is the reason for his criticisms of positions such as Virno's, which he regards as putting too much emphasis on the linguistic (Hardt and Negri 2000: 29, 364). But what does the turn to living labor mean for the issue of periodization? In a very rich philosophical reflection on the figure of the 'political monster', which begins with a critique of the 'eugenic' character of Western rationality (theory as *good breeding*), Negri has tried to depict the process whereby the monster, as a plebeian figure of commonality and power which could not be brought under the rational control of a good origin and proper breeding, moves from the margins to the system's core: 'Mobilised en masse in the wars of the nineteenth and twentieth century, the *monster* becomes the true *subject*, both *political* and *technical*, of the production of commodities and the reproduction of life. *The monster has become biopolitical*' (Negri 2001b: 191). In this same text, Negri affirms that 'power has always been power over life, biopower', and that, viewed through the lenses of antagonism, of biopolitical class struggle,

> the entirety of development has been dominated by this insubordination of life (the power [*potenza*] of life) against power [*potere*] (domination over life) .... Today however, rather than with the umpteenth revolt of *potenza* against *potere*, we are faced with common affirmation and the (probably irreversible) victory of *potenza*. The biopolitical monster is now centre-stage .... The monster has become hegemonic in biopolitics. (Negri 2001b: 192–3)

This statement, and the startling optimism underlying it, entail a move beyond the far more sober and ambivalent estimation of biopolitics in terms of capitalism and capacities put forward by Virno, and the transfiguration of the biopolitical into a kind of subjective apotheosis of the multitude. A victory, nothing less.

Whereas for Virno contemporary capitalism enjoins us to hone the tools of naturalism, linguistics, and philosophical anthropology, for Hardt and Negri, 'in the biopolitical world where social, economic and political production and reproduction coincide, the ontological perspective and the anthropological perspective tend to overlap' (Hardt and Negri 2000: 388). As Brett Neilson has suggested in a superb paper that seeks to untangle—through Virno's theoretical intercession—the dispute between Agamben and Negri, this biopolitical debate turns out to orbit far more around grounding philosophical categories, and in particular categories of modality, than it does around issues of social or political analysis. Whereas for Agamben Negri's constituent power remains caught, despite itself, in an Aristotelian matrix (and therefore in the biopolitics of sovereignty and constituted power) by its incapacity 'to think the existence of potentiality without any relation to Being in the form of actuality' (Neilson 2004: 66), Negri regards Agamben's account of bare life as an unacceptable concession to the negativity of power and a betrayal of any Spinozist politics of collective joy and desire. Virno is championed here by Neilson, then, for being able to combine a novel reading of Aristotle against the grain of Agamben's own with a radical theory of biopolitical capitalism which, though it follows Hardt and Negri's concern with the labor of the multitude, is able better to identify the 'philosophical' specificity of capitalism as a mode of social organization that 'gives the discrepancy potential/act an extraordinary pragmatic, empirical and economic importance. Capitalism *historicizes metahistory*' (Neilson 2004: 75).

Now, without going over the material admirably dealt with by Neilson, I'd like briefly to complement his treatment by touching on a couple of texts published by Negri since, which might allow us to zone in on the crux of the philosophical dispute over the biopolitical. In a critical portrait of Agamben as a figure permanently caught between an affirmative ethical moment and Heideggerian morbidity (with the latter most frequently gaining the upper hand), Negri returns to their differend in terms that should by now be familiar. First of all, skating over the rather controversial nature of the distinction itself, Negri imposes upon Agamben the dichotomous grid of biopolitics and biopower which defines his own vision of the class struggle over life:

> in his definition of *biopolitics*, Agamben not only denies that this concept can be isolated, outside and beyond *biopower*, but he also denies that the biopolitical can be conceived as a dichotomous field as well. For Agamben, the logic of the biopolitical field is, at best, a field of forces that is bipolar and transitive: home and city, *zoé* and *bios*, life and politics flow from one to the other, and are situated within an ever-reversible flow. In this way the absolute neutralisation of the biopolitical is imposed. (Negri 2006)

What does this neutralization entail? For Negri, it signifies the evacuation from biopolitics of living labor conceived of as a 'productive force', Marx's form-giving fire. Negri's opposition to this suspension of production in Agamben is couched in terms of a struggle over the very meaning of ontology. Showing the extent to which any ontology stripped of a constructive, fiercely subjective dimension is for him unthinkable, a reactionary or defeatist travesty, Negri declares that 'Agamben's exclusion of the productive determination from the concept of biopolitics not only precludes a definition of biopolitics but even prevents us from grasping the concept of being' (Negri 2006). And he fingers the culprit: Heidegger, whose incredibly influential treatment of the metaphysics of subjectivity in his Nietzsche lectures neutralized the formation of a radical political ontology, opening up a 'funereal conception of being' (Negri 2005) in which ethics is divorced from ontological construction and constitution. In Spinoza instead we have 'the only creative alternative in modernity', who grounds the conception of 'productive being, of a being as indefinite singularisation, reproduction and, therefore, construction of new being' (Negri 2006). The verdict is clear: 'One cannot place oneself ambiguously between Spinoza and Heidegger' (Negri 2005). Even Agamben's ethical gestures towards a 'coming community' and 'forms-of-life' that would subtract themselves from the lethal production of bare life by sovereign power do not seem to placate Negri's Spinozist convictions. Either ontology is both political and productive (Negri 2001b: 201), or we are left with the merely negative and formal shadow play of Power, the mystification of our collective social life.

VITALISM AND SOCIAL ONTOLOGY

Having tried to trace the key passages, and manifest tensions, in Negri's appropriation of the concept of biopolitics, I would like to conclude with some reflections on its philosophical and methodological repercussions. To begin with, we can note the explicit shift from a localized analytical register to that of a global totality, albeit an 'insurgent' one. Almost all of Foucault's methodological provisos are jettisoned, in the creation of a revolutionary grand narrative (a narrative of 'victory'!), in which, as I have sought to show, 'biopolitics' not only spans all the facets and agents within the new globalized scenario, it immerses them into a single ontopolitical continuum. Though Hardt and Negri do employ the concept in a more empirical vein, for instance to identify actors (NGOs, Indymedia, the protesters at Narmada, etc.) who seem no longer to allow themselves to be placed in a definite 'sphere'—who struggle not just over labor, but over 'life itself'—its principal role is that of 'blurring' hitherto distinct domains. Even more than the pivotal notion of 'real subsumption', for Negri biopolitics signals the impossibility of maintaining any steadfast distinction not only between domains of analysis but between explanatory stances, and even organizations (e.g. the figure of the 'party' seems to fall within the biopolitical indistinction between the social, the political and the vital). Thus it is in its internal role in Negri's own discourse—as a discourse that seeks to transcend disciplinary divisions, together with distinctions between discursive genres (e.g. the explanatory and the prophetic)—that we should look for the actual application of the concept of biopolitics (whose 'empirical' use instead rarely transcends the enumeration of biopolitical phenomena). Needless to say, besides its significant and instructive departures from Foucault, this totalizing use of the concept brings with it a whole raft of questions. Among them is of course that of whether this 'interbreeding' of the Marxian discourse of real subsumption, class struggle and living labor with the Foucauldian inquiry into the social reproduction of life doesn't have the unfortunate effect of blunting both—such that, for instance, Marxian class struggle is undermined by the microphysical dispersion of biopowers, and Foucauldian biopolitics loses its raison d'être in passing from a specific rationality of government (with its attendant and mutating technologies) to an ontological master signifier.

In line with these concerns, some commentators have sought to tar Negri with a vitalist brush (Balibar in Neilson 2004; Callinicos 2006: 144). The polemical abandonment of dialectics and the choice for a muscular ontology of immanence, driven by a strong subjectivist element, might easily lead one to such a conclusion. Thus, for Callinicos, 'central to Negri's ontology is not liberty, but Life' (Callinicos 2006: 121; see also p. 169 below). Leaving aside the fact that these two terms are incessantly conjoined in Negri's work—such that, I believe, he would find the one senseless without the other—the accusation of vitalism, with its inevitable antipolitical or even reactionary irrationalist overtones, does not quite hit the mark. First of all, contrary to what Callinicos intimates, Negri does not straightforwardly adopt Deleuze's ontological commitments (which, incidentally, are not straightforwardly 'vitalist'; see Toscano 2006). On the contrary, though Hardt and Negri (questionably) interpret Deleuze and Guattari's *A Thousand Plateaus* as 'a properly poststructuralist understanding of biopower that renews materialist thought and grounds itself solidly in the question of the production of social being', they chide them for their incapacity to really grasp the social determinations, organizations and institutions, not to mention the forms of subjectivity, which give structure to this production of social being. Enraptured by 'tendencies towards continuous movement and absolute flows', their treatment of biopower is, in the last instance, 'insubstantial and impotent' (Hardt and Negri 2000: 28). Similarly, the political deficit of the 'materialist vitalist' lineage of Nietzsche–Bergson–Deleuze is to be found in their shared incapacity to think an ontologically innovative *decision*, since, even though they 'correctly allude to the production of resistance and to the dynamic of a becoming-multitude (of singularities)', they tend to end up with 'a mere rejoicing in the banal duration of life' (Negri 2003a: 251).

This criticism of the vitalist lineage echoes in its form Negri's quarrel with Agamben, in which he declared: 'There is no bare life in ontology, like there is no social structure without ordering, or word without signification. The universal is concrete' (Negri 2001b: 193). The 'savage ontology' of vitalism, as Foucault teaches, 'discloses not so much what gives beings their foundation as what bears them from an instant towards a precarious form and yet is already secretly sapping them from within in order to destroy them'. It is (though perhaps not only) an 'ontology of the annihilation of beings' (Foucault 1989: 303). This vitalist *thanatos* is alien to Negri's democratic Spinozist vision whereby 'the political is the ontological power of a multitude of cooperating singularities' (Negri 2002c: 411). Though Negri does occasionally stray from the materialist determination of 'living labor' to speak of life 'as such', even then his position does not treat it as an independent principle (see Assoun 1999) or a mystical force in its own right. Rather, 'life is nothing other than the production and reproduction of the set of bodies and brains' (Hardt and Negri 2000: 365). In this respect, Hardt and Negri, especially when they write about the *machinic* character of biopolitics, are far closer to Deleuze and Guattari's *Anti-Oedipus*, with its equation 'NATURE = PRODUCTION', than to Deleuze's more Bergsonist texts. We should also not ignore the profound if anomalous *humanist* impetus at the core of Hardt and Negri's work, which, unlike that of Lazzarato (Lazzarato 1997), is unaffected by Deleuze's calls for a philosophy of 'anorganic life'. In the end, their notion of life is invariably social, constructed, collective. To say that the work of Hardt and Negri is not classically vitalist is not to suggest that their biopolitical recasting of the form-giving fire of living labor is unequivocal or beyond reproach. This is especially so when they frame their argument in terms of the concept of 'generation':

> Generation is the *primum* of the biopolitical world of Empire. Biopower—a horizon of the hybridization of the natural and the artificial, needs and machines, desire and the collective organization of the economic and the social—must continually regenerate itself in order to exist. Generation is there, before all else, as basis and motor of production and reproduction. (Hardt and Negri 2000: 389)

As I have suggested above, this 'always already' of generation, which, in a manner not entirely alien to a philosophy of history, is only appearing 'now', evacuates the very molecular ambivalence of a biopolitics that, at least in Foucault, had cast some doubt on the ontological anteriority of bases and motors. What's more, with its confidence in an invisible but irreversible victory, the Negrian notion of biopolitics does away with the ambiguity in Marx's own treatment of the vitality of labor, set into motion not by the impetus of its own excessive and autonomous desire but by capital. The life of laboring bodies and brains might indeed be 'what infuses and dominates all production' (Hardt and Negri 2000: 365). Even so, and especially if we take seriously Foucault's study of the capillary and subjectifying mechanisms of biopolitical 'subpower', it might be far too early to shout victory, and never too late to recognize that the vitality of many of these bodies and brains carries a very strong dose of heteronomy.

NOTES

1. Despite Hardt and Negri's foregrounding of the significance, in moving beyond Foucault, of the new political theory of value and the new theory of subjectivity they draw from the legacy of *operaismo*—formulated in terms of the centrality of immaterial and affective labor to their appropriation of biopolitics—in this paper I will opt for philosophical abstraction and deal only with the issue of 'living labor' per se, eschewing a critique of its empirical figures. I think this is warranted by Hardt and Negri's description of the dimension added by workerist and postworkerist thought as being one which examines the 'immediately social and communicative dimension of living labour in contemporary society' (Hardt and Negri 2000: 29).

2. Marx himself was not insensitive to the 'biopolitical' dimension inherent to the functioning of capital as a social relation. In the *Grundrisse* he writes of how capital must 'replace the production costs of the living labour capacities, in other words,

must keep the workers alive as workers' (Marx 1973: 359). In a recent essay which, from a critical and libertarian Marxist standpoint, provides an acute argument for the transhistorical character of capitalist 'biopolitics', Nate Holdren—making excellent use of feminist literature—has detailed, through an analysis of 'simple circulation', the way in which the very relationship between labor power as commodity, money (wages), and the means of subsistence is deeply biopolitical, and, what is more, how the continuous and violent enclosure of noncapitalist forms of life into these circuits (Marx's 'so-called primitive accumulation') provides a truly materialist insight into a critique of 'biopolitical' economy. His conclusion is that 'the expansion of value production effected by the terms biopolitics and biopower demonstrates something about the concept and material existence of capitalism itself, something true for the entirety of the epoch of capitalist production, from its beginnings to the present' (Holdren, forthcoming). Following this line of argument, one could even suggest, following David Harvey, that contemporary 'biopolitical grievances' (Hardt and Negri 2004: 285) be rethought as anti-imperialist struggle against 'accumulation by dispossession' (Harvey 2003).

3. The question of the relationship between war and biopolitics is one which exceeds the remit of this chapter. Yet we can see that Negri's characteristic oscillation between crisis/command, on the one hand, and regulation/production, on the other, is also present in this theme. Thus, though war, and in particular nuclear war, is presented as the emblem of capital's incapacity to sustain political mediations, and its terroristic resort to pure fear and command (Hardt and Negri 2004: 18; Negri 1987b; Negri 2005), Negri also tries to conceptualize what Chomsky has debunked as the 'new military humanism' in terms of a legitimating, biopolitical intervention and a new, continuous 'regulating' war (Hardt and Negri 2000; Hardt and Negri 2004: 22). It may be noted that despite the often cosmetic proliferation of NGOs—which are 'completely immersed in the constitution of Empire; they anticipate the power of its pacifying and productive intervention of justice' (Hardt and Negri 2000: 36)—and sundry biopolitical entrepreneurs, current military ventures, with the truly biopolitical misery they bring in their wake (looted hospitals, broken sewers, intermittent electricity …), hardly fit the ideal type of imperial biopolitics.

4. On government or governmentality as the 'conduct of conduct', see Foucault's lectures included in Burchell, Gordon and Miller 1991.

5. The link between biopower and the Deleuzean periodization of societies of discipline and societies of control is chronologically rather tricky. If we stick to Foucault, in fact, the disciplinary training of bodies (anatomo-politics) and the statistical governance of populations (biopolitics) are two sides of one power complex, that of biopower precisely, so that the shift is simply one of emphasis within biopower itself. Hardt and Negri instead wish to stress a shift from modern disciplinarity to postmodern biopower, which manifests itself as the society of control. As they write, 'when power becomes entirely biopolitical, the whole social body is comprised by power's machine and developed in its virtuality' (Hardt and Negri 2000: 24). Or, in a more metaphysical vein, Negri declares that in 'the period of the man–machine command becomes biopolitical control … control is inserted into the temporal ontology of the common, i.e. of life' (Negri 2003a: 256). Whilst this vocabulary of virtuality seems attractive in a temporal treatment of biopolitics (see also Lazzarato 1997), I suspect that, much as Negri's notion of productive power is not compatible with Virno's capacity or Agamben's treatment of potentiality, the notion of the virtual is far too Bergsonist to really gel with Negri's Spinozism of bodies and affects.

6
Marxist Wisdom:
Antonio Negri on The Book of Job

Ted Stolze

In memory of my mother

> The Enlightenment ... will be all the more radical when
> it does not pour equal scorn on the Bible's all-pervading,
> healthy insight into man. It is for this very reason (one not
> remote from the Enlightenment) that the Bible can speak
> to all men, and be understood across so many lands and
> right on through the ages.
> —Ernst Bloch, *Atheism in Christianity*

Louis Althusser once insisted that 'we ... have no religion, not even the
religion of our theory, still less that of the goals of history' (Althusser 1977:
9). By contrast, in a recently published autobiographical interview, Antonio
Negri has remarked that, for him at least, the problem is not religion but
transcendence:

> I have never had anything against religion, I am simply against
> transcendence. I absolutely reject every form of transcendence. But certain
> aspects of religion, and especially certain religious experiences, truly have
> the capacity to construct, not in a mystical but in an ascetic manner.
> *Ascesis* has always fascinated me: it is an interiorized construction of the
> object, whereas mysticism, on the contrary, is a distancing of the object,
> a negative theology, a theory of the margins. *Ascesis* is a constituent state,
> a transformation of the senses and the imagination, of the body and
> reason. In order to live well and in order to construct what is common,
> *ascesis* is always necessary. (Negri 2002b: 202–3, my translation)

An excellent illustration of Negri's perspective on *ascesis* and the struggle
to 'construct what is common' may be found in his newly reissued work
on the Book of Job (Negri 2002a).[1] As Negri relates in his introduction, he
began to write the book in 1982 or 1983, the beginning of his fourth year of
imprisonment (Negri 2002a: 7). Negri was only the most famous (or in the

official vilification of the time the most 'notorious') of thousands of Italian activists who at the end of the 1970s had run up against the brutal force of state repression for their participation in the decade's radical movements. During such a bleak personal and political period of his life, the relevance of the Book of Job for Negri lay not primarily in how to reconcile the reality of human suffering with the existence of a just God but instead how to *resist* suffering of a most terrestrial sort. As he explains,

> There exist dozens of readings of Job: but none had succeeded in giving a response to the theological question of evil. *Si Deus est, unde malum? Si malum est, cur Deus?* [If God exists, whence arises evil? If evil exists, why does God exist?] However, it wasn't only a matter of understanding, it was equally a matter of discovering how to construct a course of liberation: it was a practical problem, not a theodicy. (Negri 2002a: 7–8)

Negri notes that he was offering neither a detailed commentary on, nor an exhaustive interpretation of, the Book of Job but instead was merely engaging in an 'intervention' (Negri 2002a: 21). And what an extraordinary intervention! For Negri, like Ernst Bloch before him,[2] compellingly shows that the Bible is too important to be ignored by Marxists or left to believers alone.

Before considering Negri's intervention in detail, however, it is perhaps useful to provide a brief overview of the Book of Job.[3] This complex biblical text opens with a prologue written in prose that recounts a folktale about a prosperous man, Job, who, despite undergoing incredible personal adversity, nonetheless remains loyal to Yahweh (the sacred name of God in the ancient Israelite tradition). Unbeknownst to Job, the causes of his adversity are two divine tests set up by Yahweh and the 'Prosecutor' (literally, in Hebrew, the *satan*), who claims that Job would abandon his faith if he were to lose, first, his possessions and children, and, second, his physical well-being. Indeed, Job's wife from the start advises him to 'curse Elohim [God] and die', but he rejects this 'foolish' thought and accepts his complete reversal in fortune.[4] Three friends—Eliphaz, Bildad, and Zophar—come to comfort Job, who humbly and patiently accepts pain and suffering at Yahweh's hand (1:1–2:10).

The main part of the book (3:1–42:6), however, is written in poetry and depicts a strikingly different image of Job: not a man who patiently endures but one who adamantly protests against the unjust treatment he thinks he has received by divine sanction. This poetic part begins (ch. 3) with the common biblical literary form of a lament, in which Job curses the day of his birth and longs for some way to escape the misery of his life. His friends prove to be sorry comforters and offer mere theological platitudes as explanations of Job's predicament. Each of them understands God to exercise ethical control over the universe by rewarding the just and punishing the wicked. Consequently, each argues that Job himself (or his children!) must be responsible for his present dire straights. Each friend in turn affirms the conventional wisdom of divine justice—a kind of theodicy, in other words—and urges Job to make peace with God.

Job responds to his friends' arguments, accusations, and pious advice with vociferous protests that he is indeed innocent of any wrongdoing. He decries the disorder evident in a world that seems to be governed more by evil than good, and he boldly challenges God to listen to his complaint, indeed, to meet him face to face. In effect, as commentators have pointed out, Job is pressing a lawsuit against God. A dramatic—and for Negri an ethico-political and even ontological—highpoint occurs in chapter 19 when Job envisions an 'avenger' (*go'el*) who will someday come to deliver him from his present torments (19:25).

In the midst of this series of speeches and responses occurs the interlude of a lengthy, self-standing poetic meditation on the nature of wisdom (ch. 28). Wisdom is declared in this poem to be divine and thus beyond the comprehension of human beings, unless they 'fear' God and 'avoid evil' (28:25).

The next three chapters (29–31) are soliloquies in which Job recalls his previously happy circumstances and honorable position in society (29), contrasts this with his present 'miserable days' (30:16), and concludes with an oath in which he upholds his integrity and issues a direct challenge to God: 'Here is my mark: let Shaddai [the Almighty] answer me …' (31:35).

At this point a fourth, younger man, Elihu, angered by what he has heard so far, also enters into debate with Job. Elihu presents four rambling speeches in which he tries to refute the notion that suffering is necessarily the consequence of wrongdoing and rejects Job's rebellious assertion that God is acting unjustly (chs 32–7). Elihu contends that God inflicts suffering only to chasten human beings. God speaks to human beings in dreams in order to warn them against pride; those who have gone astray may hope for an intercessor to vouch for them and evoke divine grace. In the last analysis, however, Elihu maintains that God's actions are simply beyond human comprehension.

The dramatic climax of the Book of Job is a theophany. God appears and answers Job 'from the whirlwind'. In two powerful speeches (38:1–40:2 and 40:6–41:26) God directly reveals to Job the glorious expanse of the universe but only indirectly answers Job's question about the reason for his misfortunes. In these speeches the implication seems clear enough, however. At the beginning of the world God brought order out of chaos—represented by the mythical beasts Behemoth and Leviathan—but ever since has struggled to preserve this order. Chaos continually threatens to undermine that cosmic order—indeed, it invariably partially succeeds in doing so.

After God's first speech Job concedes the point: 'Oh, I am small, what could I reply to you? I put my hand to my mouth' (40:3–4). Moreover, following the second speech Job makes a crucial distinction: whereas before he had heard of God only 'with ears' hearing … now my eye sees you' (42:5a). Finally, Job utters what was once taken by many commentators to be an expression of contrition, but is more likely to be an acknowledgement that his demand has been satisfied, the time for him to lament has passed: 'I despise and repent of dust and ashes' (42:5b).

The book closes with another prose section, an epilogue that picks up where the prologue had left off. At this conclusion of the earlier folktale, the patient, humble Job prays for his friends, his former fortunes are restored—indeed, they are doubled (likely an oblique indication that he has in effect won his lawsuit against God!)—and he lives to a ripe old age (42:7–17). Especially noteworthy, however, is Yahweh's admission that Job was right all along to protest: 'He said to Eliphaz the Temanite, "I am very angry with you and your two friends, because you have not spoken truth of me, as has my servant Job"' (42:7).

For Negri the Book of Job functions as a 'theological fable' or 'parable' (Negri 2002a: 34) that can help one to construct a 'genealogy' of the 'origin of value and of the dynamic of its system, that is, also of the value of labor and of its creative aspects' (Negri 2002a: 36). Indeed, as Negri explains further, 'the reality of our misery is Job's, the questions and responses that we pose to the world are the same as Job's. We express ourselves with the same despair, by uttering the same blasphemies' (Negri 2002a: 36–7). Several themes stand out in Negri's proposed genealogy: the ethico-political significance of pain and suffering, the rejection of all forms of theodicy, and the radical openness, or *immeasurability*, of the future.

Consider, first of all, the extreme suffering and pain that Job undergoes as the result of the two divine tests mentioned above. In Negri's view, Job's experience teaches us that pain and suffering is the destiny of all human beings and can only be defined through compassion. But compassion is not simply an 'intellectual act'; it is a concrete way to 'sympathize with' or to 'suffer together' with others.[5] Here Negri's reading of the Book of Job dovetails with that of the Peruvian liberation theologian Gustavo Gutiérrez, who has pointed out that Job's 'solitude' is hardly passive or reactive. On the contrary, Gutiérrez argues, it is an active and productive solitude, in the sense that Job increasingly comes to identify with, and protest against, the various forms of pain and suffering in the world, not the least of which are due to socio-economic oppression (Gutiérrez 1987: 31–8). As Gutiérrez puts it, 'Job begins to free himself from an ethic centered on personal rewards and to pass to another focused on the needs of one's neighbor' (Gutiérrez 1987: 31). Consider in this light, then, the moving words in chapter 24 of the Book of Job, in which Job denounces those who 'snatch away boundary markers, seize flocks and pasture them ... drive off orphans' asses, take a widow's ox for collateral, shove the poor off the road', and expresses his solidarity with 'the land's destitute' who 'huddle together in hiding' and lodge naked, 'without clothing, uncovered in the cold, wet with mountain rain, [and] without shelter ... hug the rock' (24:2–4, 7–8).

Negri concludes that one of the most profound lessons of the Book of Job is precisely that

> it is not the recognition of a behavior of pain, nor the communication of a pain that furnishes us with the constitutive process of the social: pain *is* this constitutive process, and it is only by living it, by sympathizing with the world, that the world can be reconstructed by pain. Compassion goes beyond recognition, the concept, and representation. I cannot represent for myself pain if I don't live it. I cannot recognize the other who is subject to pain if I don't sympathize with him. But through this action that pushes me ... to sympathize with him, I proceed to the construction of the world. Neither God nor a meaning come down from on high constructs the very being of the world: the latter is on the contrary constructed by suffering, by pain, which come from below. (Negri 2002a: 136)

Yet none of this implies that human suffering and pain are ever theologically justifiable. For Negri the whole point of the Book of Job is not really to solve the problem of evil, rather it is to undermine the reader's confidence that there *is* any such solution and thereby repudiate every conceivable form of theodicy. The leading biblical scholar Walter Brueggemann has pointed out that nowhere in the Hebrew Bible can one find a definitive solution to the problem of evil.[6] In a real sense, then, the Book of Job only pushes an already existing biblical train of thought to its explosive conclusion. It is indeed remarkable to behold how each of Job's interlocutors in turn offers a well-worn justification for God's actions, while Job himself defiantly continues to affirm his innocence and occasionally even expresses 'a laughter that resembles sarcasm and that rejects every consoling or pacifying rhythm' (Negri 2002a: 93).

It is precisely the failure of theological justification for human suffering and evil that makes both possible and necessary what Negri regards as a 'subterranean presence' in the Book of Job that only 'gradually becomes evident and winds up exploding' (Negri 2002a: 104): the Messiah. It is only a Messiah who can come to Job's defense insofar as God has come to operate less as an impartial judge and more as a malicious adversary. It is only a Messiah who can lead Job beyond his present world of pain and suffering toward a future state of redemption. But caution is in order here.

Negri is not lapsing into yet another dubious retrospective Christian interpretation of the 'avenger' (*go'el*) to whom Job appeals.[7] Rather, again like Ernst Bloch before him,[8] he is trying to identify a powerfully materialist dimension of the Book of Job. For the kind of messianic deliverance that Job seeks can only be secured with respect to the *body*, indeed through, a 'resurrection of the flesh' (Negri 2002a: 104–8).[9]

As Negri is well aware, the idea of a resurrection of the flesh is hardly a popular idea today. Even in contemporary religious belief and practice, the 'materialist' theory of resurrection has largely been displaced by an 'idealist' theory of the immortality of the soul. Good atheist that he is, Negri is quick to add that he favors a 'secularization' of this and other theological concepts (e.g. creation or redemption), 'but only on the condition of not losing through this pseudo-rationalist conversion the practical, ethical, passional content of religious truth. It is not mystery that interests us, but grace and charity' (Negri 2002a: 114). As a result, as Negri elsewhere admits, it is not only the eschatological aspect of the concept of bodily resurrection that intrigues him, but, more importantly, it is the 'rediscovery of a materialist religion' (Negri 2002b: 231).

It is worth emphasizing at this point that adopting a messianic outlook need not imply any teleology. On the contrary, it suggests the radical openness of the historical process. For Negri at least, the Messiah 'is a surplus of Being, of materiality, original and outside of every finality, which is spread out everywhere in the world' (Negri 2002a: 146). This radical openness of the future is what Negri designates as its 'immeasurability' (Negri 2002a: 23–8). What is immeasurable is assuredly not an instance of the Burkean[10] or Kantian[11] 'sublime', for this would misconstrue the 'ontological realism' of Job's suffering and encounter with God as merely an extreme form of subjective experience (Negri 2002a: 95–6). As a result, and notwithstanding Hegel's insistence that 'mankind has revered measure as something inviolable and sacred' (Hegel 1976: 329), Negri gestures toward what is objectively beyond the possibility of even being measured, indeed, toward what is *measureless*.[12]

Yet in Negri's opinion most interpreters of the Book of Job have tended to do exactly what Job's own interlocutors do, namely, 'reduce his experience to a dimension of what is theologically known, to a given form and measure' (Negri 2002a: 139). Although Negri only briefly suggests as much (Negri 2002a: 25–6), one could point to Hegel as an especially revealing case of how *not* to interpret the Book of Job. For example, in his *Lectures on the Philosophy of Religion* Hegel admits that 'Job is guiltless; he finds his misfortune unjustifiable and so is dissatisfied' (Hegel 1988: 369). However, for Hegel this implies that

> there is an antithesis within him, the consciousness of the justice or righteousness that is absolute and of the incongruity between his fate and this righteousness. He is dissatisfied precisely because he does not regard necessity as blind fate; it is known to be God's purpose to bring about good things for those who are good. The critical point, then, occurs when this dissatisfaction and despondency has to submit to absolute, pure confidence. This submission is the end point. (Hegel 1988: 369–70)

Job's submission is, for Hegel, ultimately an expression of his complete trust in a purposeful God, in the 'harmony of the power of God with the truth' (Hegel 1988: 370). Indeed, this is why Hegel thinks that at the end God restores Job to a position of good fortune. The Hegelian dialectical method at work here could not be clearer—or more mistaken in its ability to grasp what is really at stake in the Book of Job. Misfortune, submission, restoration: Hegel has turned Job's passion into a devotional exercise.

For Job to have seen God directly means something quite different, though. According to Negri,

> Job has seen God, and he can consequently speak of and in his turn participate in divinity, in the function of redemption that human beings construct in their lives—the instrument of a death of God that is the human constitution and creation of the world. (Negri 2002a: 139)

The point here is not that an object or a being could be too large or ill-defined to be measurable. Immeasurability has nothing to do with a theoretical shortcoming in the face of immensity (such as occurs, Burke argues, when one contemplates God's 'almighty power' (Burke 1998: 111)) but instead concerns the limitless self-measurement that arises in human creative activity.

In light of this immeasurability of social practice, Negri concludes, the antagonism between life and death that runs throughout the Book of Job ultimately 'is resolved in favor of life. My life is the knowledge that I have of you—my eyes have seen you. I am. Humanity is' (Negri 2002a:

140). Although the ontological foundation of the world continues to be menaced by great forces of death and destruction (depicted as Behemoth and Leviathan), human beings can nonetheless come to resist this evil through their own acts of creation. Job's vision of God holds out the prospect of redemption, 'as the world is formed and reformed in the struggle against evil' (Negri 2002a: 140–1). In short, as Negri puts it, 'the struggle against monsters is the condition of the ordering of nature. The ordering of nature is the condition of the ordering of the world, and the latter is the condition of redemption. But these passages are neither linear nor continuous. There is no finalism, but struggle, invention, and victory. *There is constitution'* (Negri 2002a: 141).

As one would expect from the complex library of ancient Israelite traditions that it is, the Hebrew Bible contains a wide variety of modes of discourse, e.g. laws, records, genealogies, liturgies, quasi-historical narratives, love poems, prophetic injunctions, and wisdom.[13] Scholars usually categorize the Book of Job as an important example of biblical wisdom literature.[14] But there remains a crucial difference between the Book of Job and other wisdom texts such as Proverbs and Ecclesiastes (Qohelet). As Gustavo Gutiérrez has observed, there exists another 'dimension' in the Book of Job, which has a great deal in common with such prophetic books as Amos, Hosea, Micah, and Isaiah. Moreover, Gutiérrez has insisted on the inseparability of these prophetic and sapiential dimensions within the Book of Job:

> Vision of God (final stage in Job's suit against God) and defense of the poor (a role he discovers for himself because of his own innocence) are ... combined in the experience of Job as a man of justice ... .
>
> Without the prophetic dimension the language of contemplation is in danger of having no grip on the history in which God acts and in which we meet God. Without the mystical dimension the language of prophecy can narrow its vision and weaken its perception of the God who makes all things new ... . Each undergoes a distortion that isolates it and renders it unauthentic. (Gutiérrez 1987: 96)

Although Negri would clearly take exception to Gutiérrez's characterization of Job's vision of God as 'mystical',[15] he too has identified in the Book of Job a concern not only for social justice but for something more: the immeasurable. As we have already seen, for Negri what is ontologically immeasurable is not exactly 'God' but instead the radical openness of the future, always already made possible by the immanent human power to imagine and create a different world.[16] This is why I would like to argue that Negri has introduced into—or recognized as nascent within—Marxism something more than just the secularized prophetic dimension so often commented on[17]—and not always favorably, it should be said![18] To be precise, Negri has made a formidable contribution to what could be termed a distinctively Marxist wisdom tradition.[19]

By way of conclusion, let us turn again to Negri's motivation at the beginning of the 1980s for working on the Book of Job. The accumulated violence of the twentieth century had already posed, as never before, fundamental questions about the nature of human evil that echoed Job's own anguished lament. For Negri such questions included the following: 'How can one believe in reason after Auschwitz and Hiroshima? How can one continue to be a communist after Stalin?' (Negri 2002a: 27). Humanity had found itself faced with unprecedented dilemmas in which, Negri wondered,

> Why do we produce evil? And how can we orient ourselves in a world in which all dialectics have proven their disgusting non-effectiveness? In which murder and the destruction of values have attained immeasurability? And in which absolute non-Being, that is to say, total nuclear destruction of all that exists, is for the first time at the disposal of power? And what does 'salvation' mean? (Negri 2002a: 27–8)

In short, Negri admitted, 'all the certainties that we had inherited and the values for which we had struggled were put into question' (Negri 2002a: 28). This was a generalized, but *negative*, crisis of measure.

In a rather different, more hopeful, and *positive* way, though, the year 1968 had also introduced a 'crisis of measure and the laws that structure it', and a challenge to official Marxism as a 'culture of measure, a labor of measure, and a measured passion of reason of state' (Negri 2002a: 9). Indeed, by the end of the 1970s there had occurred, according to Negri, 'a mutation of labor … based on the collapse of the measure of value' (Negri 2002a: 10). As a result, both (state) socialism[20] and capitalism had become impossible; and there was a pressing need to create something new.

Such a collapse of the measure of value was, in Negri's estimation, again analogous to Job's experience, for he had once been 'loyal to all measures that regulate the world as sustained by God' (Negri 2002a: 10). But Job's singularity—and universality—was to have wound up protesting 'against measure', whether theological, ontological, ethical, or political in nature. So too, Negri proposed, must contemporary Marxist theory and practice 'move with joy beyond measure' (Negri 2002a: 10)[21] and resume a process of 'self-valorization'.[22] For Negri this was the only way to imagine communism again.

Although there is, perhaps, an inadequate anticapitalist political strategy laid out in his writings (a point made generously by Leo Panitch and Sam

Gindin (Panitch and Gindin 2002) and rather uncharitably by Alex Callinicos (Callinicos 2001a)), political strategy has never been Negri's main concern. He has always been much more interested in political *ontology*, in other words, the general conditions of possibility for envisioning any political strategy at all.[23] Negri is only half joking, I suspect, when he quips that 'my dream in life is to have a chair in ontology' (Negri 2002b: 96).

Consider in this light, then, the simultaneously political and ontological significance for Marxism of the concept of the Messiah whose incipient formation Negri discerns in the Book of Job. Negri argues that

> in Marxian discourse the Messiah is defined, revealed, and put into movement by the same contradictions that have permitted capitalist development and that have unleashed its crisis. In Marx the process is materially determined and resolved. But what then are the framework and corporeality of the theoretical struggle that are promised here? The recognition of the scientific character of Marxian discourse can, in my view, only lead us to insist on the resonance of the religious experience that traverses these pages, and that prepares the appreciation of its innovative, redemptive, revolutionary advent. Science removes from this prodigious event its mystery, but it cannot remove its passion—on the contrary, it must restore this passion to us. (Negri 2002a: 115–16)

In the last analysis, what is most impressive about Negri's intervention regarding the Book of Job is how powerfully it can help Marxists themselves to recover and sustain a passion not just to interpret but also to change the world.[24]

NOTES

1. All translations from this book are mine.
2. See Bloch's *Atheism in Christianity* (Bloch 1972), a book to which Negri refers several times, and his masterpiece *The Principle of Hope* (Bloch 1986), especially pp. 1183–311.
3. For a succinct discussion of the Book of Job that superbly indicates the current state of biblical scholarship, see Crenshaw 2001: 331–55. Perhaps the most impressive recent study is Newsom 2003. Those interested in the most authoritative, still-standard commentaries that Negri himself employs should consult the following: Pope 1965 and Habel 1975. After Negri had already completed his research, a much expanded version of Habel's commentary appeared as Habel 1985.
4. For quotations from the Book of Job I have used Edwin M. Good's vivid translation included with his commentary *In Turns of Tempest: A Reading of Job, with a translation* (Good 1990).
5. Negri develops his philosophical analysis of pain at greater length in Negri 1994.
6. See the entries for 'Suffering' and 'Theodicy' in Brueggemann 2002: 200–4, 212–14.

7. On the temptation for Christians to engage in theological 'prooftexting' of this passage, and thereby to interpret the 'avenger' as a 'redeemer' (as most English translations still indicate), see Newsom 1996: 477–9.

8. See Bloch 1972: 106–22.

9. The relationship between messianic expectation and resurrection is a dominant motif in biblical apocalypticism. On the historical emergence and development of the apocalyptic worldview, see Collins 1998.

10. See Burke 1998: 49–199. It is worth noting that Burke invokes the Book of Job as an illustration of what he means by the sublime (see pp. 106–11).

11. See Kant 2000. Kant discusses the Book of Job at some length in his essay 'On the Miscarriage of All Philosophical Trials in Theodicy', in Kant 1996: 24–37.

12. One could easily make the general case that biblical, as opposed to ancient Greek, thinking about space and time allowed for a positive appreciation of what the Norwegian scholar Thorleif Boman once characterized as 'boundlessness'. See Boman's now-classic study, *Hebrew Thought Compared with Greek* (Boman 1970: 123–83).

13. For introductions to the panoply of biblical literary forms, see Gabel et al. 2000 and Johnson 2002.

14. On the ancient Israelite wisdom tradition, and the place of the Book of Job within it, see Bergant 1997, Crenshaw 1998, and Clifford 1998.

15. Indeed, Negri identifies a mystical 'trap' laid by Job's friend Zophar (Negri 2002a: 69–70). In his recent autobiographical interview Negri likewise characterizes mysticism as 'the worst of things, because there is a negative foundation from which one believes to escape and into which one falls back again' (Negri 2002b: 134).

16. Negri does admit, however, that if he had to define 'God', it would be in terms of 'overabundance, excess, and joy' (Negri 2002b: 135).

17. For example, John Raines proposes in the introduction to his anthology *Marx and Religion* (Raines 2002) that 'like the Hebrew prophets of old, Marx knew that to speak of social justice we must become socially self-critical, and that means becoming critical of the ruling powers—whether they be kings or priests or investment bankers ... . For Marx, all ideas are relative to the social location and interests of their production. And like the prophets before him, the most revealing perspective is not from the top down or the center outward, but the view of "the widow and the orphan"—the point of view of the exploited and the marginalized. Suffering can be seen through and unveil official explanations; it can cry out and protest against the arrogance of power' (p. 5).

18. Negri himself has cautioned against 'false prophets [who] lead only to a kind of general nihilism, a destruction that ends up wiping them out in turn. Whereas to question the world is at each moment to invent; it is a constructive dimension, quite the contrary of prophetic nihilism' (Negri 2002b: 236).

19. Others who might be included within a genealogy of Marxist wisdom are Walter Benjamin and Ernst Bloch. Perhaps, too, this is one of the most important contributions made to Marxism by contemporary liberation theology. For a fine survey of the movement in Latin America and its implications for socialist renewal, see Löwy 1996. See, too, a remarkable book by the German liberation theologian Dorothee Soelle, *The Silent Cry: Mysticism and Resistance* (Soelle 2001).

20. Throughout his oeuvre Negri consistently fails, I believe, to distinguish between the former Stalinist bureaucracies and the possibility of an authentic socialist democracy. As a result, he often seems to pose an all-or-nothing alternative between capitalism and communism and thereby fails to provide an adequate theory of how *transition* to a classless society might occur. I don't mean that Negri has nothing important to say about the politics of such a transition—far from it. However, even when he does discuss transitional politics (e.g. in such works from the late 1970s as *Domination and Sabotage* (Negri 1978a) or *Marx Beyond Marx* (Negri 1991a)), it occurs at a level of abstraction that is not particularly useful for concrete struggles to win structural reforms that could in fact initiate a break with capitalist social relations.

21. Constructing such an 'immeasurable Marxism' would seem to be an important aspect of Negri's project (with Michael Hardt) in *Empire* (Hardt and Negri 2000). There is an explicit discussion of measure and immeasurability on pp. 354–9 of that book.

22. 'Self-valorization' is a key concept in Negri's theoretical lexicon and refers to workers' positive capacity through their own organizing to free themselves from capitalist exploitation and thereby transform work into freely associated production. See, for example, Negri's discussion in Negri 1991a: 162–3, 185–6.

23. The mutual implication of politics and metaphysics is, in my opinion, one of the overriding themes of his books on Descartes (*Descartes politico o della ragionevole ideologia* (Negri 1970)), Spinoza (*The Savage Anomaly* (Negri 1991b)), and the history of 'constituent power' (*Insurgencies* (Negri 1999a)).

24. Thanks to Wonil Kim for his insights regarding the Book of Job and to Tim Murphy for his astute critical remarks on an earlier version of this article—and for his patience.

Part III

Constitutive Ontology

7
Difference, Event, Subject: Antonio Negri's Political Theory as Postmodern Metaphysics

Mahmut Mutman

As Antonio Negri is the thinker of a power which exceeds representation, every representation of his philosophy is taking the risk of losing its singular power. Given the difficulty of avoiding this risk, one may perhaps try negotiating a mimetic strategy of applying to Negri the same procedure he applied to Marx: *take Negri beyond Negri*. But what is this supposed to mean? Pass Negri, leave him behind? Go further than him, get ahead of him or go away from him? Each of these would perhaps be the figure of a different journey; there is already a plurality of paths. But, according to the law of this singular figure of 'X beyond X', the direction seems to be certain: beyond Negri, there is still Negri. Is the destination the same as the departure? Will Negri be there, waiting for us at the end of the road, like Michel Foucault's 'motionless' Hegel?[1] If Negri is not a thinker of negativity but rather the thinker of a power which exceeds representation, the question then becomes how Negri could *think* this power or excess without representing and transcendentalizing it. Surely, this is also a question for ourselves, those few who read him: how could we think Negri without representing him in the sense of repeating his singular idiom, turning his (and our) productivity into exchange, circulating passwords amongst ourselves? (Negri begetting Negri!) According to the figure of excess, however, no representation of Negri can be proper to Negri, except the one which goes beyond Negri, which takes Negri beyond Negri. But this would no longer be a representation in the conventional sense. And would it not also be a certain forgetting of Negri, or the forgetting of a certain Negri? Negri beyond Negri is not simply more Negri, but perhaps also, strangely, less than Negri.

My reading will follow an oblique path through Negri's writings. It is a marginal path, emphasizing frequently used words rather than precise conceptual articulations, engaging minute critical readings by focusing on a single phrase or footnote, taking a delight in contradictions and aporias. I shall argue that Antonio Negri's philosophy is a new theory of subject as essentially displaced. This 'postmodern' metaphysics of subject offers no less than a political theory which aims to transform the present. I only aim to underline some of the limits and paradoxes of Negri's new political philosophy.

A POWER OF DIFFERENCE: FROM MARX TO SPINOZA

Negri's theoretical project in *Marx Beyond Marx* was a reinscription of the *differential* moment as irreducible in the textual economy of Marx's discourse (Negri 1991a: 52). There is an irreducible class antagonism between two social subjects in the fundamental relation that constitutes capitalism. That which seems to have a nature-like lawfulness, objectivity, and unity has therefore a political nature. The economic itself, immediately divided and dividing, *is* political. More conventional versions of Marxist theory found this a novel yet problematical approach. For instance, praising Negri's appreciation of the subjective aspect of human labor, the theorist of crisis James O'Connor has nevertheless found a 'fatal flaw' in his approach: neglecting the cultural and ideological conditions of capitalist reproduction, its institutional and cultural mediations (O'Connor 1987: 54, 91–2, 145).

For Negri, it is precisely by such a mediation that the worker's productive potential is hegemonized by capital. The law of value is the mechanism by which the capitalist captures the creative potential of the worker. (In the conventional Marxist language, capital consumes the use value of labor power.) It is the measure of value, the order of exchange and equivalence, which makes the *difference* produced by labor power identical, and this making identical of productive difference is a relationship of force and command. Therefore the workers can only negate the measure or law of value; such negation is the *affirmation* of their own autonomous subjectivity, of their own 'use values'. As capitalism is constituted by this originary difference between capital and labor, class struggle is not a privileged instance at all. It is an everyday occurrence, from absenteeism to wildcat strikes. In Michael Ryan's apt description, Negri's analysis unfolds 'a logic of separation which leads to ... the positing of an inverse world of difference emerging out of its suppressed form in the world of unity' (Ryan 1982: 207). Crisis is a structural or necessary possibility and is a result of the workers' affirmation of their autonomy, in the form of their expanding needs and new demands as well as refusal of work. As there is no formal equivalence for the kind of difference affirmed by the proletarian power, the latter means the direct appropriation of social wealth. Workers' power is the destruction of the logic of equivalence and constitutes a world of difference and plurality in which they expand their needs and their creative capacities freely. This difference or plurality is one that is immediately expressed, without mediation.

Although *Savage Anomaly* is a reading of Spinoza's work, the philosophical argument Negri finds there is not essentially different than Marx's account of capital and labor in the *Grundrisse*. Spinoza's distinction between *potentia* (power in the sense of efficacy or potential) and *potestas* (power in the sense of domination) becomes the main axis around which Negri reads his texts (see Negri 1991b). There is a complete break and no mediation between *potentia* and *potestas*. But more importantly, Negri reads *potentia* or 'potential' as both ontological and political constitution. Hence his famous thesis: Spinoza's politics is his metaphysics. This gives Negri an opportunity to answer a criticism directed at his prior work on Marx: the notions of 'autonomy' and 'self-valorization' remain captive to an identitarian logic. In Spinoza's concepts of *potentia* and *multitudo*, Negri finds a more refined concept of a pluralistic collective subject. The concept of *potentia* defines the structure of being as a constitutive collective practice which produces the world as an open-ended, dynamic activity, and informs an ethics of desire, passion, and love as well as a politics of liberation and difference. 'Multitude' is the collective subject of this constitutive movement.

Negri's Spinozian Marxism underlines a new sense of Enlightenment progressivism and gives it an ontological and political basis. In later works, this new collective subject is called 'constitutent power'. *Labor of Dionysus*, coauthored with Michael Hardt, elaborates this ontological vision by recalling Benjamin's 'nonrepresentational and unrepresentable divine violence' and rethinking it as 'constituent power' and 'constituent subject' (Hardt and Negri 1994: 294–5, 308–13). Hardt and Negri define constituent power in terms of Spinoza's notion of efficient cause as a power not separated from but internal to what it can do. This is a power, a force that comes always from below, radically alien to the negativity of domination and command (Hardt and Negri 1994: 295). Negri further develops this concept in *Insurgencies*, in the context of a theoretical engagement with the major figures of modern political theory (see Negri 1999a). Here the notion of constituent power is defined as disrupting every representation, every mediation. It is not just political but also social. Coming from below, it is also Marx's 'living labor' (Marx 1973: 361; Negri 1999a: 33). It happens, or rather it is enacted, by a collective action of the multitude. It 'takes place through nothing more than its own expression' (Negri 1999a: 16). In response, the constituted (i.e. sovereign) power captures and institutionalizes the constituent power in the form of modern political institutions and negates and absorbs it in the concepts of national or popular sovereignity. There is therefore 'an extremely close and profound link between constituent power and democracy' (Negri 1999a: 23). This obviously implies a deepening of democracy, but it is not limited to a merely democratic elaboration. Negri's ontological approach insists on 'the trajectory and motor of a movement whose essential determination is the demand of being, repeated, pressing on an absence' (Negri 1999a: 23).[2]

THE QUESTION OF IMMEDIACY: A PHILOSOPHY OF EVENT?

We should now open a parenthesis in order to make an observation and try to define a problem which will give us the key to Negri's rich and multifaceted intellectual adventure. Negri's argument so far distinguishes a certain productive and creative force as the constituent *potentia* and tries to avoid an identitarian closure by conceiving this power in terms of Spinozian 'multitude'. However, in order to further avoid this critical charge, it must be said that the workers' or the multitude's constituent power is the power of the immediate itself, the power of the event in its singular force as embodied in the subject. I would like to argue that this is the real key to Negri's theoretical trajectory. This is why for him the worker or the multitude is an *eventful* subject, by definition *in struggle*, and that is the worker's difference. If Antonio Negri would like to give event (or immediacy) priority as a materialist thinker, he does this only to the extent that the event is produced as the *property* of a figure of creative or productive subject— understood in the sense of Spinoza's concepts of *potentia* and *multitudo*, brilliantly rearticulated within Marx's analysis of capitalism.[3]

From this point of view, Michael Ryan's early criticism of Negri's 'metaphysics of subjectivity' is both important and limited at the same time. Ryan finds in Negri a residue of liberalism in the theoretical sense of an isolated, abstract notion of subject: Negri's 'expressive theory of subjectivity ... owes much to liberalism and ... marginalizes instrumental and contextual factors' (Ryan 1989: 46). For Ryan, Negri's 'decontextualized' theory of subjectivity is a theory of 'self-expression' which 'remains beholden to a notion of self-identity that is metaphysical from the perspective of the post-structuralist critique of the subject' (Ryan 1989: 57). Going further than O'Connor, Ryan argues that

[t]he subjective potential he ascribes to the proletariat, one that precedes (indeed exceeds) all social mediation, recalls the claims to interiority that grounds the very institutionality of property that Negri wants to eliminate. It is not shaped or given content by 'external' instruments or cultural representational forms. (Ryan 1989: 57)

By giving form or rhetoric and context a secondary and accidental place, Negri risks 'conceiving of social construction as a matter of pure content' and despite his important merit of giving capitalism a political meaning, 'his commitment to the *immediacy of self-determination* remains captive to metaphysics' (Ryan 1989: 58–61, my emphasis). The philosophical question here is *not* the priority Negri gives to the immediate or the event, *but* perhaps his desire to locate immediacy in a productive collective subject as its property. Although it can and must be argued that the productive and subordinate subject has a different relationship to the event, by virtue of its place in the system of power and production, and that this is evident in the eventful historical nature of a collective subject such as the working class, it does not follow that this is its *privilege*. The immediate or the event escapes. It is a relationship, not a property. The lure of locating the event in the subject is powerful but it is equally misleading, for it leaves us with a notion of subject that is unquestioned and unconstituted. In Negri's approach *the event takes the form of the subject as ontological constitution*. The problematical implication is the subject's possession and control of the event. This gives Negri's philosophy a powerful paradox which is never resolved but is further carried away and proliferated in the unfolding of his work: while the event is *determined* in and as the subject, the latter is by the same reason the site of *creativity* in the sense of a productive power which exceeds representation. This aporia traversing Negri's discourse can only be seen from the edge of this discourse, taking Negri *beyond* Negri.

A CERTAIN TENSION

Like that of every great philosopher, Antonio Negri's work too is characterized by a singular idiom as well as rhythm and style of unfolding. Just thinking his unique vocabulary would be sufficient to see this: not only organizing and constitutive concepts such as autonomy, constituent power, or multitude, but also a series of descriptive terms such as 'open', 'expansive', or 'productive' are given singular meanings in his text. I would like to focus on another such frequently found word in Negri's text. It seems to be the one that is least noticed and perhaps the least noticeable, for it does not easily or calmly fit Negri's apparent argument. On the contrary, it reveals a certain kind of restlessness and agitation, and indeed the force of a conflictual passage. I am talking about the word and perhaps the concept of 'tension', especially in *The Savage Anomaly*.[4] This text is written in and by tension, which keeps coming back to it, asserting itself through its lines and pages.

For instance, when Negri reads Spinoza's definition of *cupiditas* (desire), he often refers to a certain 'tension' that seems to be an essential aspect of being as desire. The constructive power of being is identified with 'the actuality of the constructive tension of *cupiditas*' (Negri 1991b: 155). There is no sense in which it is defined as lack:

> *Cupiditas* is ... a power, its *tension* is explicit, its being full, real, and given. The actual growth of the human essence, then, is posed as *a law of the contraction and expansion of being in the tension of the spontaneity to define itself as a subject*. (Negri 1991b: 156, my emphasis)

Similarly, Spinoza's 'disutopian' ethical project approaches the concept of constitution on a horizon of absolute immanence. Yet again this ethical projectivity is made by a 'progressive tension, without resolution in continuity'. In the constructive tension of being, 'being and nonbeing affirm and negate each other simply, discretely, immediately. There is no dialectic' (Negri 1991b: 219–20). To give a last example, speaking of Spinoza's metaphysics of time as the time of further constitution, Negri writes that 'the essential *tension* wants existence' and 'being is temporal *tension*' (Negri 1991b: 228).

There is *no affirmation of being without this essential, constructive tension of being, which is also a temporal tension*. While concepts such as crisis and antagonism are given an important place in readings of Negri, such a small word as tension seems to have been forgotten. It is understood immediately and forgotten, lost in reading. But the affirmative power of productive difference, *potential*, desire or being are never without tension. The constitutive, *essential* and *temporal* tension of being is internal to the power it expresses. If there is no mediation in Antonio Negri's philosophy, then there is a strong tension. In the *Oxford English Dictionary*, we find that the word has several senses: bodily, affective, mental, and electric. Following the *OED*, we might say that tension occurs in a *force field* and names many relations which constitute it: contracting as well as expanding ('law of being in tension' as Negri said above), pulling a body in opposite directions, pulling apart as well as pulling together, swelling or tightening as well as extending, etc. It is a term that involves an oppositionality and the movement of its complementary poles. As a term functioning in the context of an ontology of constitutive desire, 'tension' has an affinity with 'intensity' as understood by Gilles Deleuze and Félix Guattari (see Deleuze and Guattari 1987: 150–66).[5] In their approach, intensities (flows, thresholds, gradients, intensive differences) are always on the move, as they are distributed on the surface of a body without organs by which one desires. In this Spinozian problematic, the notion of the fullness of desire should not be confused with fulfillment or stasis. It is better understood as an abundance or excess which exceeds itself in and by its movement. 'Tension' is thus without *aufhebung* and can be read as expressing the movement of this fullness, its disquiet and dynamicity, its unstable and fluctuating nature. What is the lesson of attending to the functioning of the notion of tension in Negri's text? A reading which opposes the affirmative to the negative 'simply, discretely, immediately', to steal Negri's own expression, would be a poor reading which behaves as if mere negation (of the negative) were possible. Affirmation always involves tension; it does not inititate a struggle to which it is prior as the property of a subject, it is itself the struggle which it opens up in a *force field*.

REVERSAL OF HUMANISM AND POSTMODERN SUBJECT

If this is an important reminder, then it shows once more that Negri's political theory is more *a theory of subject* than a theory of event. Negri's reversal of transcendental humanism with an *immanent* one puts him in strange company with what might be described as (and often what he himself describes as) 'postmodern' thought. For, if there is something that can be called postmodern, it can only be a *reversal* of humanism which remains, being a reversal, humanism, i.e. a philosophy of subject. In this respect, Negri's thought is close to Anglo-American postmodernism, developed as a response to the postwar French radical philosophical conjuncture. Inspired by psychoanalysis and semiotics, the Anglo-American postmodern thought is a *replacement* of the concept of an essentialist category of human subject with that of a human subject constituted in displacement. This is why, from Homi Bhabha to Judith Butler and Donna Haraway, this postmodern thought remains a theory of (split, hybrid) subject and thus a reversal of humanism.[6] It is important to underline that the *unity* of the subject is always maintained in this split and hybrid constitution. Despite the fact that Negri's analysis does not have much to do with psychoanalysis, nor with a notion of founding lack, his general argument joins this predominant theoretical tendency of postmodern humanism. Negri's use of the notion of 'tension' as a conflictual passage which defines the productive being of desire is clearly a figure of *displacement*—'intensities on the move' would have been Deleuze and Guattari's definition of displacement. To this we should also add his understanding of *potentia* as 'counterfinality' as another clear instance of the figure of an essentially and constitutively displaced human subject. Other major articulations of this figure are the notion of hybridity in *Empire*[7] as well as certain prominent features of the concept of multitude in both *Time for Revolution* and his most recent work with Michael Hardt, *Multitude*, as I shall show below.

It is not sufficient to argue that the subject is split, displaced, in tension, or hybridized as long as this remains a theory of subject, for such a theory assumes the principle and unity of its object, i.e. the subject. In the context of Negri's theorization, the crucial concept becomes that of affirmation. The question is always: What makes affirmation affirmative? In whatever I affirm, if I have not at the same time affirmed all of that with which my affirmation is involved, my affirmation is weak. (For instance, for any force or power, affirmation is immediately the affirmation of a struggle.) In other words, what the politico-philosophical gesture of affirmation affirms is the whole force field in all its complexity. *This force field cannot be readily translated into a collective subject.* It is not that the force field is simply greater than the subject or that it is infinite while the subject (individual or collective) is finite. We should go back to the notion of the immediate here. The concept of the force field implies that the immediate or the event is not simply appropriable and containable.[8] Contrary to a kind of philosophy of mediation which denies the immediate any right to exist, we should insist on the relevance of the immediate as that which happens: the event in its irreducible singularity. But if the event is singular, it remains other. For when the singular is known and mastered, it is no longer singular. (This is why the constituent power of the multitude always remains other to the constituted power of representation.) As is often emphasized, there is something that always remains unactualized in every event. In everything that happens, there remains something that is yet to happen. The concept of force field refers to the impossibility of ultimately locating and appropriating the immediate.[9]

KAIRÒS

As the notion of the 'immediate' occurs in the historical vocabulary of revolutions (we often find it in expressions such as 'the immediate abolition of slavery'), there is also always something of the question of 'timing' in every revolution. This brings us to Negri's recent major philosophical contribution: *Time for Revolution* (Negri 2003a). '*Kairòs*' is the name he gives to the 'time for revolution'. In ancient rhetoric, *kairòs* (the right moment of speech) involves the account of the contextual particulars and the specificity of the audience as well as good timing for saying something. Rethinking a rhetorical concept which refers to the contextual and temporal considerations of effective action, Negri's concept is inevitably a response to criticisms such as Ryan's. But Negri also gives this old concept a new sense and develops a new theory of time.

The second part of *Time for Revolution, Kairòs, Alma Venus, Multitudo,* presents a complicated philosophical theory of time and revolution. It deserves a much more detailed reading than the one I am capable of giving here. In the first chapter, titled 'Kairòs', Negri develops a theory of (common) name and naming according to which marking the thing in space (or expressing a common name) occurs at the same time as the event of the thing. As 'transcendental' theories focus on space and consider time as extrinsic modality, Negri wants to theorize the *event* of adequate naming or the *'this here'*. The 'this here' is an event, that is the truth or the adequation of the act of naming and of the thing named when they are produced or called into existence *at the same time*. This is an absolutely singular relationship, nonordinary and nonrepetitive. The 'at the same time', the time of the *kairòs*, is seen as a restless and vacillating temporality, closer to the sense of tension in the reading of Spinoza. The old concept of *kairòs* as instant is reconstructed by Negri as a singular and open present in which innovation is produced in the sense of creation of *new being* rather than in the restricted sense of scientific or technological innovation. It means a grasp of the immediate in its very occurring, conceived by Negri in terms of the adequation of the name and the thing named, the truth of their occurrences at the same time. It is in the restless, vacillating temporality of *kairòs*, between the eternal (the time of the before) and the *to-come* (the time of the after), on the edge of the void that new being is created. Once more, politics and ethics are ontology.

What is the philosophical status of the notion of adequation here? No doubt, it should be read as an event or occurrence by which something new is brought into existence in a productive process of naming.[10] The question is whether one can have a philosophically adequate *theory* of the nonidenticalness of time, that is an adequate theory of the singular adequation of *kairòs*, the 'timing' of innovations or revolutions. It is certainly not a question of denying the singular and immeasurable nature of *kairòs*, the event of a decision. But the more one theorizes this, the more one tends to forget that, for exactly the same reason, there can be no general theory of the singularity and incommensurability of *kairòs*.

Or better, every theory of the singular and the immeasurable is taking the risk of reducing it to the general and the measurable, that is the transcendental.[11] Can there be a philosophical theory that guarantees how 'the imperatives of the immeasurable for the singularities that constitute the multitude: do not obey, that is be free; do not kill, that is generate; do not exploit, that is, constitute the common' (Negri 2003a: 258) will not turn into transcendental, empty signifiers which begin to justify that which is established (be it an academic or political group or state apparatus or party or movement or movement of movements, and be it left or right) rather than create new being? I am not overlooking a necessary political moment here in the name of some irresponsible intellectual deconstruction, but I am trying to see the *specificity* of a moment of decision. The moment of decision can only go through a most careful calculation in a force field to which theory is not just external and upon which it cannot just be applied. If, in Negri's words, 'the decision is always multilateral, "impure" and monstrous', this is because it is always made in a *force field* characterized by an essential *undecidability*. If there are 'imperatives' of the immeasurable, this 'immeasurable' is clearly a Levinasian Other which is defined as giving birth to the transcending force of the imperative (see Levinas 1969). And, if the imperatives are '*for* the singularities that constitute the multitude', how to read this Levinasian moment, in which, in an undecidable genealogical emergence of the imperative, the otherness of singularity might give way to the transcendental truths of moralistic identity in a prescriptive mode? Surely, the point here is *not* to deny the constitutive, inscriptive force of the imperative at all, *but* to underline that no philosophical theory can control the displacement of otherness into identity in the rapidly shifting terrain of writing immediacy.

An insistent theoretical and political theme traversing Negri's work is the question of *organization*. In *Time for Revolution*, he rethinks it by new concepts of constellation and cooperation: 'co-operation is a constellation of differences in the heart of the multitude; it is that *clinamen* that productively organizes the chaos of a multitude of singularities' (Negri 2003a: 230). This is an important philosophical formulation, and indeed a classic one. The clear implication is the concept of a *prior* chaos (a chaotic multitude) that is organized *afterwards*. This introduction of linear temporality typical of the discourse of metaphysics establishes hierarchy. Further, Negri speaks of a specifically *productive* constellation: 'a constellation is more productive than the sum of the productive singularities (taken separately) that co-operate with them' (Negri 2003a: 231). The obviousness of this is a bit risky, given the philosophical concepts and political issues at stake: a singularity itself might well be a constellation, just as every constellation and/or cooperation is singular.[12] Gilles Deleuze and Félix Guattari spent a good deal of philosophical effort to dismantle just this concept of the whole as more than the sum of its parts:

> ... the Whole itself is a product, produced as nothing more than a part alongside other parts, which it neither unifies nor totalizes, though it has an effect on other parts simply because it establishes aberrant paths of communication between noncommunicating vessels, transverse unities between elements that retain all their differences within their own particular boundaries. (Deleuze and Guattari 1990: 42)[13]

Negri's concept is *a step back* from Deleuze and Guattari, for, being more than the sum of its singular parts, it should transcend and therefore begin to command them. Further, if in Deleuze and Guattari the whole is called whole by virtue of a specific power of communication between noncommunicating parts, then these communications are *aberrant*, as they carefully emphasize (therefore not necessarily cooperative).[14] That is to say, they are *not* communications that are controlled and managed by a center which will therefore have to transcend them as having more than the sum of their powers. Negri's way of constructing productive cooperative constellations puts his concept of constituent power in crisis. If the constitutent power is defined by its power of *exceeding* representation, this is the critical moment of its turning to constituted power.

But why does the classic concept of the whole return in the middle of Negri's discourse?[15] While Negri is keen on a philosophically sensitive point such as the complexity of origin,[16] his concept of immanence is still opposed to that of transcendence in a binary way. Dismissed from all philosophical consideration and politicized immediately, transcendental thinking can return with a vengeance. From a deconstructive point of view, this is an elementary problem: the beginning or origin is always complex, there is no 'elementary', no simple. But 'complex' here surely does not mean 'many', 'plural', not even 'multiple'; it means the complexity of a *relationship*. No theoretical discourse and no political organization which merely opposes immanence to transcendence can ever be complex. Such political and theoretical assemblages or constellations will remain vulnerable to the return of intellectual and political hierarchies. This is the undecidability which inscribes the decision at stake: the more immanent immanence is, the more transcendent it becomes. If, for instance, the multitude were *entirely* immanent so that it would require no form of representation (that is to say, no form of organization), then would it not become transcendent to all representation? A mere refusal of this kind of *moving limit* between the immanent and the transcendent is simply untenable.[17]

MULTITUDE

Does the concept of multitude go beyond the postmodern reversal of humanism? Does it displace the very system of subject instead of making the notion of displacement a slave of the category of subject, such as we find in the Anglo-American translation of French radicalism?

I have argued that a project of theorizing the singular and the immeasurable risks the tendency of transcendentalizing itself. Every such theorization also has to be a theory of *subject*. The concept of the multitude, borrowed from

Spinoza, is developed by Negri as a response to the question of the subject. It is impossible to discuss all the aspects of Negri's complicated understanding of this concept, which also involves an analysis of current configurations of global capitalism, especially in his coauthored works with Michael Hardt, *Empire* (Hardt and Negri 2000) and *Multitude* (Hardt and Negri 2004). Here I will mainly focus on the more philosophical and theoretical aspects of the concept of multitude.

I should begin by drawing attention to Hardt and Negri's description of multitude as 'living flesh' in *Multitude*: 'what we experience is a kind of social flesh, a flesh that is not a body, a flesh that is common, living substance' (Hardt and Negri 2004: 192; see also the whole passage, 189–96). Or, common social being as an 'amorphous flesh that as yet forms no body' (Hardt and Negri 2004: 159). This opposition between flesh and body is familiar from metaphysics as the opposition between unformed matter and form (or body and mind). Indeed, Hardt and Negri describe the flesh as 'unformed life force' and 'elemental power' (Hardt and Negri 2004: 192) and body as organized form. This opposition between the unformed and the form has been radically criticized in post-1968 radical thinking, especially by feminist theorists (for it is part of a whole patriarchal chain of oppositions: body vs. mind, nature vs. culture, woman vs. man).[18] In a way which resonates with Negri's opposition between chaos and form in *Time for Revolution*, Hardt and Negri describe their task as 'to investigate the possibility that the productive flesh of the multitude can organize itself otherwise and discover an alternative to the global political body of capital' (Hardt and Negri 2004: 189). It is precisely at the moment of emergence of such an important and urgent political task of 'alternative' that the system of binary oppositions (flesh vs. body, chaos vs. form, body vs. mind) operates its logic: when given a new form or new body, the multitude is *no longer* multitude. The 'flesh' is no longer 'flesh', but now 'body' which, by the nature of this division, should indeed produce a new 'flesh' while forming itself into 'body'. There is multitude beyond multitude; the multitude is in excess of itself (as going beyond itself and creating a form of itself). By the same logic, there is also multitude left behind multitude (in order to maintain itself as multitude, to maintain its 'living flesh'—as there is no body without flesh).

It is not that Hardt and Negri are totally unaware of this question of the multitude's *dividing itself up* (flesh and body, now and future, the unformed and the form) at the moment they touch it. If the multitude is thus difficult to represent or express, perhaps this is because *it* has already touched them: their writing is the way it survives by *multiplying* itself in and through it. If the multitude is described as *'living* flesh', its form of life must be defined as *survival* or *living-on.*

This is also the question of the image or imaginary. As Negri and Hardt are involved in the generation of a new political imaginary, we assume for the sake of argument that the multitude is a better political image of the social or the popular than the ones we had so far (leaving aside its social analysis or political economy, which I find problematical from the point of view of the North–South distinction). What needs to be kept in mind is Gilles Deleuze's fine warning to Negri when the latter questioned the 'tragic note' in the former's work. Moved by his friend's feeling, Deleuze begins to answer by remembering that 'any political philosophy must turn on the analysis of capitalism and the ways it has developed' and ends his prudent answer by an important reminder: 'How any group will turn out, how it will fall back into history, presents a constant "concern". There's no longer any image of proletarians around of which it's just a matter of becoming conscious' (Deleuze 1995: 171–3).[19] If, following Negri, we accept that it is necessary to construct a new image of proletarians such as the multitude, then, after poststructuralism, we have to be careful about the nature of the image. If the multitude is always beyond itself, if its very form of life is survival or living-on, then this form must be described as a *formless form*, a form without form, in other words, a paradoxical form rather than the unformed or the elemental.[20] Therefore, for instance, what Negri calls 'transvaluation of values' (the sense of languages and decisions created by the living labor of the multitude), which is essential in the production of new being, is *not* recognized 'by the fact that it has *no model*', as he writes in *Time for Revolution* (Negri 2003a: 235, my emphasis). On the contrary, languages, decisions, or senses are *never simply without a model*, but this 'model' is a model without model.[21]

This is not a minor point at all, for what we encounter in the above discussion is again the question of *undecidability*, which is clearly inscribed in Hardt and Negri's discussion of multitude. As they understand, the multitude is also a decision and a *project* since it is not a political body in the modern sense at all.[22] If therefore the multitude is *both* the flesh that is yet to be formed into a body *and* the form or the project, i.e. the (projected or modeled) body itself, then there is a fundamental undecidability which characterizes this concept. This must be acknowledged and engaged openly.[23] The paradox implies that the multitude is never simply given in its image or concept, as it is clearly without synthesis. It is not therefore a matter of saying that no image can be fixed or no decision can be given, but rather of acknowledging that all decision is taken in a force field characterized by a fundamental *undecidability*—especially if a decision is something different than a categorical choice (such as accepting the immanent and rejecting the transcendental).

Both Negri's *Time for Revolution* and *Multitude*, coauthored with Michael Hardt, emphasize aspects of cooperation, communication and dialogue *within* the multitude as well as the notion of the *common*.[24] As this absolutely important concept takes us away from the identitarian and totalizing procedures of classic essentialism, while enabling us to think similarity of the conditions of existence of the oppressed and the exploited, in their immense variety, it is also taking the serious risk of offering a facile solution of the problem. Describing the multitude as singularities in common is an image of plurality rather than a (non-)image of complexity. If the multitude is without synthesis, this is not necessarily because it is composed of a plurality of singularities ('composed of radical differences, singularities, that can never be synthesized in an identity' (Hardt and Negri 2004: 355)) nor necessarily because there are many multitudes ('multitudes intersect with multitudes' (Hardt and Negri 2004: 349)), but because of its paradoxical nature, which I have described as 'form without form' and which has to do with the undecidability inherent in the force field in which it lives-on or survives. The quasi-liberal *sociologistic* image of a decentralized, pluralistic network is *inadequate* for accounting for this complexity. It needs to be supplemented with the materialist concept of force field. While regarding plurality as a necessary moment, a genuinely radical perspective has to work differently with an image of plurality *precisely because of the singular nature of each and every decision.* Negri writes, for instance:

> when a name is said and heard, when it lives in language, every *kairòs* will be open to other *kairòs*—and altogether these events of naming will, in facing one another, in dialogue and perhaps clashing, constitute common names. It is in relation to alterity that the name spills into the common. (Negri 2003a: 155)

There is no happy production together of common names 'in dialogue, perhaps clashing'. The *alterity* Negri has to refer to here disturbs the notions of network, constellation, cooperation, and communication and gives the commonness a new sense, for it is other than the common to which it is immanent—it is indeed the force that always changes the common and that makes it keep going, survive. The relationship that constitutes the common is not merely dialogical, communicative, and cooperative. To shift to a different philosophical idiom here, 'even before speaking in one's own name, before all responsibility', Jacques Derrida writes:

we are caught up, one and another, in a sort of heteronomic and dissymmetrical curving of social space—more precisely, a curving of the relation to the other: prior to all organized *socius*, all *politeia*, all determined 'government', *before* all 'law'. Prior to and before all law, in Kafka's sense of being 'before the law'. (Derrida 1997: 231)

The heteronomic and dissymmetrical curving of a law of originary sociality is 'also a law, perhaps the very essence of law'. It implies an experience of impossibility, hence a *possibilization*. Derrida continues: 'what is unfolding itself at this instant—and we are finding it a somewhat disturbing experience— is perhaps only the silent deployment of that strange violence that has always insinuated itself into the origin of the most innocent experiences of friendship and justice' (Derrida 1997: 231). This careful thinking of sociality might help to save the multitude from a certain naivité.[25] If, from a *political* perspective, a multiplicity of struggles (class, race, gender, ecological, national, sexual, etc.) *traverse* and *interrupt* each other, since each is singular, other than the other, then the real theoretical need beyond emerges as a thinking which will transform the necessary possibility of interruption (of one struggle by another) into an *enabling* moment. This might be a beginning point for a contemporary rethinking of the Spinozian 'art of organizing encounters'.[26] Is it not also what Deleuze so delicately described as 'constant concern' above? Precisely *kairòs*, the event of a decision which is always produced in a complex force field, requires an eye for openness or otherness, for the enabling power of the undecidable. Assuming that it is accepted as a better image of the people, the image and concept of multitude should be supplemented minimally by the concepts of alterity, force field, and undecidability. It is in this sense that affirmation affirms the whole force field, and complexity is the complexity of a relationship rather than just a reference for the 'many'.

EXODUS, OR DISPLACEMENT

Negri's theory of multitude is both a theory of production of new being (politics as ontology) and a theory of subject which emphasizes a new pluralistic unity. The notion of event occupies a strategic place at the juncture of these two aspects. We have seen that the concept of *kairòs* is an attempt to think the singular nature of the innovation of new being. For Negri, the event always involves the *decision*. With the common event decision, 'the event becomes subject' (Negri 2003a: 255). Or, 'the decision, in so far as it is the event of the subject, is the "this here"—that is, "at the same time" the decision of the name and of the event—which is to say, the presentation of the body to the common' (Negri 2003a: 259). This is the climax of Negri's singular theoretical argument.

What is there at the climax, beyond Negri? When the event becomes the subject, what is the decision taken? If Negri's decision is 'exodus' defined as 'taking leave of domination' (Negri 2003a: 259), and if the most explicit and strategic form of domination is sovereignty, then we are perhaps strangely close to Bataille's 'sovereign operation'. Of course Negri's and Bataille's concepts of sovereignty are different. Further, it might be objected that in Negri's Spinozian absolute democracy the multitude governs itself, while in Bataille's sovereign operation no such self-government is possible (as we shall see in a moment). But 'taking leave of domination' is *not* the same as self-government (unless the self—or some part of the self which is thus more self than the alienated, othered self—is seen as outside domination, i.e. transcendental, sovereign, and free to govern itself, in which case there is no need for taking leave, nor for self-government). To put it in other words, when the event becomes the subject, it is not simply that the event (as *kairòs* or decision) is productive or constitutive of new being in the sense of just another being. *The decision is a decision to take leave of sovereignty*—otherwise what is new? Since what is at stake cannot be a new system of sovereignty, the subject, who is by definition a sovereign system and a sovereign unity, can therefore no longer remain as subject. At the moment the event becomes the subject, the subject becomes the event, insofar as the latter is the event of a decision to take leave of sovereignty. To put it in other words, the decision to take leave of sovereignty cannot be a project or program at all.

This is very close to Bataille's sovereign operation. Bataille subjected Hegel's notion of the master to a fascinating *displacement* by taking the fight for recognition to an extreme. In Hegel's dialectic of master and slave, the master *retains* the life that he exposes to risk. Bataille thought of a strange, excessive moment of mastery which he named 'sovereignty'—an impossible 'mastery' which destroys mastery. Unlike Hegel's dialectic, in which meaning and truth is always preserved, this excessive sovereignty has to do with an absolute expenditure or loss, a negativity without reserve, without measure, and without discourse (and therefore a negativity that can no longer be called negative). Sovereign operation (laughter, drunkenness, eroticism, sacrifice, poetry) is outside dialectic, without *Aufhebung*. As an affirmation of loss, sovereignty neither maintains nor governs itself. It is already displaced, on the move, without gathering itself in concepts such as displacement or sovereignty. This implies that sovereign operation is impossible. It is nevertheless experienced as paradox, as an experience that cannot be experienced. For instance, the rebel is put in the position of having to take the power against which she/he is fighting (Bataille 1998:

191–2). Comparing Breton's concept of automatism with Sartre's notion of freedom, Bataille writes: 'If I do not seek to dominate it, liberty will exist' (Bataille 1998: 198).[27] It might be said that this subjectless, impossible liberty is a liberty *to-come*.

If Negri is so close to Bataille, he also seems to be far from him when he slightly shifts the sense of exodus a few pages later, defining it as 'to take leave while constituting', that is constructing common machines, 'turning the technological monster into the angel of the *to-come*' (Negri 2003a: 261). Since exodus is also 'taking leave of representation' (Negri 2003a: 260), these common machines should be outside representative institutions and mechanisms. Characterized by the openness and chance of the *to-come*, they could only have been machines which work by a kind of sovereign operation—impossible machines which work by breaking rather than working, dominating, or governing themselves, perhaps a bit like the paradoxical form I have mentioned above.

This is no doubt an irrepressible philosophical implication of Negri's argument, whether it is acknowledged or not, and even though it seems to remain somewhat marginal or subliminal. The more visible tendency in Negri's recent texts is a result of his intense reading of and alliance with Anglo-American postmodernism. Here the notion of exodus emphasizes not the displacement of the (category of) subject as in the above reading but a figure of 'displaced subject', that is to say, clearly a reversal (rather than displacement) of humanism, hence maintaining the principle and unity of the subject.[28] In *Multitude*, Hardt and Negri call this figure the new republican race of hybrids and cyborgs. Hence the predominant sense of exodus in Negri's argument:

> It is a case then of hybridizing in a cosmopolitan fashion the world of life, that is appropriating global mobility through the generation of new bodies. 'Proletarians of all countries, unite' is an injunction that today means: mix up races and cultures, constitute the multicoloured Orpheus who generates the common from the human. (Negri 2003a: 260)

The new, cosmopolitan and globally mobile race of hybrids and cyborgs constitutes the humanist figure of displaced subject. This is *the model* or *the type*.[29] The most powerful and privileged example of this paradigm of displaced postmodern subject is of course the migrant, for this figure can bring together both theoretical and geographical senses of displacement. Although Hardt and Negri see migrants as one category of the multitude among others, it is a *special* category for them. For in the case of the migrant, '[the] combined act of refusal and expression of desire is enormously powerful' (Hardt and Negri 2004: 133). They are not unaware of the fact that migrants are upwardly mobile: 'they roll uphill as much as possible, seeking wealth and freedom, power and joy' (Hardt and Negri 2004: 134). Nevertheless, their singular condition is almost actualizing an ideal: 'the experience of flight is something like a desire for freedom' (Hardt and Negri 2004: 134). Would it be too unfair to Negri and Hardt to say that the real social subject of exodus is the migrant?[30]

To the extent that this can be said, this is no doubt a highly problematical position, especially from the point of view of the political economy of global capitalism. The point is not that there is a necessary conflict between the metropolitan migrants and the peripheral workers and peasants, but the question of the *social implications* of the image of resistance. It is not for nothing that Hardt and Negri see the peasant as the greatest challenge to their project, because theirs is an urban, metropolitan project. It is also not for nothing that the issue of 'cultural difference' comes up at this point, and is comfortably answered by referring to Gilles Deleuze's philosophy of difference: 'India, however, is not merely different from Europe. India (and every locality within India) is singular—not different from any universal standard, but different in itself' (Hardt and Negri 2004: 128). Since this is an 'application' of Deleuze, a theoretical parenthesis is necessary: in his reading of eternal return in the context of the Platonic dialectic, which distinguishes between copies and simulacra (good and bad copies),[31] Deleuze argues that there is no ultimate ground, no universal standard by which we can measure simulacrum or difference in itself. In the 'parodic' eternal return, 'each thing exists only in returning, copy of an infinity of copies which allows neither original nor origin to subsist' (Deleuze 1994: 67). There is a shift here from emphasizing the power of simulacra to the concept of 'no origin'. If liberating the same from the tyranny of the identical and relating it to the different meant abolishing the same together with the identical,[32] then perhaps we would have had no original (whether this original be conceived as ground, referent, model, or form). But if this were the case, how would we have had 'copy of an infinity of copies'? Relating the same to the different implies 'a reference without a referent', as Jacques Derrida carefully argues in his double reading of Plato and Mallarmé (Derrida 1981: 206).[33] That is to say, not simply the absence of a reference or origin, but rather the complexity or differentiality of origin.

To go back to the case in question, *there is always a universal*, but, rather than constructing some ultimate ground, this 'universal' is a space of writing and iterability, and a site of political and social struggles. This is the only condition in which we can approach India's singularity. On the one hand, we should not leave any territory or population simply outside measure—how can one argue for the poor if you have no measure of GNP or ecological footprint? On the other hand, singularity of such places cannot just be recognized by a transcendentally correct benevolent consciousness or philosophical theory.[34] For this would, quite simply, be a politics of recognition. The 'good' of recognizing India's singularity solves no problem, except taking the risk of a different form of desire for exoticization in the absence of political economy. At the moment I recognize something as singular, it must have already left my field of recognition. Otherwise the universal (i.e. the subject who recognizes something as singular) would be able to establish an ultimate ground according to which it would then be able to assign and govern singularities.

Far from recognizing no universal standard, indeed Negri's (and Hardt's) theory is that of a universal form of the subject, the displaced subject of exodus. This is why the peasant and the native are challenges for this approach. These subjects are *foreclosed* from the power of displacement, while the concept of displacement is conveniently reduced to that of a spatial movement.[35]

These two figures of exodus, one that is close to Bataille's sovereign operation (which is desubjectifying) and the other a new humanist theory of displaced subject, cannot be brought together or synthesized. When interpreted in Bataille's sense, 'taking leave of domination' is the return of the unlocatable and inappropriable *immediacy*, for the impossible experience of sovereignty rejects external goals. It is a radical loss of access rather than direct access. This unlocatable singular event which returns (call it revolution) communicates with what Derrida has described above as 'the heteronomic and dissymmetrical curving of the social', which I have related to the transversal and interruptive nature of a multiplicity of singular social struggles.[36] A political decision is always this going through (or experience of) the otherness of the event of the social, that which lies beyond a deciding subject. Conventional politics, left or right, tends to totalize the transversal, straighten the curve, and erect it as an upward constitution (sometimes in terms of a 'type'). To decide and to act in view of the undecidable is to change the relationship to this necessary contamination so that the *to-come* keeps coming. This permanent awareness and permanent interruption is the *enabling* power of the undecidable.[37] This is not theorizing democracy at all, even though democracy is the most reasonable form of collectivity today. It is only a supplement to it.

GOOD CONSCIENCE

What happens when democracy is theorized? Negri approaches democracy in terms of Spinoza's '*omnino absolutum imperium*' or 'absolute democracy', in an essay titled 'Reliqua Desiderantur: A Conjecture for a Definition of the Concept of Democracy in the Final Spinoza' (Negri 1997b).[38] Democractic theory is hegemonized by 'contractarianism' which relativizes freedom and redefines it juridically. For contract theory, absolute freedom means a situation of war and chaos. If democracy is constitutive of absoluteness as the government or the sovereignity of the *entire* multitude, Negri asks, then how can it be simultaneously a regime of freedom? The metaphysical answer is the absolute as *potentia*. The political answer is given in the different forms of the projection of *potentia* of the multitude (tenure or magistracy of each citizen, etc.). If there are necessarily 'organizational phases, functions of control and representative mediations', from the perspective of absoluteness, these 'do not form dialectical interruptions; they do not organize passages of alienation', but these mechanisms articulate the open horizon of *potentia* (Negri 1997b: 228). Whereas Hegel sees the absolute in terms of an infinite and indivisible totality, there is a double movement in Spinoza: toward absoluteness, the unity and indivisibility of government, *and* toward plurality, the singular powers of the multitude. The relationship between the absolute and the multitude is an open process, not a presupposed unity as in Hegel. But multitude is both an elusive subject (for it is the entire multitude) and a juridical subject, constitutive of civil right. If reason requires the absolute, it also has to confront the variable effects of the will, *fluctatio animi*. When the necessity of governing the fluctuations of the multitude (its 'animal life' according to Spinoza) arises, this is not turned into Rousseau's general will. The multitude is a multitude of singularities in Spinoza. But this also means that its duality is never resolved:

> So that it seems that the *multitudo* can be a political subject only as an idea of reason or as a product of the imagination. By contrast, concretely, the *multitudo* is a continuous and contradictory mixture of passions and situations—and then across a new dislocation, an accumulation of will and reason, which, as such, constitute institutions. (Negri 1997b: 234)

If, when the reason is confronted with the fluctuating soul, the absolute fails to embrace freedom, it can still 'permit the life in common of singularities, reciprocal tolerance, the power of solidarity' (Negri 1997b: 235). Hence the Spinozian rewriting of republican *tolerance*: the multitude is the foundation of democracy insofar as it *allows* singularity. But what guarantees that a citizen will realize that his or her interest is tolerating the other? Negri looks for a further reason and finds it in the concept of '*pietas* that forms and constitutes the reciprocal relations that are established among the multiplicity of subjects that constitute the *multitudo*' (Negri 1997b: 237). *Pietas* is defined by Spinoza as the 'desire to do good generated in us by our living according to the guidance of reason' (Spinoza 1985: IV P37 S1, 565). For Negri it is an instance of *love* of universality (what is called 'love' in *Time for Revolution*, and 'public love' in *Multitude*).[39]

The opposition between the demand for reason and the fluctuating soul is of course the one between the flesh and the body, the unformed chaos and organized form, the multitude as social practice and the multitude as political project. Spinoza must certainly be credited for leaving the process open, but it must at the same time be admitted that his difference from the liberal tradition is undecidable, for he works within the very opposition which forms the essence of this tradition: body vs. mind, nature vs. culture, violence vs. civility. The danger of 'chaos', of a chaotic multitude that must be organized, returns in the middle of his discourse, and Negri's as well. Does one just go ahead, dialectically as always, and create new forms, new syntheses? Or keep an eye on the formation of collectivities and multitudes so that their paradoxical forms at the threshold of the undecidable are in touch with the *to-come*? The point here is precisely that such undecidability must be recognized and engaged in ways other than a rhetoric of openness and plurality. The image of good, plural unity is *necessary but insufficient* in the essential work of imagination. If *pietas* is 'the desire that no subject be excluded from universality' (Negri 1997b: 238), this concept or principle offers no guarantee, as it is always subjected to writing or practice. I have just tried to show that Negri's privileging of a figure of displaced subject maintains the exclusion of peasantry and natives.[40]

My criticism is not made in the name of dismissing the public notion of love, found especially in various religious discourses. In *Multitude* as well, Hardt and Negri draw our attention to the political significance of Christian and Judaic notions of public love. These are not merely precapitalist, backward belief systems. Such traditions 'conceive love as a political act that constructs the multitude'.[41] But interestingly, Islamic and Buddhist traditions are not mentioned. Is this because, unlike Christianity and Judaism, they are backward, peasant religions? Questions multiply: who then are the multitude? What about the desire that *no subject* be excluded from universality? There is no need to tell how tragic the consequences of forgetting the great Islamic tradition of Sufism will be in today's world—a great mystical tradition from Hallaj-i Mansur to Rumi, with its singular notion of love characterized by an immanent reading of the concept of God. The application of philosophically correct notions in political writing (as we have seen in the case of the application of Deleuze's concept of difference-in-itself) might perhaps be much less important than a minimal attention to the complexity of the force field, so that its almost mad plurality, which is the real democratic strength of a transformative politics, shall not be forgotten.

A cursory look at these traditions will show how complex the notion of love is in the so-called 'traditional' social register. These formations might be the site of new deterritorializations and a much less violent subjectivity; they are also patriarchal formations. This leads us to repose the question of public love and the alterity it involves without forgetting the singularity of love along the gender dimension. For instance, Gayatri Spivak defines love in terms of 'ethical singularity': a relationship in which responsibility is mutual, while there is also the sense that something has not got across, a secret which the lovers want to reveal rather than conceal:

> *In this secret singularity, the object of ethical action is not an object of benevolence, for here responses flow from both sides* .... This encounter can only happen when the respondents inhabit something like normality. Most political movements fail in the long run because of the absence of this engagement. In fact, it is impossible for all leaders (subaltern or otherwise) to engage every subaltern in this way, especially across the gender divide. This is why ethics is the experience of the impossible. Please note that I am not saying that ethics are impossible, but rather that ethics is the experience of the impossible. *This understanding only sharpens the sense of the crucial and continuing need for collective political struggle.* For a collective struggle *supplemented* by the impossibility of full ethical engagement—not in the rationalist sense of 'doing the right thing', but in this more familiar sense of the impossibility of 'love' in the one-on-one way for each human being—the future is always around the corner, there is no victory but only victories that are also warnings. (Spivak 1995: xxv, my emphasis)[42]

Public love guided by reason cannot 'form and constitute the reciprocal relations that are established among the multiplicity of subjects that constitute the *multitudo*' unless it is supplemented by a thought of impossible ethical singularity. This is why perhaps we should now go back to tolerance, which appeared as a result of aporia. Negri argues that if we cannot perfect the relationship between absoluteness and freedom, this is still no reason not to act (Negri 1997b: 242). This clearly implies that aporia is not just resolved in tolerance, but it is *experienced*. I have emphasized this aporetic and undecidable nature of the political in my reading of Negri in several instances: the question of immediacy and event, the heteronomic and dis-symmetrical nature of the social, the transversal and interruptive nature of struggles, taking leave of sovereignty, exodus, and love. Speaking of the duties of democracy, Jacques Derrida writes:

> How to justify the choice of *negative form* (*aporia*) to designate a duty that, through the impossible or the impracticable, nonetheless announces

itself in an affirmative fashion? Because *one must avoid good conscience at all costs*. Not only good conscience as the grimace of an indulgent vulgarity, but quite simply the assured form of self-consciousness: good conscience as subjective certainty is incompatible with the absolute risk that every promise, every engagement, every responsible decision—if there are such—must run. To protect the responsibility or the decision by knowledge, by some theoretical assurance, or by the certainty of being right, of being on the side of science, of consciousness or of reason, is to transform this experience into the deployment of a program, into a technical application of a rule or a norm, into the subsumption of a determined 'case'. All these are conditions that must never be abandoned, of course, but that, as such, are only the guardrail of a responsibility to whose calling they remain radically heterogenous. The affirmation that announced itself through the negative form was therefore the necessity of *experience* itself, the experience of the aporia (and these two words that tell of the passage and the nonpassage are thereby coupled in an aporetic fashion) as endurance or as passion, as interminable resistance or remainder. (Derrida 1993, my emphasis)

Hence the necessity of going through the aporia as an affirmative, enabling (non)passage, on the way to transform impossibility into possibility. Derrida's insistence on avoiding the good conscience at all costs might be a much more radical and critically useful gesture than a new humanist theory of displaced subject, for the latter is never independent of conscience and its assurances. Antonio Negri's exemplary aporetic embrace is between metaphysics and politics, giving one to the other. It is an impossible passage that, nevertheless, he keeps passing, always leaving himself beyond himself. It is to this experience of impossibility that we owe the greatness of his work.

NOTES

1. 'We have to determine the extent to which our anti-Hegelianism is possibly one of his tricks directed against us, at the end of which he stands, motionless, waiting for us' (Foucault 1972: 235).
2. Interestingly this is also a passage in which Negri gives reference to Bataille, Blanchot, Nancy, and Aristotle; see Negri 1999a: 340. See also Georges Bataille, 'On Sovereignty' in Bataille 1993; Blanchot 1988; Nancy 1991; Aristotle 1941. The possible agreement or disagreement between Negri's constituent power and Bataille's sovereignty, Blanchot's 'unavowable' or Nancy's 'inoperative' community need to be discussed. Negri offers a political–philosophical theory of subject, whereas in writers like Blanchot and Nancy, we find a deconstructive engagement with concepts of subject, community, and work, and certainly not a philosophical (ontological) theorization of these. I will discuss Bataille's concept of sovereignty below.

3. This admirable philosophical move liberates Spinoza from academic philosophy and rearticulates his philosophical significance in a new social, political and historical context.
4. Indeed one should mention yet another such word: 'rhythm'. 'Constitutive rhythm' or the 'rhythm of being' are frequent expressions in *The Savage Anomaly*. Not unsurprisingly, Negri uses it especially where he talks about Spinoza's concept of the fluctuations of the soul (*fluctatio animi*), see Negri 1991b: 154. Considerations of space disallow me to point to the philosophical significance of the notion of rhythm, which is indeed more important than that of tension.
5. I thank Timothy S. Murphy for suggesting that I make this connection.
6. For a criticism of Homi Bhabha in this context, see Cheah 1998: 290–328; and for excellent criticisms of Judith Butler and Donna Haraway, see Kirby 1997: 100–28.
7. I have already argued this in a critical reading of *Empire*; see Mutman 2001: 43–60, especially 56–8.
8. Jacques Derrida's concept of 'generalized writing' can be understood in this sense; see 'From Restricted to General Economy: A Hegelianism without Reserve' in Derrida 1978: 251–77.
9. Is it because the immediate or the event is not containable that Spinozian *veritas norma sui* ('truth is its own norm') often runs the risk of what Jon Beasley-Murray once described as 'the re-inscription of faith performed by Negri in the course of his analysis'? See Beasley-Murray 1994.
10. Negri gives the most beautiful descriptions of this singular act: '. . . the name presents itself in the vacillation of *kairòs*, and it is through this vacillation that the true is revealed. As Leopardi says, it is in the instant that the young man, vacillating, appropriates the name; and in the same way, he who invents approaches the new; and that the poet, vacillating, fixes the verse. The solution of the vacillation, its necessary decision, is the presentation of the name' (Negri 2003a: 153).
11. Although in Negri's coauthored book with Michael Hardt the authors underline that 'a philosophical book like this is not the place for us to evaluate whether the time of revolutionary political decision is imminent' (Hardt and Negri 2004: 357), the question is not limited to a philosophical book's timing of revolution, but depends on the critical and radicalizing force of its argument.
12. Negri's implicit claim seems to be that we are not simply talking about society and individual. We should also note that when Negri defines the result of this cooperative constellation as 'surplus value', this should not be confused with Marx's theory of value.
13. For an excellent discussion of the concept of whole in Althusser as well as in Marx and Deleuze and Guattari, see Plotnitsky 1993: 273–95.
14. We should add that such communications are *also* secret, subterranean, unconscious, etc.
15. Just a few lines above, speaking of the classic critique of reformism as changing the parts without changing the whole, Negri writes: 'once outside the transcendental illusion, the whole is nothing other than the ensemble of the parts' (Negri 2003a: 22). Is whole not the way to the transcendental illusion when conceived classically as more than the sum of its parts? How is a nonsovereign whole so easily attainable? How is it 'once outside'?
16. He carefully speaks of 'a complex genealogy of sequences of co-operation' (Negri 2003a: 232).
17. Negri writes: 'Some postmodern authors look for an opening on the margins of the model that is emerging. But the margin is a liminal transcendence—an immanence that is almost a transcendence, an ambiguous location where materialist realism must bow to mysticism. Some endlessly pursue this margin (Derrida); others fix on it as though it were a case of gathering up the power of the negative that has at last been seized (Agamben). This thinking of the common, in the anxiety of awaiting the other (as in Levinas), results in mysticism' (Negri 2003a: 192). Is mysticism not too harsh a judgment by a thinker who himself makes a good deal of religious (and

specifically Christian) references and who is criticized in similar ways in orthodox left circles? For instance, Derrida's endeavor should not be reduced to a romantic, endless pursuit of the margin, but it is more usefully read as a *rigorous thinking* on the margin or limit beyond straight dismissals, affirmations, or crossings, whatever particular period, text, or philosophy is at stake. Interestingly, while none of these thinkers has a historical characterization such as postmodernity, it is Negri himself who does indeed admirably look for an *opening on the margins* of what he describes as the postmodern period.

18. I do not need to refer to the writings of Gilles Deleuze, Jacques Derrida, or Luce Irigaray. A recent and brilliant feminist and poststructuralist discussion of this philosophical issue can be found in Kirby 1997. Although Hardt and Negri give reference to Kirby's work, they have not articulated her argument.

19. I am grateful to Bulent Eken for drawing my attention to this source.

20. If it were not for the opposition it makes to 'being', I would have added: 'becoming-form of the form'. I could also have written 'a difference without reference, or rather a reference without a referent' (Derrida 1981: 206). But of course, in a much more relevant way I could have written 'spectral' in Jacques Derrida's sense again; see Derrida 1994. I cannot follow the full implications of the spectrality, i.e. the alterity of the multitude here.

21. This is of course constantly contradicted in the *actual practice* of imagining and constructing, i.e. *writing* the multitude. For instance, *Multitude* itself ends with a reference to Madison's and Lenin's projects. Another example is Negri's concept of love (which is like a Gramscian cement holding the multitude together—otherwise why mention it at all?). This is modeled on the earlier, traditional model of Judaeo-Christian religious love (Hardt and Negri 2004: 351–2), and so on.

22. For instance, 'only when every discipline of labor, affect and power that makes gender difference into an index of hierarchy is destroyed ... Only then will gender difference become a creative, singular power and only then *will the multitude become possible*, on the basis of such differences' (Hardt and Negri 2004: 355, my emphasis). Or more explicitly: 'what we need *to bring the multitude into being* is a form of grand politics that has traditionally been called Realpolitik or political realism' (Hardt and Negri 2004: 356, my emphasis).

23. The Pauline concept of 'the power of the flesh' only reproduces the same problem; see Hardt and Negri 2004: 159.

24. An interesting comparison for further discussion might be Jean-Luc Nancy's work on community, especially his discussion of 'communication' as well as his concept of the 'share'; see Nancy 1991.

25. And also from a highly problematical naturalism, as we find in Hardt and Negri's description of Spinozist absolute democracy as the basis of every society. According to this, our daily interactions and practices are 'civil process of democratic exchange, communication and cooperation', otherwise 'society itself would be impossible' and consequently while other forms are distortions of human society, democracy is a 'natural fulfillment' (see Hardt and Negri 2004: 311). There is no doubt a sense of truth in this. But what happened to Félix Guattari's brilliant concept of microfascism, or Foucault's microphysics of power? And in what sense really is empire an 'immanent' power?

26. The expression is Deleuze's; see Deleuze 1990a: 260–2. Michael Hardt mentions Deleuze's formulation in his commentary (Hardt 1993: 108–11). I do not discuss here problems of Spinoza's notion of usefulness, his understanding of transformation of natural into civil state, etc. I only need to underline Deleuze's careful remark, reflecting his awareness of finitude (Negri's 'tragic note'): 'This endeavor does of course have its limits: we will still be determined to destroy certain bodies, if only in order to subsist; we cannot avoid all bad encounters, we cannot avoid death' (Deleuze 1990a: 261).

27. See also Jacques Derrida: 'From Restricted to General Economy: A Hegelianism without Reserve' in Derrida 1978: 251–76.

28. This also implies that Spinoza's philosophy is not really an alternative to psychoanalysis as is often claimed, even though it might be superior to it in certain respects.
29. This concept figure of the 'type' is of course very, very old. So the new race of the hybrid subject is as new as a philosophical reversal of race as natural distinction. For the concept of 'type' in Western metaphysics, see Lacoue-Labarthe 1989, especially pp. 43–138.
30. In this, they are in complete agreement with Jacques Derrida's recent work which emphasizes the migrant in the context of the concept of the '*arrivant*'.
31. See Deleuze 1994: 28–69, especially 66–9; Deleuze 1990b: 253–66.
32. 'In reality, the distinction between the same and the identical bears fruit only if one subjects the Same to a conversion which relates it to the different, while at the same time the things and beings which are distinguished in the different suffer a corresponding radical destruction of their *identity*' (Deleuze 1994: 66).
33. This is also why for Derrida text means that 'every referent, all reality has the structure of a differential trace' and *not* that 'all referents are suspended, denied or enclosed in a book' (Derrida 1988: 148).
34. This is as old as Edward Said's introductory warning: 'One ought never to assume that the structure of Orientalism is nothing more than a structure of lies or of myths, which, were the truth about them to be told, would simply blow away' (Said 1978: 6).
35. Deleuze and Guattari's concepts of 'schizo' or 'nomad' too had a sense of spatial displacement. But they also emphasized that schizos' or nomads' movements are *not necessarily* tied to a journey from one place to another. 'The schizo knows how to leave ... but at the same time his journey is strangely stationary, in place' (Deleuze and Guattari 1990: 131); 'The nomad distributes himself in a smooth space; he occupies, inhabits, holds that space; that is his territorial principle. It is therefore false to define the nomad by movement' (Deleuze and Guattari 1987: 381).
36. This use of the notion of the transversal is different than Félix Guattari's more specific social-psychological sense in the context of psychiatry; see Guattari 1984: 11–23. But it is perhaps closer to Gilles Deleuze's use in his *Foucault* (Deleuze 1986: 22–5).
37. My formulations are inspired by Gayatri Spivak's discussion of Derrida's *Politics of Friendship* in her *Death of a Discipline* (Spivak 2003: 27–31).
38. The essay is published in Italian in *Studia Spinoza*, 1 (1985), 143–80.
39. See Negri 2003a: 209–24 and Hardt and Negri 2004: 351–2.
40. I think women as well, in the sense that the opposition between flesh and body is a patriarchal opposition. But this would require a much more detailed reading.
41. Hardt and Negri 2004: 351–2.
42. For Spivak, literature appears as a singular space of singularity; see especially her argument that it should supplement knowledge in her *Death of a Discipline*.

8
Antonio Negri and the Temptation of Ontology[1]

Alex Callinicos

The late Jacques Derrida accused Antonio Negri of being 'confined, out-of-in-it, within the walled perimeter of a new ontological fatherland, a liberated ontology, an ontology of self-liberation. In, for example, a Spinozist sense of the word "liberty"' (Derrida 1999: 269). It isn't obvious how damaging a charge this is. Many would say that an ontology, in the sense of a philosophical conception of the structure of the world, is unavoidable: indeed, the founding assumption of Derrida's practice of deconstruction is that it is simultaneously both impossible to escape metaphysics and necessary to employ various devices aimed at keeping it at arm's length. What is perhaps more interesting to explore is the nature of a particular theorist's ontological commitments.

Contrary to what Derrida suggests, central to Negri's ontology is not liberty, but Life. He writes, with Michael Hardt:

> From one perspective Empire stands clearly over the multitude and subjects it to the rule of its overarching machine, as a new Leviathan. At the same time, however, from the ontological perspective, the hierarchy is reversed. The multitude is the real productive force of our social world, whereas Empire is a mere apparatus of capture that lives off the vitality of the multitude—as Marx would say, a vampire regime of accumulated dead labour that survives only by sucking off the blood of the living. (Hardt and Negri 2000: 62)

A little later on in *Empire*, discussing the antihumanism of Althusser and Foucault, Hardt and Negri write: 'Anti-humanism, then, conceived as a refusal of transcendence, should in no way be confused with the negation of the *vis viva*, the creative life force that animates the revolutionary stream of the modern tradition' (Hardt and Negri 2000: 91–2). The revolutionary version of modernity—the Renaissance humanism that culminated in Spinoza—is the subject of Negri's best book, *Insurgencies* (Negri 1999a). In *Empire* Hardt and Negri return to the subject of ontology in the key late chapter 'Generation and Corruption'. Here they criticize both the apologetic affirmation that capitalism is natural and the 'mysticism of the limit' that, denying the possibility of revolt, 'leads merely to a cynical attitude and quietistic practices' for having 'lost track of the fundamental productivity of being'. This productivity is realized in living labor, which is conceived in Deleuzian terms: 'Desiring production is generation, or rather the excess of labour and the accumulation of a power incorporated into the collective movement of its singular essences, both its cause and its completion.' Indeed, say Hardt and Negri, generation thus understood is the 'first fact of metaphysics, ontology, and anthropology'. Corruption, by contrast, 'is not an ontological motor but simply the lack of ontological foundation of the biopolitical practices of being'. It is 'the substance and totality of Empire. Corruption is the pure exercise of command without any proportionate or adequate reference to the world of life' (Hardt and Negri 2000: 387, 388, 389, 391).[2]

Here we have outlined the key concepts that constantly recur in Negri's recent writings—productivity, creativity, life, labor, desire, and multitude. I shall have some critical reflections to offer about them towards the end of this chapter, but I want to concentrate on how they came to occupy the prominence they currently enjoy. Rereading Negri's writings of the 1970s, one is struck by the extent to which some at least of these themes are already present at least in embryo. From this perspective, *Marx Beyond Marx* is an emblematic text, one that points both back towards Negri's more avowedly orthodox writings of the 1970s and forward to the later work, in which Marx is more and more read through Foucault and Deleuze.

In considering this book I take two reference points: first, some themes in some of Negri's writings of the 1970s, and, second, Marx's own economic theory. Though my own position is much closer to the classical Marxist tradition than Negri is, my purpose in using this second reference point is not to put him on trial for heresy. Even if that were ever an interesting exercise, Negri has suffered too many trials as it is. But there is something very striking about the way in which he invokes the authority of one of Marx's key economic texts, the *Grundrisse*, to offer a reading of Marx that it is fairly easy to show is quite at odds with the latter's central theoretical claims. This discrepancy may tell us something about the driving forces of Negri's thought, or at least about themes that have become ever more powerfully articulated in recent years.[3]

NEGRI'S *GRUNDRISSE*:
REVOLUTIONARY SUBJECTIVITY VERSUS MARXIST 'OBJECTIVISM'

The significance of the *Grundrisse* for Negri is that it allows us to conceptualize the capitalist mode of production primarily as a power relation constituted by the irreducible antagonism between labor and capital: 'We thus see, throughout the *Grundrisse*, a *forward movement in the theory*, a more and more constraining movement constituted by the *antagonism between the collective worker and the collective capitalist*' (Negri 1991a: 4). Indeed: 'The *Grundrisse* represents the summit of Marx's revolutionary thought' (Negri 1991a: 18). That this is so is indicated by the fact that it starts, unlike *Capital*, not with the commodity, but with money:

> Money has the advantage of presenting me immediately with the lurid face of the social relation of value; it shows me value right away as exchange, commanded and organized for exploitation. I do not need to plunge into Hegelianism in order to discover the double face of the commodity, of value: money has only one face, that of the boss. (Negri 1991a: 23)[4]

Or, as Negri puts it more succinctly, 'in this Marx, money is a *tautology for power*'. The merit of starting with money is closely related to another, that in the *Grundrisse* the theory of surplus value is not presented as it is in *Capital*, on the basis of an initial discussion of the theory of value (to which the first chapter of *Capital*, volume 1, 'The Commodity' is devoted):

> The difference between the *Grundrisse* and the later works of Marx resides in the fact that, in the first, *the law of value is presented not only mediatedly, but also immediately as the law of exploitation*. There is no logical way which leads from the analysis of commodities to that of value, to that of surplus-value: the middle term does not exist; it is—that, yes—a literary fiction, a mystification, pure and simple which contains not a word of truth. (Negri 1991a: 35, 24)

Negri thus explicitly thematizes the discrepancy between the *Grundrisse* as he reads it and *Capital*:

> Marx beyond Marx? The *Grundrisse* beyond *Capital*? Maybe. What is certain is that the central character of the theory of surplus-value puts an end to every scientific pretension to derive any centralization and domination from the theory of value. The theory of surplus-value breaks down the antagonism into a microphysics of power. (Negri 1991a: 14)

This latter reference to 'a microphysics of power' indicates that here already Foucault has become an important reference point for Negri. But he appropriates poststructuralism in his own way. In an interesting passage that anticipates the discussion of antihumanism in *Empire*, Negri praises Althusser for attacking '[t]he orgy of totality, rebirth, and plenitude to which we gave ourselves over', but continues:

In avoiding humanism, some would also seek to avoid the theoretical areas of subjectivity. They are wrong. The path of materialism lies precisely through subjectivity. The path of subjectivity is the one that gives materiality to communism. The working class is subjectivity, separated subjectivity, which animates development, crises, transition and communism. (Negri 1991a: 154)

This privileging of subjectivity forms the basis of the opposition that Negri draws between the *Grundrisse* and *Capital*:

it is not a question of an abstract polemic against *Capital*: each of us was born in the reflection and the theoretical consciousness of the class hate which we experience in studying *Capital*. But *Capital* is also that text which served to reduce critique to economic theory, to annihilate subjectivity in objectivity, to subject the subversive capacity of the proletariat to the reorganizing and repressive intelligence of capitalist power. We can only reconquer a correct reading of *Capital* (not for the painstaking conscience of the intellectual, but for the revolutionary conscience of the masses) if we subject it to the critique of the *Grundrisse*, if we reread it through the categorical apparatus of the *Grundrisse*, which is traversed throughout by an absolutely insurmountable antagonism led by the capacity of the proletariat. (Negri 1991a: 9)

So, on the one hand, *Capital* is the privileged site of an 'objectivist' understanding of capitalism, but, on the other, it can be read 'correctly' (i.e. presumably in a way that follows 'the path of subjectivity') with the help of the *Grundrisse*. This passage reminds us of the extent to which the interpretation of *Capital* was a central feature of the intellectual revival of Marxism in the 1960s and 1970s, most famously in the form of *Reading Capital* in France, but in Germany through the study circles and discussions that gave rise to the capital-logic school, and in Italy under the aegis of *operaismo*. Already in 1955 Mario Tronti could write: 'One returns to *Capital* each time one starts from capitalism and vice versa: one cannot speak of the method of *Capital* without transferring and translating this method into the *analysis* of capitalism.'[5]

Marx Beyond Marx is a contribution to this discourse that constantly moves between *Capital* and capitalism, a contribution that operates at the limits of this discourse by summoning up the *Grundrisse* to correct the defects of Marx's later 'objectivism'. An example of this procedure is Negri's discussion of the tendency of the rate of profit to fall (TRPF), which

bespeaks the *revolt of living labor* against the power of profit and its very separate constitution; a revolt against the theft and its fixation into a productive force for the capitalist against the productive force of the worker, into the power of social capital against the vitality of social labor: because of this *living labor reveals itself as destructive*. (Negri 1991a: 91)

Thus necessary labor—that is, the portion of the working day devoted to the reproduction of labor power—is *'a rigid quantity'* that constitutes

a limit to valorization. A limit increasing to the extent that any increase in productivity and in the sum of profit is faced with a force less and less willing to be subjected, less and less available for compression. Such rigidity imparts its primary sense to the law of the tendency of the rate of profit to decline. In this law we must read what Marx had acknowledged in the *Grundrisse* immediately before the first formulation of the law, that is, the radical estrangement, *the autonomy of the working class from the development of capital*. (Negri 1991a: 100–1)

The rate of profit falls, therefore, because of capitalists' inability, thanks to working-class resistance, to increase the rate of surplus value (the ratio between surplus and necessary labor) or perhaps even to maintain it at its previous level. This is an interpretation of the TRPF that in effect displaces the explanation that Marx gives in *Capital*, volume 3, where the main mechanism responsible for the falling rate of profit is the tendency for the organic composition of capital—the value ratio that reflects the growing role of dead labor relative to living labor in capitalist production—to rise, something that can in principle take place even if the rate of surplus value also rises. Negri dismisses this as so much 'economism' and 'objectivism':

The law of the tendency to decline represents, therefore, one of the most lucid Marxist intuitions of the intensification *of the class struggle* in the course of capitalist development. The confusions on the subject will emerge later on when Marx, *reformulating the law*, instead of proposing the ratio between necessary labor and surplus labor, proposes the formula of *the organic composition of capital*—or that of the ratio between profit and wage. These two formulae are obviously present in the *Grundrisse* as well, but here they are subordinated to the quantities defined by the law of surplus-value. Whenever, on the contrary, they become prominent or exclusive, the entire relation will be dislocated on an economistic level and objectified improperly. (Negri 1991a: 101)

Consistent with his view of capitalism as a pure power relation, Negri thus attributes to the Marx of the *Grundrisse* a view of crises as a consequence of 'the working class struggling against work under capitalism and for its own self-valorization' (Negri 1991a: 102). This is, of course, precisely the view that Negri had developed in his earlier writings. Thus he wrote in 1968 that the Marxist theory of the business cycle conceptualizes

> this cycle-form as the form of a power-relation between classes in struggle (a power-relation which was originally described by Marx in a context where capital was extremely powerful, but which can be and has been overthrown by the course of working-class struggle).

This same text articulates another long-standing theme of Negri's writing, namely that the progressive socialization of both capital and labor reduces the relation between classes to one of open and unmediated political violence:

> The new state-form corresponding to the socialization of capital does not succeed in reactivating mechanisms that the class struggle had closed off; rather it plays a (necessary and exclusive) role of political repression, and does so in ways functional to the new situation of a levelling out of the rate of profit. The antagonistic stance that capital always assumes when faced by the emergence of the working class as a productive social force here reaches maximum proportions. 'Political violence' has always been 'the vehicle of capital's economic process' [Luxemburg], but here the ideal notion of capital as a social mediating force becomes pure abstraction: it is now represented as a pure repressive force.[6]

Another text, this time dating from 1981, at once radicalizes and reaffirms the idea that capitalist economic relations are becoming comprehensively politicized:

> *The conditions for the extraction of surplus-value now exist only in the form of a general social relation.* Profit and the wage become forms of the division of a value content which no longer relates to any specific mechanisms of exploitation, other than the specific asymmetry of command within society.

Indeed, '[e]xploitation consists in command. It is violence against the antagonism of social subjects that are fighting for liberation.'[7] This last passage resonates with Hardt and Negri's portrayal of the corruption of Empire as the pure exercise of command.

The significance of the *Grundrisse* for Negri is that it is the text of Marx's that, on his view, anticipates the formation of social capital: 'while in *Capital* the categories are generally modeled on private and competitive capital, in the *Grundrisse* they are modeled on a tendential scheme of *social capital*'. Marx's analysis of the monetary crisis of 1857–58 provided him with a lens through which to survey the future evolution of capitalism:

As if in an enormous effort of anticipation, the crisis comes to figure the historical tendency of capitalist development. And it is in this historical projection that the crisis becomes a crisis of the law of value. Within the historical projection of a form of production which becomes increasingly more social, in which the modern function of value is transformed into a function of command, of domination, and of intervention on the social fractions of necessary labor and accumulation. The state is here the 'synthesis of civil society'. (Negri 1991a: 25; see also 187ff.)

This process culminates in the fusion of an increasingly socialized capital and the state:

Marx indicated, and often too frequently, especially in the *Grundrisse*, that to say State is only another way of saying capital. The development of the mode of production leads us to recognize that to say State is the *only* way to say capital: a socialized capital, a capital whose accumulation is done in terms of power, a transformation of the theory of value into a theory of command, the launching into circuit and the development of the state of the multinationals. (Negri 1991a: 188)

FROM THE *GRUNDRISSE* TO *CAPITAL*: VALUE, EXPLOITATION, AND COMPETITION

The theory of capitalist development outlined in *Marx Beyond Marx* is in many ways a familiar one, in which what Negri calls 'private and competitive capital' progressively transformed, as a result of processes of centralization and concentration, into a single collective entity that comprises both capital and the state. In a celebrated early essay he had developed a reading of Keynes as an entry point for analyzing this transformation.[8] In *Marx Beyond Marx*, he cites Hilferding and Lenin, but there are plenty of others who argued something similar, from Bukharin to Castoriadis (Negri 1991a: 27).[9] Negri's conclusion that the socialization of capital has rendered the law of value inoperative is also far from unique:

The Law of Value dies ... Once capital and global labor power have completely become global social classes—each independent and capable of self-valorizing activity—then the Law of Value can only represent the power (*potenza*) and violence of the relationship. It is the synthesis of the relations of force. (Negri 1991a: 172)

There are two distinctive features of Negri's version of this theory. First, the progressive socialization of capital is often seen as a relatively benign process: for Hilferding, for example, a more organized capitalism could both avoid economic crises and admit its gradual and negotiated reform. As the passage just cited indicates, this is not Negri's view. The politicization and socialization of the relations of production implies their reduction to straightforward relations of force, and capitalist domination is reduced to 'pure command'. This development is both stimulated by and helps to promote the constitution of the working class as a revolutionary subject that, refusing work, practices 'self-valorization', appropriating the resources required to meet its own independently determined needs (see especially Negri 1991a, Lessons 7–9).

Second, Negri, as we have seen, uses the *Grundrisse* in order to legitimize his version of the theory. He reads the manuscript as a prophetic text, one that somehow succeeds, against the grain of Marx's own later economic writings, in summing up the subsequent course of capitalist development. There is a sense in which this utilization of the *Grundrisse* is perfectly intelligible. The socialization of capital involves, according to Negri, the latter's transformation into a collective subject:

'Social capital' is the form in which the expansive power of capital is consolidated through and upon circulation. An expansive power, which, as we have seen, is also and above all a collective power. In this relationship *social capital is the subject of development*. In operating circulation, capital posits itself as sociality, as the capacity to engulf within its own development, in an ever more determined manner, every socially productive force. The subjectivity that this synthesis confers on capital represents what capital itself has achieved through the process of subsumption, through the ever more coherent and exhaustive acts of subjugation of society. *The very mode of production is modified.* (Negri 1991a: 121)

What is interesting about this stress on the subjectivity of social capital is that it connects up with a point that commentators have often made, usually as a criticism, about the *Grundrisse*, namely that Marx tends there to hypostatize capital as a collective subject that automatically produces its own conditions of existence. Consider, for example, the following passage:

Thus e.g. while the process in which money or value-for-itself originally becomes capital presupposes on the part of the capitalist an accumulation— perhaps by means of savings garnered from products and values created by his own labour etc., which he has undertaken as a *not-capitalist*, i.e. while the presuppositions under which money becomes capital appear as given, *external presuppositions* for the arising of capital—[nevertheless,] as soon as capital has become capital as such, it creates its own presuppositions, i.e.

the possession of the real conditions of the creation of new values *without exchange*—by means of its own production process. These presuppositions, which originally appeared as conditions of its own becoming—and hence could not spring from its *action as capital*—now appear as results of its own realization, reality, *as posited by it—not as conditions of its arising, but as results of its presence*. (Marx 1973: 459–60)

Edward Thompson calls this 'an extraordinary mode of thought to find in a materialist, for capital has become Idea, which unfolds itself in history', a case of '*unreconstructed* Hegelianism' on Marx's part (Thompson 1978: 253). Other critics have pointed to a tendency of Marx to rely, notably in his discussion in the *Grundrisse* of the crucial transition from money to capital, on a speculative dialectic that seeks to deduce the self-expansion of value from the concept of money itself.[10] It is in part for this reason that many commentators see Marx's economic thought undergoing between the *Grundrisse* and *Capital* a process of what Jacques Bidet calls '*rectification*' that involves the progressive (though incomplete) liberation of Marx's discourse from, as Bidet puts it, 'the Hegelian heritage of a dialectical form of exposition' (Bidet 1985: 124, 161).[11]

Negri himself is dismissive about the problem of Marx's relation to Hegel: 'That Marx was Hegelian has never seemed to me to be the case: on the sole condition of reading Marx and Hegel.' But he has, tacitly at least, a response to the question posed above about Marx's tendency in the *Grundrisse* to hypostatize capital: '*If capital is a subject on one side, on the other labour must be a subject as well.*' In the era of social capital the relations of production are reduced to the struggle between two autonomous and antagonistic collective subjects:

> The relation of capital is a relation of force that tends toward the separate and independent existence of the enemy: the process of workers' self-valorization, the dynamic of communism. Antagonism is no longer a form of the dialectic, it is its negation. (Negri 1991a: 57, 123, 186)

One might wonder how satisfactory it is to replace one hypostasis positing its own presuppositions with two conjoined in endless conflict. To begin to bring out difficulties with both Negri's interpretation of Marx and his analysis of capitalism in *Marx Beyond Marx*, let us consider the significance of the process of conceptual 'rectification' that culminates in *Capital*. Why then does Marx start with the commodity rather than money in *Capital*?[12] The short answer is that doing so allows him to conceptualize two central features of the capitalist mode of production, *exploitation* and *competition*.

In the *Grundrisse* Marx draws a celebrated distinction. On the one hand, '[c]*apital in general*, as distinct from the particular capitals', consists in 'the specific characteristics which distinguish capital from all other forms of wealth—or modes in which (social) production develops'. On the other hand, '[c]apital exists and can only exist as many capitals, and its self-determination therefore appears as their reciprocal interaction with one another', that is, in competition (Marx 1973: 449, 414).[13] To put it another way (borrowed from Robert Brenner), capitalist relations of production involve both the 'horizontal' antagonism between capital and wage labor that is constitutive of 'capital in general' and the 'vertical' conflicts among competing capitals (Brenner 1998: 23). A proper understanding of these two dimensions of the capitalist mode of production and of their interrelationship presupposes an analysis of their structural conditions of possibility.

This analysis is provided by the treatment of the commodity in *Capital*, volume 1, chapter 1.[14] Here Marx presents the labor theory of value by constructing the model of a system of generalized commodity production, in which the mass of products of labor take the form of commodities exchanged on the market. Autonomous but interdependent producers are compelled to exchange the products of their labor in order to meet their needs. As a result of the competitive interaction of rival producers on the market, these products tend to be sold at prices that oscillate around a level that reflects the socially necessary labor time required to produce them. Hence the dual nature of the commodity, the 'elementary form' of the 'wealth of societies in which the capitalist mode of production prevails': every product both is a use value, namely the human need that it meets, and has a value, the socially necessary labor time required to produce it, whose 'form of appearance' is the price for which the commodity would be exchanged at any given moment on the market (Marx 1976: 125, 139).

This analysis of the commodity allows Marx to make three decisive breakthroughs in his account of capitalist exploitation once, in part 2 of *Capital*, volume 1, he extends the model of generalized commodity production to cover labor power.[15] First, the distinction between use value and value, and that (closely related) between labor and labor power, allow him to solve the conundrums about how to explain capital's self-expansion with which he had grappled in the *Grundrisse*. The valorization of capital is possible because labor power when used through the actual expenditure of labor creates more value than the value it has as a commodity—that is, the socially necessary labor time required to reproduce labor power, largely (though not wholly) represented by the wages offered to workers on the market.[16] Second, conceptualizing labor power as a commodity allows Marx to formulate clearly the historical specificity of capitalist exploitation. The transformation of labor power into a commodity implies, as its historical presupposition, the separation of the direct producers from the means of production. Consequently the extraction of surplus labor does not, as in the case of earlier modes of production, require the direct application of political coercion: lacking direct access to the means of production, the worker finds herself without an acceptable alternative to selling her labor power on terms that lead to her exploitation. 'The silent compulsion of economic relations sets the seal on the domination of the capitalist over the worker. Direct extra-economic coercion is still of course used, but only in exceptional cases' (Marx 1976: 899).

Third, his analysis of the commodity permits Marx to locate capitalist exploitation at its proper level, in the relations of production. One motive behind the *Grundrisse*'s initial focus on money was what he regarded as the need to develop a critique of the theory of labor money developed by Proudhon and his followers, for whom 'the degradation of *money* and the exaltation of *commodities* was the essence of socialism' (Marx 1971: 86).[17] In other words, for Proudhon the problem with capitalism lay in the corruption of the commodity system introduced by money and banking. Monetary reform, including the introduction of labor money, would help to establish a just market economy. Marx comments: 'One might just as well abolish the Pope while leaving Catholicism in existence' (Marx 1976: 181 n.4). Exploitation for him is a consequence of the commodification of labor power, that is, of the normal workings of a system of generalized commodity production, not that of a deformed or corrupted market economy.

At the same time, Marx's analysis of the commodity allows him to treat competition as a constitutive dimension of capitalist relations of production. Competition among decentralized but interdependent producers is an inherent feature of a system of generalized commodity production. This is the sphere of what he calls in the *Grundrisse* 'many capitals'. Coexisting in that text with the propensity noted above to hypostatize capital in general into a collective subject that produces its own conditions of existence is the idea that competition plays a critical role in bringing into operation the characteristic tendencies of the capitalist mode of production: 'The influence of individual capitals on one another has the effect precisely that they must conduct themselves as *capital*; the seemingly independent influence of the individuals, and their chaotic collisions, are precisely the positing of their general law' (Marx 1973: 657).

Such formulations are ambiguous between the attribution of causal powers to competition among 'many capitals' and the treatment of this sphere as an external phenomenal expression of the inner tendencies of capital in general. The latter approach is evident in the following passage:

'Conceptually, *competition* is nothing other than the inner *nature of capital*, its essential character, appearing in and realized as the reciprocal interaction of many capitals with one another, the inner tendency as external necessity' (Marx 1973: 414). The critical issue analytically here is whether the 'inner tendencies' of the capitalist mode of production can be specified independently of competition or whether the causal mechanisms responsible for these tendencies necessarily involve competition. The successive conceptual recastings that Marx's economic writings underwent in the decade between his starting the *Grundrisse* and publishing the first volume of *Capital* involves his giving increasing causal significance to competition. Bidet presents this through a contrast between the tendencies of capitalist development and the structure of class struggle and competition:

> The system only has *tendencies* (to relative surplus-value, to rising productivity, to accumulation) because of its *structure*. The latter concerns *simultaneously* the relations between classes, between the opposed elements of classes (entrepreneur/employees) and between elements within each class, here the relation of competition between capitalists. This is what is partially hidden by the theme of 'essence/surface'.
>
> The reference to the tendencies of the system and to the interests of the dominant class would be purely metaphysical if it did not refer to the question of the *interests* of the 'individuals' who compose it and of the constraints that weigh on these individuals, that is to say individual capitals 'personified', as Marx puts it, by their holders. Capitalism does not possess any general tendency except in relation to what motivates individual capitals, with this structure of interests and constraints that defines the competitive relationship. (Bidet 1985: 135)[18]

The significance of competition can be seen in Marx's explanation of the technological dynamism of capitalism. In volume 1 of *Capital*, this figures in Marx's discussion of relative surplus value, where the rate of surplus value is increased thanks to rising productivity of labor. Already here Marx (somewhat uneasily) introduces competition: a capitalist who introduces a new labor-saving technique can sell his products at a price somewhere between their 'individual value', that is, the actual labor time used to produce them, and their 'social value', the socially necessary labor time required to produce them in the sector in question, which, by definition will be higher, allowing the innovator to make a surplus profit. Here the differences between individual capitals competing in the same product market have become an essential dimension of the analysis (Marx 1976: 433–6).

This argument is greatly extended in *Capital*, volume 3. First, in the key chapter 10 of part 2, 'Equalization of the General Rate of Profit Through

Competition', Marx greatly develops his analysis of the difference between the market price of commodities and their market values, what in volume 1 he calls 'social value', that is, the value that reflects the average conditions of production in the relevant branch of production, and of the surplus profits that derive from individual capitals achieving levels of productivity that are higher than the average. Then in part 3, when Marx develops the theory of the tendency of the rate of profit to fall, he makes the search for surplus profits the mechanism responsible for the rising organic composition of capital: when other capitals copy the innovation responsible for surplus profit, a new market value is established for that sector equivalent to the individual value of the innovator's commodities. His surplus profit is thereby eliminated, but also, since higher productivity is usually bought with a higher organic composition of capital, the generalization of the innovation produces a fall in the rate of profit. That capitalism is defined by a *dual* conflictual relationship—between capital and labor and among competing capitals—is well brought out in a passage at the end of Marx's discussion of surplus profits, which he argues offers 'a mathematically precise proof why capitalists form a veritable freemason society vis-à-vis the whole working class, while there is little love lost between them in competition among themselves' (Marx 1981: 300).[19]

THE TEST OF HISTORY

The argument of *Capital* is, of course, conducted at a very high level of abstraction. Much of the subsequent development of Marxist political economy has involved the position of more concrete levels of analysis designed, on the basis of the more abstract conceptualizations of *Capital*, to explain the course of capitalist development in the twentieth century (see Callinicos 2001b). Negri's own stance is at an oblique angle to this intellectual process. He barely adverts to the capital-in-general/many capitals distinction in *Marx Beyond Marx*: this is hardly surprising since he believes that contemporary capitalism is constituted by politicized relations of force between two antagonistic class subjects. Harry Cleaver accurately reflects his view of competition when he writes:

> in the development of this clash of subjectivities the continual development of the working class from dominated labour power to revolutionary class ... increasingly undermines capitalist control and imposes its own directions on social development. Because of this, competition among capitalists is less of a driving force and more what Negri calls 'sordid family quarrels' over which managers are best at imposing discipline on the working class. (Cleaver 1984: xxii)

Beyond a certain point, there is little to be gained in simply confronting Negri's highly selective appropriation of the *Grundrisse* and the interpretation of Marx's intellectual evolution between 1857 and 1867, briefly outlined in the preceding section. I think that my interpretation is more accurate, but the history of creative misreadings of canonical texts is long and rich enough for this claim to be easily dismissed as mere pedantry. The interesting questions are rather these: To what extent did *Marx Beyond Marx* capture the subsequent evolution of capitalism and the class struggle? How useful did Negri's subjectivist appropriation of the *Grundrisse* prove to be? In my view, the answer that any serious appraisal of the history of the past 25 years must give to these questions is: Not much.

This claim can be considered at two levels. First, is it the case that competition among capitals has been supplanted through the comprehensive politicization of the relations of production, as rival collective subjects are locked in combat? The answer, surely, must be, No. Whatever theoretical perspective one adopts, it is undeniable that economic competition, particularly at the international level, has increased very significantly over the past generation. In the face of this intensification of competition, the idea, essential to Negri's assertion that the 'Law of Value dies', that prices are no longer the outcome primarily of economic processes but are politically determined, is untenable. When competition occurs at the international level between rival capitals, no individual capital or nation state is in a position autonomously to set prices.[20] At the national level, the consequence has been to force a series of large-scale capital restructurings that have eliminated some firms and drastically disrupted the institutionalized relations that previously existed between specific capitals that sometimes enjoyed a monopoly or semi-monopoly position within their domestic market and the nation state.

One might indeed say that the era of neoliberalism has seen a partial depoliticization of economic relations. Of course, these relations are still constituted by exploitation, and in that fundamental sense remain political. Moreover, the 'depoliticization' that has occurred has been in part the outcome of a series of highly ideological interventions at the national and international level (in the latter case, the Washington Consensus enforced by the US Treasury, the International Monetary Fund, and the World Bank) that have sought to present the economic as a neutral sphere whose mastery is purely technical and dependent on understanding the 'natural' laws of the market. All the same, if we understand the politicization of economic relations in the terms in which it is presented in *Marx Beyond Marx*—that is, as a process whereby economic relations are increasingly the resultant of the conflict between collectively organized and politically self-conscious class subjects, then this process is less advanced than it was a generation ago. The intensification of international competition has made it harder for individual capitals to weld themselves into collective subjects at the national level, both because this competition encourages firms to invest and trade at the global level and because nation states have to deal not just with 'native' capitals but with foreign multinational corporations that have invested in their territories. It is important not to confuse this relative dis-articulation of capital at the national level with the idea that globalization has rendered the nation state impotent. Nevertheless, a consequence of this disarticulation is that individual capitals, including the biggest multi-nationals, find themselves subject to processes of primarily international economic competition that they cannot control (see Harman 1991 and Harman 1996).

This shift is registered by Negri in his more recent work. After all, what is empire but 'a *decentralized* and *deterritorializing* apparatus of rule that incorporates the entire global realm within its open expanding frontiers' (Hardt and Negri 2000: xii)? The metaphor of the network that Hardt and Negri, like many other analysts of contemporary capitalism, use implies at the very least a decentralization of power, its dispersal among rival centers. Indeed, '[i]n this smooth space of Empire, there is no *place* of power—it is both everywhere and nowhere' (Hardt and Negri 2000: 190). Such a view of capitalism seems hard to square with Negri's earlier conception of capital as a collective subject. The same would seem to be true of the '*trifunctional*' Polybian constitution of Empire involving

> a functional equilibrium among three forms of power: the monarchic unity of power and its global monopoly of force [the United States and the G7 in particular]; aristocratic articulations through transnational corporations and nation-states; and democratic–representational *comitia*, presented again in the form of nation-states along with various kinds of NGOs, media organizations, and other 'popular' organisms. (Hardt and Negri 2000: 314–15)

Yet the older idea of the state as the instrument of the collective subject social capital continues to figure in *Empire*. Hardt and Negri interpret Marx's famous declaration in the *Manifesto* that '[t]he executive of the modern state is but a committee for managing the common affairs of the whole bourgeoisie' (Marx and Engels 1998: 37) in precisely these terms: 'by this they mean that although the action of the state will at times contradict the immediate interests of the individual capitalists, it will always be in the long term interests of the collective capitalist, that is, the collective subject of social capital as a whole' (Hardt and Negri 2000: 304). The form taken by this relationship varies as capitalism changes in the course of its development.

As capital becomes transnational, so the functions of the state are taken over by the Polybian mixed constitution. What binds together 'the diverse functions and bodies of the hybrid constitution' is Guy Debord's 'society of the spectacle', 'an integrated and diffuse apparatus of images and ideas that produces and regulates public discourse and opinion'. In turn, however: 'The spectacle of politics functions *as if* the media, the military, the government, the transnational corporations, the global financial institutions, and so forth were all consciously and explicitly directed by a single power even though they are not' (Hardt and Negri 2000: 321, 323).

So, despite the fact that, 'in this smooth space of Empire, there is no *place* of power', the imperial constitution operates as if 'the collective subject of social capital as a whole' were in command. It is not clear whether we are supposed to conceive this as a paranoid collective fantasy or an objective functional relationship (or perhaps both). As is often true of functionalist theories of the state, Negri easily slips into more instrumentalist formulations, for example, declaring after 9–11 that the United States was acting on behalf of 'collective capital' (Negri 2001a; see also Hardt and Negri 2004: 177). Alternatively one might take seriously Marx's declaration: '*Capital in general*, as distinct from the particular capitals, does indeed appear (1) *only as an abstraction*' (Marx 1973: 449).[21] In other words, rather than seek to hypostatize capital in general as a collective subject, 'social capital', it might be more useful to analyze the concrete forms of competition and cooperation among 'many capitals' at both the national and the international level and how these articulate with the processes of geopolitical competition constitutive of the interstate system. The outcome of such an analysis would in my view be a much more complex picture that the transfer of political power to a set of transnationally organized institutions that Hardt and Negri claim has taken place (Callinicos 2002; Callinicos 2003a: ch. 5; Wood 2002).

The second level at which history has judged *Marx Beyond Marx* harshly is that of the class struggle itself. The intensification of international economic competition and the consequent disarticulation of national capitalisms have involved also a number of serious defeats for the organized working class from the late 1970s onwards. If these were most severe in the United States, where the partial recovery of profitability was made possible by an unprecedented twenty-year compression of real wages, in Europe they were most spectacular in the two advanced capitalist societies where working-class combativity had been most developed in the early 1970s, Italy and Britain. Exploring the causes of these severe setbacks for the workers' movement is not the function of this chapter. Nevertheless, it is clear enough that they involved, on both sides of the class divide, the interrelation of objective and subjective factors (see Harman 1988).

On the part of capital, the harsher competitive pressures on established industries both demanded and facilitated the dismantling or weakening of what had hitherto been strongholds of working-class organization, but the realization of such objectives required the construction of national capitalist coalitions with the ideological will and political capacity to wage the necessary class battles. On the side of the working class, the demoralizing effect of mass employment, the economic fragmentation produced by the processes of capital restructuring themselves, and the bureaucratization of workplace organization interacted with the general commitment to class collaboration of both the political and trade-union leaders of the workers' movement and the marginalization of more militant groups of workers and of the revolutionary left, partly self-induced, but partly the product of larger forces and strategies.

These changes, to varying degrees, and generally in a partial and confused form, registered in the consciousness of the left. In Britain, for example, debates were provoked by the recognition, from otherwise very different perspectives, by Tony Cliff of the Socialist Workers Party and by the right wing of the Communist Party grouped around *Marxism Today* that the initiative had decisively swung back to capital's favor.[22] In Italy, within the autonomist movement of which Negri was a leading member, Sergio Bologna wrote in 1977 a celebrated essay, 'The Tribe of Moles', seeking to trace the concrete economic and social processes that were fragmenting the left produced by the Hot Autumn but also, he believed, producing new political subjects, above all in the shape of the student rebellion of that year (Bologna 1977).[23] Negri too, in one of his most notorious texts, 'Capitalist Domination and Working-Class Sabotage', also written in 1977, acknowledged these processes of fragmentation, but analyzed them in terms of the thesis of the politicization of the relations of production. His argument repays close examination since it represents a crucial test of the capacity of the version of Marxism most fully expounded in *Marx Beyond Marx* to anticipate the course of the class struggle.

Consistently enough, Negri argues that 'the crisis of the Planner State'—of the managed capitalism that emerged in the era of Keynes and the New Deal—means that 'never before has the capitalist state been so politically autonomous! ... The source and the legitimation of power are no longer the law of value and its dialectic, but the law of command and its hierarchy' (Negri 1978a: 248). So far, so familiar. But Negri argues further that the death of the law of value means that incomes are now politically determined, rather than being the result of economic processes. The state is now the *State-based-on-Income-as Revenue*, the Income-State [*Stato-rendito*]—a state of political income. The one absolute value against which all other hierarchical values must measure themselves is political power. And this one absolute value is the foundation for the construction of a scale of *differential incomes*, whose value is calculated on the basis of one's greater or lesser distance from the center, from the site of production of power. (Negri 1978a: 248)[24]

There are two particular consequences of this development that are worth noting here. First, the labor market becomes segmented on the basis of the political rewards allotted to specific groups of employees: 'the indifference to the value you produce is equalled by the attention paid to the extent of your faithfulness to the system' (Negri 1978a: 249). Second, this politicization of the labor market implies that wages cease to reflect economic determinants:

at this point, *the wage is no longer*, in its economic identity, an *independent variable*. It is completely subordinated to the entire dynamic of power, to the entire framework of the political autonomy of the state. The wage is reduced to the hierarchy of command, in a process that is the counterpart, the obverse of the repression of proletarian unity at the social level. (Negri 1978a: 249)

I shall address the sociopolitical conclusions that Negri draws from this analysis in a moment. It is first worth emphasizing that the idea that the wage has ceased to be 'an independent variable' represents the apparent reversal of his normal position. This position, reaffirmed a year or so later in *Marx Beyond Marx*, is that the wage *is* an independent variable: 'When the wage actually does appear in the first volume of *Capital*, taking over a number of themes explicitly launched in the *Grundrisse*, it appears as an "independent variable"' (Negri 1991a: 131). Rereading this passage still surprises me, since it is precisely and blatantly the opposite of what Marx actually wrote in *Capital*: 'To put it mathematically: the rate of accumulation is the independent, not the dependent variable; the rate of wages is the dependent, not the independent variable' (Marx 1976: 770).[25] Marx's theory of wages affirms that any tendency for the money price of labor power to rise about its value will be counteracted by a rise in the rate of unemployment, either because of the profit squeeze that starts the downward phase of the business cycle or as a result of longer-term technological changes produced by the tendency for capital to rely more on relative surplus value to increase the rate of exploitation (see Rosdolsky 1977: 282–313).

Once again, the point of noting the gap between Negri and Marx (so extreme here that Negri reads in *Capital* the opposite of what Marx actually writes) is not to denounce a deviation from orthodoxy but to get a clearer idea of the driving forces of Negri's own theory. To return to *Marx Beyond Marx*:

> *The wage is an independent variable in so far as the quantity, the quality, the value of necessary labor 'must' be a fixed dimension for capital* ... Its value is not determined once and for all in exchange, but is *the result of the class struggle*, when it fails to become the dictatorship of the proletariat. Independence determines the struggles, fixes the possibilities and the development. It is the struggle which consolidates the values of necessary labor and poses them as historical entities: the sign of a totality of needs, of behaviours, of acquired values that only the struggle succeeds in modifying and developing—and this according to the possibilities that living labor contains, as a result of the transformations that it has undergone, possibilities that are always linked to the productive transformation of capital. (Negri 1991a: 132)

The wage thus reflects the '*power of living labor*', of autonomous proletarian subjectivity (Negri 1991a: 132). As we have seen, Negri believes that this power, expressed through the 'rigidity' of necessary labor, its incompressibility by capital, is responsible for the tendency of the rate of profit to fall. From this perspective, Negri's claim that the politicization of the relations of production means that 'the wage is no longer an independent variable' is less a contradiction of his theory of the wage than its flip side. For the assertion of working-class subjectivity and the response of the 'collective capitalist' have now reached such a point of crisis that they have broken economic relations loose from any objective determinants and reduced them to the contingent consequences of the clash of antagonistic class wills. Because in '*the prevalence of the subjective* in the explanation of the current dialectic of capital', 'it is the productivity of the proletarian subject that structures the destructuring, that is, negatively determines its own opposite', the political determination of the wage by capital reflects the same 'power of living labor' responsible for the rigidity of necessary labor (Negri 1978a: 239).

In the specific context of Italy in 1977, however, Negri saw the transformation of the wage into a 'dependent variable' fixed by the collective will of 'social capital' as the source of the divisions within the working class:

> There is also direct action to be taken. Some groups of workers, some strata of the working class, remain tied to the dimension of the wage, to its mystified terms. In other words, they live off this political income. Inasmuch as they are living off this political income (even some who work in the large factories), they are stealing and expropriating proletarian

surplus-value—they are participating in the social-labor racket on the same terms as their bosses. These positions—and particularly the union practice that fosters them—are to be fought, with violence if necessary. It will not be the first time that a procession of the unemployed has entered a large factory so that it can destroy the corruption of the labor aristocracy along with the arrogance of political income! This was what the unemployed were doing in Britain in the 1920s, for example—and quite rightly so.[26] Here, however, it is no longer simply a matter of the unemployed. Here we are dealing with all the protagonists in the social production of value who are rejecting and refusing the operation that capital has set in motion in order to destroy their unity: *the workers of the large factories need to be brought back again to this front of the struggle.* This is fundamental. The *social majority of the proletariat*, of socially-productive labor-power, must impose the issue and practice of unity, bringing it once again to the attention of the workers in the large factories. The *mass vanguards* of the large factories must struggle, in conjunction with the proletarian movement, to destroy the parasitic filth celebrated and guaranteed by the unions in the large factories. This is fundamental. Here, in fact, we are dealing with the project—the living, effective project—of workers' self-valorization, which refuses, and must destroy, the vacuity of the *rentier* logic of capital, and all of its apparatuses. (Negri 1978a: 251)

I make no apologies for quoting this extraordinary passage at some length. Nor do I apologize for not mincing my words: this must be among the most foolish and irresponsible statements to be produced by a social theorist with the kind of reputation now enjoyed by Negri. Where does one start? In the first place, Negri's premise is false. As we have seen, it is not the case that prices and therefore also incomes have become politically determined quantities: the intensification of competition, particularly at the international level, means that economic actors are not free to set prices and incomes according to their political priorities. Of course, the division of value between labor and capital is the outcome of class struggles, and in that sense is political, but these struggles unfold in the context of economic constraints inherent in the structure of global capitalism. Secondly, even if it were the case that incomes were now politically determined, this would surely be true of all recipients of 'income-as-revenue'. So why pick out 'the workers of the large factories' as a privileged beneficiary of the distributive policies of the Italian state?

The answer is that here at least politics was in command. Negri's portrayal of these workers as a labor aristocracy served to legitimize the political strategy being pursued by sections of the autonomist movement in 1977–79, who welcomed confrontations such as the notorious clash between their supporters and Lucio Lama, general secretary of CGIL, supported by Communist Party and union stewards, at Rome University in February 1977. Immediately after the passage just cited, Negri responded to 'those jackals that I already hear howling: I am not saying that the Mirafiori worker is not an exploited worker' (Negri 1978a: 251). Why then talk about 'even some who work in the big factories ... stealing and expropriating proletarian surplus-value' and about 'parasitic filth'?[27] These equivocations seem less important than Negri's call for 'direct action', even 'violence', against such workers, talk that nullifies his assurances that he seeks 'unity'. What we have here is a theoretical rationale for a policy of polarizing the Italian left between a self-declared 'proletarian movement' and those sections of the organized working class that remained loyal to the PCI and CGIL leadership—a group that was growing in 1976–77, as Bologna had the prescience to recognize at the time.[28]

Here the judgment of history has of course been particularly harsh. Nemesis came for workers in the big factories in the autumn of 1980 but it was not inflicted by a Negri-led 'proletarian movement'. The management of Fiat, which had taken on 12,000 new workers (mainly women and young people) two years earlier, succeeded in sacking 14,000 workers, many of them established militants. This crushing defeat, from which the Italian workers' movement is only now beginning to recover, depended in large part on the Fiat bosses' success in manipulating divisions within the workforce and the wider left. A heavy responsibility lies on all those who contributed to the development of these divisions. On the side of the workers' movement, the lion's share must be taken by the leaderships of the PCI and CGIL, whose pursuit of the 'historic compromise' with Christian Democracy laid the basis for the employers' offensive that, too late, they sought to prevent. Negri himself was by the time of the Fiat struggle himself a political prisoner, in effect a victim of the historic compromise. All the same, he cannot avoid his share of the blame insofar as in widely read texts such as 'Capitalist Domination and Working-Class Sabotage' he produced a triumphalist Marxist rhetoric that sought to consolidate and radicalize the divisions in an already highly fragmented movement. This seems to me, politically at any rate, to be a much more serious charge than the apparently unending debate over Negri's alleged complicity in armed actions associated with the Red Brigades.[29]

THE FLIGHT INTO ONTOLOGY

It would be unfair to demand of *Marx Beyond Marx* critical reflection on a defeat that only took final form after it was published in 1979. This text is an extended theoretical argument for the version of *operaismo* that Negri had developed in the course of the 1970s, one that increasingly located proletarian subjectivity outside the factory among the diverse subjects oppressed by a social capital whose politicized 'command' operated in every sphere of life. Negri himself summed up this shift as reflecting the transition 'from the working class massified in direct production in the factory, to social labour-power, representing the potentiality of the new working class, now extended throughout the entire span of production and reproduction'.[30] This theme of the 'social worker' replacing the 'mass worker' is still present in *Empire*, though it is now overlaid by the new concept (taken from Spinoza) of the multitude.[31]

Neither *Empire* nor any other later texts by Negri of which I am aware develop anything that amounts to a serious critique of the positions that he took in the 1970s. He seeks to differentiate the version of autonomism that he had developed from the Red Brigades' terrorism, while insisting: 'The sharp, definitive defeat of the political organizations of the movement at the end of the 1970s by no means coincided with any defeat of the new political subjects which had emerged in the eruption of 1977'.[32] This way of putting it sidesteps the larger wave of defeats suffered by the organized working class in Italy and the rest of the advanced capitalist world that were a necessary condition for the process of capital restructuring driven through under the banner of neoliberalism. Hardt and Negri actually claim this process as a victory for the working class: 'The power of the proletariat imposes limits on capital and not only determines the crisis but also dictates the terms and nature of the transformation. *The proletariat actually invents the social and productive forms that capital will be forced to adopt for the future'* (Hardt and Negri 2000: 268; see generally chapter 3.3). This claim is a direct echo of the primacy of proletarian subjectivity affirmed by Negri in the 1970s, for example, thus:

> The whole of capitalist development, ever since the working class established itself at a high level of composition, has been nothing other than the obverse of, a reaction to, a pursuit of proletarian self-valorization—an operation of self-protection, of recuperation, of adjustment in relation to the effects of self-valorization, which are effects of sabotage of the capitalist machine ... here the methodology of the *critique of political economy* has to be modified, taking as its starting point proletarian self-valorization, its separateness, and the effects of sabotage that it determines. (Negri 1978a: 241)

This argument is a hyped-up version of a longstanding theme of *operaismo*: Tronti also tended to portray each phase of capitalist development as a response to new forms of working-class autonomy. But the question one must ask is this: To what extent does the idea capture the tortuous—sometimes indeed tortured—reality of the kind of 'recomposition' that the working class experienced during the Great Depression of the 1930s or the long phase of economic crises that began in the early 1970s? Certainly these processes involve very powerful assertions of working-class subjectivity— sometimes full of combative self-confidence, at other times, more heroic but desperate fights with backs to the wall. But it seems unconvincing to describe the outcomes of such struggles as 'invented' by workers and 'forced' on capital. What would the members of former mining communities in Britain, now often given over to drugs and despair, say if we told them that their present plight was a consequence of their own practices of 'proletarian self-valorization'? To say this is not to ignore or diminish the forms of resistance that the oppressed and exploited are able to achieve even in desperate circumstances (something well captured by Ken Loach in films like *Raining Stones*). But it is to recognize that some circumstances are better than others, and these differences in situation are not simply a consequence of which collective subject is able to assert its class will more effectively, but reflect, among other things, the structurally determined capacities that workers and capitalists can bring to bear against each other (Callinicos 2004).

Here we can appreciate the merits of Marx's rather than Negri's theory of wages, according to which, as Roman Rosdolsky puts it,

> it is simply not the case that labour and capital represent two autonomous powers, whose respective 'shares' in the national product merely depend on their respective strengths; rather, labour is subject to the economic power of capital in capitalism from the start, and its 'share' must always be conditional on the 'share' of capital. (Rosdolsky 1977: 284)

This imbalance reflects the fact that, should wages rise sufficiently to bring about a serious fall in the rate of profit, capitalists may react by using their control over the means of production to reduce investment and output, thereby, by raising the rate of unemployment, undermining workers' bargaining power. It was precisely for this reason that Marx argued that the wage struggle must be transformed into a political movement whose aim is to expropriate capital. Given the role that mass unemployment had played over the last generation in weakening organized labor and increasing the room for manoeuver of capital, this reasoning seems of more than theoretical import, though philosophically it does make Negri's tendency to counterpose revolutionary subjectivity to 'objectivism' otiose.

Rather than reconsider the primacy that he had accorded to subjectivity in his writings of the 1970s, Negri has preferred to transform it into an ontological principle. Already in *Marx Beyond Marx* he had put forward 'the principle of constitution', which

> introduces into the methodology the dimension of the qualitative leap, a conception of history reduced to collective relations of force, thus a conception that is not sceptical, but dynamic and creative. Every constitution of a new structure is the constitution of a new antagonism. (Negri 1991a: 56)

Here we have *in nuce* the idea of constituent power that plays such a central role in Negri's recent writings. His fullest development of this concept appeals to the 'second Foucault' of the *History of Sexuality*:

> In Foucault humanity appears as a set of resistances that produces an absolute capacity for liberation, outside any finalism that is not an expression of life itself and its reproduction. Life liberates itself in humanity, and opposes itself to everything that limits and imprisons it. (Negri 1999a: 27, 341 n.103, translation modified)

Negri's account of constituent power seeks, in fact, to marry Foucault to Marx as the theorist of 'the all-expansive creativity of living labor' (Negri 1999a: 326):

> living labor incarnates constituent power and offers it the general social conditions through which it can express itself: constituent power establishes itself politically on the basis of that social cooperation that is consubstantial with living labor, thus interpreting its productivity or, better, its creativity. In the immediacy, the creative spontaneity of living labor, constituent power finds … a way to massify its creativity. One must carefully examine this nucleus of living labor, this creative tension that is simultaneously political and economic, productive of civil, social and political structures, and which is thus constituent tension. Cooperative living labor produces a social ontology that is constitutive and innovative, an interweaving of forms that touches economics and politics; living labor produces an indistinct mixture of politics and economics that has a creative figure. (Negri 1999a: 33, translation modified)

Here we are back in the same circle of concepts—creativity, productivity, living labor, etc.—with which we began. It is not to diminish the brilliant critical history of Renaissance humanism to which the bulk of *Insurgencies* is devoted to say that the actual theorization of constituent power in that book, notably in the concluding chapter, does little more than play the changes on these concepts. But one doesn't have to be a card-carrying follower of Derrida to think that terms such as 'creativity' and 'productivity', which are endlessly used to specify the content of the concept constituent power, are badly in need of deconstruction. To say, for example, that '[t]he dynamic, creative and continuous constitution of the process of power [*potenza*] is politics' is less the solution of any problem than an invitation critically to examine the concepts in terms of which politics is being defined (Negri 1999a: 335, translation modified). This observation is not intended to deny that any philosophical argument must find a resting point somewhere, in a set of premises whose truth is left unquestioned at least for the task in hand, or to demand that Negri pursue an infinite regress of justifications, but rather to point to the fact that the particular resting point he has lighted on is especially liable to crumble beneath him, since it consists in a set of concepts that radicalize his subjectivization of the social by grounding it in a subjectivized nature.

The name often given to nature so conceived is Life. It is striking, for example, how the concept of social cooperation that Negri takes from Marx in order to specify the concept of living labor is itself redefined: 'Cooperation is life itself, insofar as it produces and reproduces itself.' Negri also says that Marx is best understood from the standpoint of 'Foucault, the genealogist of subjectivity' (Negri 1999a: 332, 222).[33] As we have seen, what Negri takes from Foucault is the idea that resistance is an expression of Life. This is not so much Foucault's idea as Deleuze's. The latter's *Foucault*, which Negri cites, is more reliable as an exposition of Deleuze's own views than of those of Foucault. As Alain Badiou has suggested, this is a fairly typical procedure:

> in starting from innumerable and seemingly disparate cases, …, Deleuze arrives at conceptual productions that I would unhesitatingly describe as *monotonous*, composing a very particular regime of emphasis or almost infinite repetition of a limited repertoire of concepts, as well as a virtuosic variation of names, under which what is thought remains essentially identical. (Badiou 2000: 15)[34]

Life certainly doesn't go unanalyzed in Deleuze's work. *A Thousand Plateaus* (Deleuze and Guattari 1987) in particular is, among other things, the development of a highly distinctive ontology of Life. There is a strong case for saying that the influence of this text on *Empire* is systematic, and that the theoretical construction of Hardt and Negri's book cannot be fully understood unless it is set alongside *A Thousand Plateaus*. Properly to demonstrate this and to explore its implications would be a substantial study in its own right.[35] In the absence of such a work, one can still wonder whether the best strategy to rescue a version of Marxist political economy that had been found historically and politically wanting is to subsume it into the kind of vitalist ontology that, whatever its precise derivation, demonstrably organizes texts such as *Insurgencies* and *Empire*. In them one finds concepts and themes from Negri's earlier work petrified in the more articulated philosophical framework that he has now built to support them. He writes for example, 'True political realism does not consist in recognizing the decisive character of physical force and acquiescing to it; on the contrary it consists in considering how this domination is always indefatigably undermined by the *constituent sabotage* of the multitude' (Negri 1999a: 333–4, translation modified). Sabotage, already transformed in Negri's writings of the 1970s from a tactic into the dynamic source of capitalist development, is now promoted further to the status of a trans-historical reality.

The ontological carapace in which such essentially political concepts are now encased makes it difficult to involve them in the normal interchanges of debate. Perhaps this helps to explain why *Empire* is, as Daniel Bensaïd puts it, so 'strategically mute' (Bensaïd 2002). For strategy concerns itself, not with the nature of being, but with the necessarily hazardous calculations that political actors must make as they grapple with an objective context (including the strategies and actions of others) whose current state and future course are riddled with uncertainties, in part because the interactions among the antagonists produce unexpected transformations.[36] There is no great dishonor in the fact that Negri's theoretical work of the 1970s supported a failed political strategy; that was a decade from which the entire left, reformist and revolutionary, emerged defeated. But themes from that decade survive in his current work, somewhat changed but still preserved in philosophical aspic, in the way, for instance, that the 1970s idea of 'the refusal of work' finds its continuation in Negri's contemporary preoccupation with 'exodus and desertion' (for example Negri 2001a).

The metaphysical abstraction with which such themes are formulated helps to immunize them from critical examination. This is a pity. *Empire* has captured the imaginations of some of the best activists in the movement against capitalist globalization—generally for good reasons—for example, Hardt's and Negri's willingness to stare capital in the face, recognizing both its destructive potential and the possibilities for liberation that it secretes, and the serenity with which they affirm the actuality of communism. But what Derrida calls 'the walled perimeter of a new ontological fatherland' that surround the testable—and contestable—economic and political propositions that *Empire* advances is an obstacle to the development of the debate that the movement needs to have about its future.[37]

NOTES

1. Portions of this chapter first appeared in Callinicos 2006. I am grateful both to Polity and to the editors and publishers of the present collection for permitting the publication of this present chapter.
2. See generally Chapters 4.1, 'Virtualities', and 4.2, 'Generation and Corruption'.
3. In this chapter I develop aspects of the critique of both *Empire* and Negri's earlier thought first advanced in my article 'Toni Negri in Perspective' (Callinicos 2001a), which discusses *Empire* in much more detail than I do here.
4. See also p. 138: 'At the heart of this relationship, the capitalist relation is immediately a relation of power.'
5. Quoted in Wright 2002: 28. This book is a valuable study of the origins and development of *operaismo*.
6. Negri, 'Marx on Cycle and Crisis', in Negri 1988: 66, 72.
7. Negri, 'Archaeology and Project: The Mass Worker and the Social Worker', in Negri 1988: 224, 225.
8. Negri, 'Keynes and the Capitalist Theory of the State post-1929', in Negri 1988.
9. See, for example, Bukharin 1971 and Castoriadis 1988.
10. See Marx 1973: 239–376, and, for critical commentary, for example, Mepham 1979, Bidet 1985: ch. 6, and Bidet 1990: 67–73.
11. See generally Bidet 1985: ch. 7. For other important studies of the progressive recasting of Marx's economic concepts and of the critical role in this process of the *Economic Manuscript of 1861–3*, see Vygodsky 1974, esp. chs 5–7, and Dussel 2001.
12. In pursuing this theme I have benefited from reading Daniel Bensaïd's critique of *Marx Beyond Marx*, 'A la recherche du sujet perdu (Negri corrige Marx)' (Bensaïd 1995).
13. The distinction between capital in general and many capitals is one of the main themes of Roman Rosdolsky's classic commentary on the *Grundrisse*, *The Making of Marx's Capital* (Rosdolsky 1977). See also Arthur 2002.
14. The interpretation of this chapter in its successive versions raise many issues that I cannot discuss here, but that I first addressed in my doctoral thesis, 'The Logic of *Capital*' (Callinicos 1978). I have also greatly benefited from Bidet's discussions of the market and competition in Marx's thought in Bidet 1985 and Bidet 1990. I should make it clear that I do not agree with the conclusion drawn by Bidet, both in the latter text and in Bidet 1999, that Marx should have posited the market as a 'metastructure' common to both capitalism and socialism: see Callinicos 1994 and Callinicos 2006: §1.2.
15. It is important to see that, by the stage of *Capital*, the commodification of labor power is not treated as somehow implicit in the very concept of a market economy. As Bidet puts it, its introduction involves 'a constructivist initiative, which consists in adding a new determination to the antecedent categorial system, the commodity system. Marx "determines" a commodity of the system as being "labour-power"' (Bidet 1990: 71–2). This is an example of how in *Capital* Marx proceeds by what Althusser calls 'the position of concepts', the progressive introduction (rather than conceptual deduction) of new theoretical determinations that permit the elaboration of more concrete levels of analysis; see Althusser 1978a.
16. The concept of labor power does emerge first in the *Grundrisse* (Marx 1973: 267), but, as John Mepham notes, 'Marx's difficulty in expressing the relation between labour, "labouring capacity" and surplus-value (pp. 333f.) testifies to the fact that this crucial distinction does not stabilize conceptually nor receive definitive terminological expression in the *Grundrisse*' (Mepham 1979: 170).
17. See Rosdolsky 1977: ch. 4, and Vygodsky 1974: ch. 3.
18. The ambiguity of Marx's treatment of competition in the *Grundrisse* is perhaps partly a consequence of a similar ambiguity in one of the main influences on that text, Hegel's account of essence and appearance, where appearance is an externalization of essence, which might seem to reduce it to merely epiphenomenal status, but at the same time essence is nothing but the relationship among appearances. As Charles Taylor puts

it, for Hegel, 'the more essential reality is externalized, the more the relatedness of reality is developed and the more inwardness it has' (Taylor 1975: 278).

19. See, on the role of the struggle for surplus profits in the TRPF, Marx 1981: 373–4 and, in the law of value more generally, Marx 1981: 1020.

20. See, for example, the detailed evidence of the impact of international competition on costs, prices, and profits especially in the manufacturing sectors of the US, Japanese, and German economies assembled by Robert Brenner in Brenner 1998 and Brenner 2002.

21. Under (2) Marx does go on to assign 'capital in general ... a *real* existence', namely as money capital, an idea that is developed in *Capital*, volume 3, part 5, where the circuit of money capital is analyzed as, among other things, where '[t]he capital relationship assumes its most superficial and fetishized form' as 'self-valorizing value, money breeding money' (Marx 1981: 515–16).

22. For the SWP's part, see Cliff 1979 and the special issue of *International Socialism* on the 1984–85 miners' strike and its aftermath (1985); compare, for *Marxism Today*, Jacques and Mulhern 1981 and Hall and Jacques 1983.

23. See Wright 2002: 203–11 on this text and the debate it provoked.

24. See also Negri, 'Crisis of the Planner State', in Negri 1988.

25. Elsewhere Negri cites another passage where Marx supposedly treats both surplus value and wages as independent variables: Negri, 'Marx on Cycle and Crisis', in Negri 1988: 66. In fact what Marx says in the passage in question is this: 'With the division between surplus-value and wages, on which the determination of the profit rate essentially depends, two quite different elements are involved, labour-power and capital. It is the functions of two independent variables which set limits to one another, and the *quantitative division* of the value produced emerges from their *qualitative distinction*' (Marx 1981: 486). But labor power and capital, not wages and surplus value, are the independent variables here; moreover, to affirm the qualitative difference between labor power and capital implies nothing about the precise form of the interaction between them responsible for the wage rate and hence (other things being equal) the rate of surplus value. The passage comes in any case from Marx's discussion of the rate of interest, which he is trying to show, unlike the rate of surplus value, has no long-term determinants—an argument that goes against Negri's entire interpretation of capitalism as progressively disjoined from any objective anchorage.

26. The original English translation by Ed Emery includes a parenthesis just before this sentence: '(See the accounts in Wal Hannington's *Unemployed Struggles*)' (Negri 1978b: 110). I am grateful to Tim Murphy for pointing out that this is an interpolation added to Negri's original. This source in any case offers no support for Negri's strategy. *Unemployed Struggles* is a quasi-autobiographical work by Wal Hannington, Communist leader of the National Unemployed Workers Movement in Britain between the wars. The book does indeed describe 'factory raids' that the newly formed NUWM organized during the postwar slump in the early 1920s. Far, however, from attacking 'the arrogance of salaried income', the NUWM, led largely by activists whose role in the wartime shop stewards' movement had cost them their jobs in the subsequent recession, acted, as Hannington puts it, in a 'spirit of working-class solidarity ... We were urging the employed workers to stand firm everywhere against any attempt to lower their conditions and we were assuring them of the support of the unemployed in such a fight.' The raids were directed, not at those workers still with jobs, but at employers who were increasing overtime during a time of mass unemployment. The NUWM's concern to win the backing of the workers at the factories it occupied is reflected in one clause of the agreement that ended a raid on an Islington factory in January 1922: 'Also that the girls will not be stopped for time lost by this raid carried out by the unemployed.' As a result of the NUWM campaign, a proposal for an overtime agreement was overwhelmingly rejected in a ballot by the Amalgamated Engineering Union, still then largely an organization of skilled male workers and therefore often called a 'labor aristocracy'. The NUWM's efforts to unite unemployed and employed workers was shown by the demonstrations it organized

in support of the engineers during the great 1922 lockout and by its unsuccessful attempts to affiliate to the Trade Union Congress. See Hannington 1936: chs 2, 3, and 6 (quotations from pp. 25 and 50).

27. Even in Negri's own theoretical terms this seems like a nonsensical statement. If '[p]rofit and the wage [have] become the forms of the division of a value-content which no longer relates to any specific mechanisms of exploitation', what basis remains for distinguishing necessary labor (i.e. the social labor required to reproduce labor power and therefore determining its value) from surplus labor? Once the division of the social product is politically determined it makes no sense to talk about surplus value as an objective quantity that is capable of appropriation.

28. See the texts cited in Wright 2002: 170, 216.

29. I have discussed Negri's political role in the 1970s further in Callinicos 2001a: 35–45; see also the texts cited there. Wright 2002 has a good discussion of Negri and the shipwreck of Italian autonomism in the 1970s in chapters 7 and 9. Toby Abse has given an unusually severe judgment (on the left) of Negri's role in the 1970s (particularly with respect to the activities of the armed groups) in Abse 2000.

30. Negri, 'Archaeology and Project', in Negri 1988: 209.

31. Thus see Hardt and Negri 2000: 409.

32. Negri et al., 'Do You Remember Revolution?', in Negri 1988: 242. Negri does more directly confront the reality of defeat (though primarily as a personal experience) in Negri 2004b: 39–57.

33. See Negri 1999a: 262ff. for Negri's more detailed discussion of Marx's treatment of cooperation in *Capital*.

34. For a discussion of the differences between Deleuze's and Foucault's conceptions of power and resistance, see Callinicos 1989: 80–7.

35. I briefly discussed some of the analogies between the two texts in Callinicos 2001a: 47–8.

36. For a brilliantly dialectical exploration of these issues in a military context and from a conservative perspective, see Luttwak 2001, and, for an equally fine Marxist treatment, Bensaïd 2003.

37. For my own thoughts on this subject, see Callinicos 2003b. Negri's ontology and the development of his and Hardt's analysis in *Multitude* are subjected to detailed critical examination in Callinicos 2006, especially chapter 4.

9

Materialism and Temporality
On Antonio Negri's 'Constitutive' Ontology

Charles T. Wolfe

> Materialists, if at all intelligent, should speak of power
> rather than of bodies.
>
> G. Deleuze

In what follows, I shall not consider the work of Antonio Negri as a whole, but rather in some of its recent manifestations,[1] from *Macchina tempo* and the work on Spinoza in the early 1980s to the recent work on *pouvoir constituant*, on empire, and on a Lucretian strand of materialism, connoted by the expression *Alma Venus*, from the second line of *De rerum natura*. I shall presuppose the existence of something like a doctrine of materialism and a theory of temporality in this body of work, and thereby ignore certain questions of genre which might compel the reader to distinguish between a properly political project and a philosophical one. As we shall see, however, it becomes impossible here to dissect the whole and surgically remove an inquiry into matter and time, brain and intellect, power and possibility, nature and ontology, without also having to consider the additional pair of praxis and action. By examining and assessing these conceptual 'regions', I shall seek to determine what is new in Negri's treatment of these old themes. This implies pinpointing the moments at which his understanding departs from a more 'canonical' understanding of these themes ... or from my own. Since this is not an exercise in comparative textual analysis, I will not speak of Negri as a 'reader' of Lucretius, Spinoza, Marx, or Deleuze, but rather seek to emphasize some of the shared features in this heretical tradition, in order to arrive, as it were, at its essential *Denkform* or what in French is called a *portrait robot*, the hypothetical portrait of a suspect, which can then be evaluated.[2]

The argument itself runs as follows. I start (§1) with the varieties of materialism, summarily presented as atomism, Spinozism, and mechanism, and then gradually narrow the focus so that we arrive at Negri's idiosyncratic materialism in which machines are intermingled with intellects (§2), on an infinite horizon of production and desire, in the name of 'the common'.

So clearly this materialism is not a metaphysical doctrine of the primacy of matter, or a biologistic appeal to vital forces. It is much more a materialism of action and of relations, in a world where nature is already lost (§3), where machines structure our reality, a reality which is given over to the production of subjectivity. So already one can ask, why is it a materialism? In order to understand his intention(s), it is necessary to dwell on Negri's appeal to ontology (§4). Presumably due to an underlying nominalism which is never too far from the surface, ontology here is not what we might expect; it is 'constitutive ontology', a discourse on transformation and liberation, rather than an explanation of the world by means of a *reductio*. Constitutive ontology does not seem to resemble materialist ontology (even if the passions play an important role in both), except in a very particular understanding of materialism as a negative, destructive doctrine, which, by invoking the rule of Nature and denying the existence of the soul, normativity, etc., represents a significant threat to the social order. Finally (§5) we come to the other pole of his thought, temporality. In many ways this would seem to be the very opposite of a materialist doctrine, especially when one considers the typical lack of philosophies of time in the materialist tradition. Thus I try (§6) to investigate the 'operator' within matter, the true source of activity or real ground of productivity, according to Negri. I conclude (§7) by confronting materialism and temporality while recalling the naturalistic project, and seeking to evaluate the consequences.

1. MATERIALISM

The metaphysics presented in the classical figure of ancient atomism and the Epicurus-Lucretius complex is not a metaphysics of order, nor a reduction to the constituent particles of atomism, which are eternal. Instead, it is a metaphysics of decomposition, built upon a world smaller than the phenomenological world of our experience, which at the same time is full of consequences for our own human practice. The apparent unity of the forms of our experience is decomposed into a welter of microentities. The traditional problem with this atomistic reduction is how to reconcile it with human freedom; in response, one can claim that the *clinamen*, the deviation or swerve of the atoms, allows precisely (in a kind of micro–macro identity) for freedom qua indeterminacy. Instead of a brutal denial of the texture of our experience, and, more importantly for Negri, instead of a denial of our possibility of acting, 'A tiny yet enormous glow shines through the rainfall of atoms' (Negri 2000b: §11; Negri 2003a: 186).[3]

In Lucretian atomic turbulence, Negri diagnoses a struggling against the 'monolith of materialist metaphysics', an attempt to 'carve it into a physics, an ethics, and a theology'. And here (as well as in Spinoza, surprisingly enough) he feels that the actualization of powers in the natural world does not leave enough room for freedom qua innovation; recalling the Aristotelian relation between *dunamis* and *energeia*, actualization seems like merely a filling-out of the dotted lines in matter. In the language which I hope to explicate later in this chapter, Negri says that

> the progression of the common, that is, the unity of eternity and innovation, is not granted a creative dimension. The problem lies precisely here: to produce freedom by the same token as eternity, and to make the common the active key of the construction/reconstruction of the world, and not just its flat result. (Negri 2000b: § 13; Negri 2003a: 187)

If what is fundamentally common to us and to the world is that we are both made up of atoms, their swerves, and their collisions, how can the new emerge? How can the common ever be *produced*?

In fact, this productive challenge, this 'clash' which ultimately is at the root of all great phantasmagorias of material transformation of the cosmos, 'worlds made of atoms and chance', of vortices or animalcules, germs, seeds, spores, microbes ... infinitesimal parcels of life and information, this clash or encounter reveals itself to be a source of *the new*. And this experience of the new is located *in our world*, not in the world of the atoms themselves. At an unspecified, undetermined place and time (*nec regione loci certa nec tempore certo* (Lucretius 1916: bk.2, 216ff.)), a minute deviation of atoms in their fall causes them to undergo a series of sudden, random encounters. It is only when the atoms come together in these encounters that they come into Being, while at the same time, 'hanging' or 'hooking' onto one another in accordance with a blind, mechanical causality, they create a *world* through which they come into being. 'The encounter doesn't create any of the reality of the world, which is nothing but agglomerated atoms, but it grants reality to the atoms themselves' (Althusser 1982b: 555–6).[4] The same portions of Epicurus and Lucretius are read by two thinkers who have much in common, Althusser and Negri, yet Althusser chooses to emphasize the randomness, the sudden encounters, which ground existence in contingency; Negri emphasizes the moment of innovation, the production of the new, which will be a central feature of what he calls 'constitutive ontology': ontology tied to a process of constitution.

With Spinoza, we leave the problems of microscopic reduction and the universe of chance, and arrive at a materialism that is grounded on *desire*, a desire which 'knows neither death nor negation',[5] an immanent '*vis viva*, a living force, that unfolds from a physical *conatus* to human *cupiditas*, to divine *amor*' (Negri 2000b: §12; Negri 2003a: 186). A rather perfidious challenge to this operational history of philosophy comes to mind at this point: can't one find a powerful account of desire in Hegel too, one that goes as far as to include *animals* and their drive or appetite which leads them to devour what is in front of them, even if they are convinced of its ultimate nothingness?[6] The answer would be the invocation of *hope*, ethically, and *plenitude*, ontologically (there is always more, the world can always become ever more common, it is maximally full). Hegelian desire and self-overcoming, in a movement towards totality, are not popular refrains in these parts, for therein 'there is no longer anything that strives, desires, or loves; the content of potentiality is blocked, controlled, hegemonized by finality' (Hardt and Negri 2000: 82).[7] This notion of potentiality will be associated with a theory of temporality explicitly intended to counteract any sense of teleology or historicity, as we shall see when discussing Negri's theory of 'political time'. Nonetheless, desire, whether the desire of the multitude or desire *tout court*, presents a rather difficult problem for genuine materialist discourse, as does time: if the world is always maximally actual, full, energized, productive, where is time? In the more specific terminology which I discuss in §5: if the world is maximally full because it is traversed by incessant transformations (thus allowing for 'living labor', for the inherent movement of artificiality, of the transformation of Nature into second Nature), how is it that these transformations are not tantamount to a *spatialization* of time? If Negri's 'transfigured' materialism of desire allows him to escape the typically impoverished situation of materialism with regard to time, we can also turn the question around and say, in what way are we still in a materialism?

Let's note, in any case, that for both the Epicurean–Lucretian thinker and the Spinozist thinker, *there is nothing outside of nature*, nothing 'more' or beyond the natural realm. The fascinating (and sometimes maddening) trait Negri imposes on this naturalistic trajectory is that he includes all forms of artifice, technology, transformation, and political change within this natural realm, under the heading of 'the common'; it is, after all, an extremely consistent move. But, as we shall see, Nature is hardly recognizable underneath all its *travestissements*![8] So the present brand of materialism is neither a reductionist project, nor an ontology in the ordinary sense, nor, lastly, an ethically motivated invocation of Nature over and against society.

It is often noted that we need a new history of materialism, some 150 years after the publication of Lange's work, and Negri expresses the same wish (Negri 1982a: 326 n.11/Negri 1991b: 268 n.11; Negri 2000a: 8, 60/ Negri 2003a: 140, 177–8)[9]—but in his case, it is in order to invent a new history of materialism as the 'other' of power (*potere*).[10] This is why it is difficult here to define a metaphysics apart from a politics. Similarly, he has recently spoken of his ongoing project as a 'materialist ontology of power' (*potenza*) (Negri 2000a: 9; Negri 2003a: 140). Materialism as the 'other' of power (*potere*) means the denial of power as rule, as overarching authority; as such, it is an immanentism. Politically, this gives rise to the opposition between *pouvoir constituant* and *pouvoir constitué*, between constituting power and constituted power,[11] between the democratic upsurges which produce constitutions (reminiscent of Arendt's 'moments of freedom') and the written constitutions which result from them. The assertion of immanence is also an assertion of the *common*; the ultimate goal of this materialism is not a 'naturalized epistemology' in which the old metaphysics is replaced with science as we know it, but rather an assertion of the common. Common notions are the instruments by which we participate in the structure of reality, structuring it and being structured by it; they are social forms of knowledge, Negri says. His desire to assert the common and ground it in a power belonging to the multitude, a power which denies the transcendence of power-as-rule or authority, was reawakened, he says, by the 'ethical', 'humanitarian', 'just' wars of the 1990s.

2. MACHINES AND INTELLECT

When invoking a doctrine such as materialism, one ordinarily assumes that it rests on a substrate which we might call 'matter'. So far, nothing much has been presupposed or predetermined: brute matter or living matter, matter as recipient of artificial transformations (grafts, hybridizations, 'prostheses', etc.), or possessor of 'powers' which ultimately take on the guise of these transformations ... ? But the tradition to which Negri belongs, whether we consider it from the historical angle of *operaismo*[12] or the cultural context of his French companions, is one which asserts that *agencements* are more primary than matter itself; this can be traced back to the Spinozist insistence that bodies be understood as composites, and hence all ultimate understanding of a world of bodies, all materialist ontology, will be an understanding of *relations* between these compositions. Bodies are not merely defined by their chance encounters and shocks, but by the *relations* between the infinity of parts which composes each body.

With this emphasis on relations, networks, *agencements*, and 'metabolic' exchanges of matter, we come to the 'high-water marks' of post-Marxist thought: even Deleuze is less of a materialist than he is a philosopher of networks, of hidden forms which he calls, for example, 'folds'; even Foucault, who does speak of a 'materialism of bodies' as the fundamental level of his historical project, always seems obsessed with the overarching danger of a kind of generalized Fordism, in which materialism is no longer the issue at all.[13] The quotation from Deleuze that served as an epigraph can now be stated in full: 'One recalls Plato saying that materialists, if at all intelligent, should speak of power rather than of bodies. But it is true, conversely, that intelligent dynamists must first speak of bodies, in order to "think" power' (Deleuze 1990a: 257). The first option seems to correspond more clearly to the work of Negri; the second, to work such as Foucault's.

In a brief sketch of the idea of matter in Western philosophy, Negri distinguishes between the total depreciation or devalorization of matter in antiquity, modernity's claim that it is not *knowable* (or that it can be known only phenomenally, which amounts to admitting that one does not come into contact with matter itself), and lastly, the revised claim of postmodernity that matter cannot be part of *communication*. His response to all of this is to assert that matter is productivity itself (Negri 2000a: §6 *bis*, p. 60; Negri 2003a: 177–8); if it is indeed true that the word 'matter' comes from Indo-European roots for 'wood', 'house', or 'construction material',[14] it seems easy enough to say: matter is making (*poiesis*), and this is a handy way to dissolve the difference between matter and intellect. We can think here of the early Marx's emphasis on 'metabolic change', with the posit that what is first, as a kind of ur-predicate of matter (recalling the attribution of motion to matter by the first modern materialists such as Hobbes and Toland), is a *poiesis*, a capacity for and process of production, a 'fabricational' process. But once this is posited, we have of course lost matter, we are on the slippery slope leading to industry, to a 'remechanization' of matter. This is the confusing nature of 'mechanism': as terrible as the creation of 'mechanistic materialism' was,[15] we must also acknowledge the force of the machine, as an explanatory model, but also in itself. Of course, the fact that all bodies are related to and with other bodies, mechanically or rather 'machinically', to use Félix Guattari's neologism, means that the problem of a mechanistic reduction of the world as we experience it is a false problem. Referring to Spinoza's transformation of the Cartesian idea of mechanism, Negri emphasizes that while mechanism governs infinitely composite existing bodies, it cannot be understood without reference to a dynamic theory of the capacity to be affected (ultimately, the *conatus*): no mechanism without dynamism (Negri 1982a: 94 (also n.92), 128–9, 234, 247 and in general all of ch. 7, §1; Negri 1991b: 42 (also 243 n.50), 66–7, 144–5, 154 and in general all of ch. 7, §1). Moreover,

Machines, the reality constructed by capitalism, are not phantasms of modernity after which life can run unscathed—they are, on the contrary, the concrete forms according to which life organizes itself, the world transforms itself, and the material connections within which subjectivity is produced. (Negri 1995b: 99)

Not only does the production of our subjectivities take place in interaction with a world of machines, but machines are the very forms according to which life organizes itself; hence Nature wears many masks, as Diderot would say. The philosophical background for this highly futuristic-sounding world of living machines is the idea of a materialism of relations, and more specifically, Spinoza's statement of identity between the order and connection of ideas, and the order and connection of things: *ordo et connexio rerum idem est ac ordo et connexio idearum* (Spinoza 1992: *E* II P7 and V P1 D). So despite all repudiations of earlier mechanistic deviations, we are nonetheless in a certain kind of mechanistic materialism, but an extremely vitalized one.

There is only matter, no spirit; spirit, *Geist*, is the brain, and furthermore, no brain exists in isolation, the brain is always part of a 'General Intellect', it is always a *social brain*.[16] In the metaphorically charged language of *Alma Venus*, 'there is no merchandise that is not a service, no service that is not a relation, no relation that is not a brain, no brain that is not common' (Negri 2000b: §16b; Negri 2003a: 189). Are we in the presence of a particularly Harlequinesque form of panpsychism? As a reader of Spinoza, Negri does not want to reduce thought to extension, nor even *explain* thought by appealing to extension (or extension by appealing to thought). Thus again one notices that it is a strange kind of materialism that is operative here. At times the author speaks in exalted tones of pantheistic, Neoplatonic or Renaissance understandings of power, interiority and creativity, and opposes them to a bland, colorless, merely intellectual appropriation of Nature characteristic of the Enlightenment (Negri 1982a: 86; Negri 1991b: 36).[17] Yet to be fair, if there is a panpsychism, it is one in which the soul does its best to imagine what increases the power of the body (Spinoza 1992: *E* III P12). And in any case, to fully understand the unity of soul and body, we must *first* know the nature of our body (*E* II P13 S).

So if there are only bodies and relations between bodies, only different planes of composition, lines, planes and solids, forces and powers, we can make two observations. One, this is a strange kind of materialism, filled with scorn for mere 'spatialism'; two, there does not seem to be room for any kind of subjectivity. Or is there? As we shall see below, there is certainly a process by which subjectivity is produced, and indeed, there are many *subjectivities* in the plural. Both observations can be pacified: the matter seems strange because it is saturated with language, and thereby it does not exclude subjectivity. 'Subjectivity is not something "internal" set before something "external"', such as language; 'the production of subjectivity, that is, the production of needs, affects, desire, activity and *techné*, takes place through language and, better yet, the production of subjectivity is language—in the same way that language is subjectivity' (Negri 2000b: §16c; Negri 2003a: 190). So, in contrast to philosophies of the subject, even ones which mask their identity by claiming to speak about cognition or perception, here subjectivity is not *first*, it is something *produced*.

How could there be a philosophy of praxis, of transformation, of action, if there were only matter? Materialism could happily exist as a *negative* moment—the materialist is not a thinker of equilibrium, of the norm, even a dynamical norm; not a thinker of the *re*composition in a harmonic system of all organic fibers. When she stares at a pond full of fish, tadpoles, insects on the surface and pools of algae, she does not see organisms and ecosystems everywhere, as the holist does. Holists, from Aristotle to Hegel, hide behind the 'spectacles' of organism or structure. In contrast, the Romantic (and already Lucretian) emphasis on decomposition, whether in the form of the world of atoms, or of the assertion of generation and corruption as the ceaseless movement of Nature, grants materialism the power of a negative moment, which also functions as a powerful denial of existing regimes; but how could it ever become 'constitutive' or 'productive' ('active' or 'affirmative', in an earlier vocabulary)? Because this encounter between humans and machines—this inscription of humanity into the mechanical world of relations and artifice and prostheses, or better, this commingling of the two, such that artifice can no longer be distinguished from nature, 'the tool is no longer something different from the agent', having been replaced by 'a set of prostheses that have accumulated, adding up and thereby multiplying the productive potential of the agent' (Negri 2000b: §16b; Negri 2003a: 189) ... —is immediately a *production of subjectivity*, as Guattari tirelessly repeated throughout his life, whether in the context of clinical, political, or aesthetic practice, or even on ontological grounds. 'If production is communication, then the world of nature and artifacts must be wholly related to the production of subjectivity, and that subjectivity establishes production in the bio-political' (Negri 2000b: §16f; Negri 2000a: §16 *sex*, p. 79; Negri 2003a: 191).

Thinking, speaking, and acting are traceable back to a common root, *poiesis*. We are parts of Nature, but our acts of creation or fabrication, of production or transformation, are also parts of Nature. The world of the intellect is linked to the world *tout court* by the productive imagination. It is precisely through imagination that the body can participate in the totality of being (Negri 2000a: §4 *quater*, p. 56; Negri 2003a: 174–5), and it is only due to the workings of the imagination that we can escape the crude monism in which, to use Spinoza's image, a mouse might be the same as an angel, and suffering a kind of joy.[18] How can one reconcile the goal of a profoundly monistic philosophy with the increasing emphasis on a 'materialism of language'? (That is, a materialism predicated on an understanding of matter—of the world which surrounds us, our *Umwelt*— which includes language.) Well, the world must be full, and language is part of this plenitude. Since reality and perfection are the same (Spinoza 1992: *E* II D6), 'the existence of the world does not require any mediation to be ontologically validated' (Negri 1982a: 119; Negri 1991b: 60). The more it can be said that we live in a world of language, the more our laboring capacity is connected to a capacity to live within sign-systems and transform them ... the more the brain replaces *Geist*, the more we are in a common world. 'The multitude not only uses machines to produce, but also becomes increasingly machinic itself, as the means of production are increasingly integrated into the minds and bodies of the multitude' (Hardt and Negri 2000: 406). Negri combines metaphysical arguments and diagnoses of sociotechnological transformations to assert that materialism may be about what is common, but this must then include language; better still, in an even more exciting challenge for the materialist, he includes the brain:

> The tool in the relationship between man and nature, or between man and man, has entirely changed. We no longer need tools in order to transform nature ... or to establish a relation with the historical world ... we only need language. Language is the tool. Better yet, the brain is the tool, inasmuch as it is common. (Negri 2000b: §16b; Negri 2003a: 189)

3. NATURALISM WITHOUT NATURE (THE CENTAUR'S SMILE)

Nature is already a lost, inaccessible realm here, for we are governed by second, third, and *n*th natures. In his most recent book, Negri speaks about a transition from the figure of the centaur, in which man is fused with nature, to that of the 'man–man', or man doubling his essence through praxis, and finally to the stage of the 'man–machine', where the organic integrity of the human being has become suffused with artifice (one recalls Richard Lindner's painting 'Boy with Machine', which is reproduced at the beginning of *Anti-Oedipus*, or the films of David Cronenberg). Ostensibly regarding Spinoza, Negri will say 'There is no nature, ... only a second nature, the world is not nature but production', i.e. there is not a causality of principle and consequence, a cause and an effect or result, but rather a process of *production* (Negri 1982a: 338–9; Negri 1991b: 225–6 (and Negri 1997a: 428; Negri 1999a: 326–7)).[19]

Not only is nature lost, but there appear to be no regrets! No nostalgia for a world of nature, neither a state of nature which would serve as a ground from which to criticize the corruptions and deviations of society, nor a meta-physically infused Nature with a capital N which serves as the ground, the 'seat' of all possible production, creation, transformation, and life. On the contrary, there is a kind of hunger for artifice, in its liberating capacity. As we know from his reactions to *A Thousand Plateaus* and later, *What is Philosophy?* Negri was particularly sensitive to Deleuze and Guattari's call for a 'new philosophy of nature, *at a time when all difference between nature and artifice is fading away*'.[20] Perhaps for personal reasons, Deleuze seemed increasingly hostile to this world of artifice at the end of his life. In contrast, Negri is delighted that the world is 'invested by the teleology of linguistic and subjective prostheses' (Negri 2000b: §16e; Negri 2003a: 191). The prosthesis is a figure of innovation here: in a world where all differences between nature and artifice are vanishing, prostheses are simply another moment of the creative activity of the human intellect and its transformation of nature. Nature is taken as process of production, materialism is materialist production, and both are about the establishment of the common: 'life and politics, these two old fetishes which had been separated by the dis-ciplinarization of the transcendental knowledge of modernity, become indistinguishable from each other' (Negri 2000b: §16d; Negri 2003a: 190). Nature and politics mingle in a process of recomposition (I think that the figure of the irremediably *social* brain is the best image here, in preference to the slippery invocation of 'biopolitics').

Nature is thus the 'world well lost', including naive, Feuerbachian-type appeals to the senses, which Marxist thought wished to eliminate from the outset. A slogan for Marxism here might be 'Le naturalisme est le professeur de natation de l'insuffisance' (Kraus 1975: 144). As we have seen, matter becomes nothing more than a substratum for *labor*, for transformation. 'Labor is the productive activity of a general intellect and a general body outside measure', it is simply the '*power to act*' (Hardt and Negri 2000: 358, authors' emphasis).[21] Thus the materialist sense of the common is not enough for Negri, at least as it is understood in a 'naturalistic' sense. The world of artificiality, the world in which technology has already become fused with nature, is not something to be rejected—it *cannot be*—but serves rather as Negri's 'epistemological horizon'. In a witty and trenchant piece entitled 'The Specter's Smile' (Negri 1999b), Negri had invoked the subversive force of laughter against some of the defeatist versions of 'spectral' Marxism circulating around the globe. Here, all the explanatory force of naturalism (as epistemology) is present, without any 'pastoral' residues of Nature: the centaur must be smiling.

4. CONSTITUTIVE ONTOLOGY

Instead of an appeal to a first ground of Being, or a hierarchical structure which allows the philosopher to move from the entitative horizon of beings (as entities) to a more 'powerful' horizon of Being, the appeal to ontology here is always an appeal to 'the ontological weight of the desires and practices of existing subjects' (Hardt and Negri 1994: 288) ... where desire is understood in rather Arendtian fashion as the collective will to begin a project, the will for renewal. Hardt and Negri give this a biopolitical cast and say that desire is 'productive space, the actuality of human cooperation in the construction of history. This production is purely and simply human reproduction, the power of generation'; 'we are masters of the world because our desire and labor regenerate it continuously' (Hardt and Negri 2000: 388). Similarly, 'ontology is not an abstract science. It involves the conceptual recognition of the production and reproduction of being and thus the recognition that political reality is constituted by the movement of desire and the practical realization of labor as value' (Hardt and Negri 2000: 362). Presumably, 'ontology' is being used here synonymously with the more specific 'constitutive' ontology, i.e. the result of the dilution of ontology in the pool of ethicality and historicity (Negri 1982a: 154; Negri 1991b: 84).

There *must* be ontology, as there are *real* subjects engaged in *real* conflicts. Furthermore, ontology essentially means *freedom* for Negri: the freedom to say what is, is tautologically already freedom. To be able to say 'what is' and thereby introduce difference into what is, is ontology; it is freedom. 'Perfection' equals 'Liberation' (Negri 1982a: 250/Negri 1991b: 156; Spinoza 2000: II, §7), perfection is not transcendence but rather the totality of being as given (yet Negri still grafts a kind of 'futurity' onto this being). Here ontology instantly becomes political, since freedom amounts to the positing of difference within an already unified world, and thus a rejection of a certain kind of order (see 'Letter to Félix Guattari on Social Practice' in Negri 1989: 166). Constitutive ontology is tied to liberation (indeed, they are equivalent); the political significance of the 'constitutive' element can also be expressed in classic Rousseauian language as follows: if what there is, is *constituted*, the foundations of authority are weakened. In the title of the Spinoza book, *The Savage Anomaly*, 'savage' refers precisely to this *ontological* dimension of liberation. Negri associates the 'savagery' of Spinoza's thought with the 'multiplicity' of being, the ceaseless production of the new, whereas 'anomaly' refers primarily to the historical and social context. The anomaly only becomes savage once we enter the terrain of ontology.

It may come as a surprise, with all this, to detect a strange lingering Heideggerianism in Negri's thought. As much as we hear about the expanses of Being, in its fullness, plenitude, completion, perfection, etc., we must be aware too that Negri also describes this Being as 'the substantiality of all that it posited' (Negri 1982a: 264; Negri 1991b: 167). It is the word 'posited' which should attract our attention, and, as discussed below, 'projectuality'. If human existence is always ahead of itself, if its fundamental character is to be projected into Being (and to 'make projects', to plan ahead), what distinguishes this thought from Heidegger's insistence that possibility stands higher than actuality (*'Höher als die Wirklichkeit steht die Möglichkeit'* (Heidegger 1929: §7, p. 38))? Well, if we distinguish between potentiality and possibility, the former is then to be associated with 'constitutive ontology', an ontology of praxis, whereas the latter mainly has to do with the constitution of the *subject*. The tendency to emphasize *possibility*, the future (i.e. the sum of possibilities to come), 'projectuality', 'desire', and other elements which have a Heideggerian tonality to them, must be understood in Negri's case as a utopian political project (or 'dystopian', as he says): the originary productive ground of 'constituting power' is not, he declares, 'an *élan vital* which could be fulfilled within institutions' (Negri 1997a: 33; Negri 1999a: 22).[22] I must confess to some perplexity, here again: if the movement of constituting power is not something that can be fulfilled in institutions, isn't it then a kind of 'remainder', or something always lying ahead, in the wings? And if that is the case, why isn't it *Möglichkeit*, then? In fact, it is always the same element of confusion for me: how can materialism harbor temporality? how can nature harbor artificiality? how is potentiality not the same as possibility? how are political upsurges not subsumable under a logic of conflict? how is the common not a process of 'making the same', as in a logic of communication? Leaving these questions open, let's apply the balm of a slogan and say: for Negri, possibility means the possibility of change.

In more technical terms, this notion of possibility as possibility of change, or better, possibility understood as *potentiality*, that is, as power, is described by Negri as 'constitutive temporality' (or, in his earlier works, 'antitranscendence' and especially 'antimodernity'),[23] i.e. 'a conception of time as an ontologically constitutive relation which breaks the hegemony of substance or the transcendental, and therefore opens onto power' (Negri 1995a: 7). Another name for this, which appears in passing in the Spinoza book, and is developed at greater length in *Le pouvoir constituant*, is 'dystopia'. Negri's desire always to define the moment of sociopolitical 'emergence' in opposition to a sense of limit, emphasizing its existence solely in the Now (in accents reminiscent of Marx and Benjamin's 'revolutionary temporality': an *acceleration* of time, in which history becomes the present, and the present becomes an intensified, productive Now), is partly a standard rejection of

Hegelian determinate negation. Hence *dismisura* (incommensurability) and the movement towards the common, instead of an identification between actuality and rationality; hence dystopia instead of utopia. But if Negri relies on a fundamental opposition between power, possibility, or dystopia on the one hand, and transcendence on the other hand, what should we make of the other opposition between act/action/plenitude in the Spinozist vein and Heideggerian *Möglichkeit*? How can one put forth a philosophy of power-as-potentiality in a Spinozist context in which everything is always *actual*?

From the materialist standpoint, there is no real distinction between potentiality and actuality; rather, there is a distinction between the natural capacities of something and its actual exercise of these capacities: in Spinozist terms, the power to act and the power to be acted on—*both of which are actual*. For Spinoza, there is always a relation between *potentia* and *potestas*, such that there is always a capacity to be affected; again, *no such capacity ever remains inactualized*, there is 'no power that is not actual' (Deleuze 1990a: 93).[24] Essence and existence, actuality and possibility are but modes of something more primary. So we can say that there is a special prestige attached to the notion of potentiality in this tradition, particularly with reference to Spinoza, and further back, to the Renaissance notion of *posse*. The above depreciation of possibility in favor of actuality means that the philosophical horizon here is necessarily one of plenitude, materiality, determinacy, and passion (Negri 1982a: 137–8; Negri 1991b: 72–3), terms which are invoked throughout Negri's works like incantations. This depreciation also relies on the notion of perfection (cf. Spinoza 1992: *E* I P11 S: if the power to exist equals power itself, then the more existence is contained within the nature of a thing, the more power to exist it will have ...). Since there is no flirtation or 'tarrying' with the negative, there is not even room for a notion of the possible 'as mediation between the positive and the negative' (Negri 1982a: 249; Negri 1991b: 155).

If Being is equivalent to Perfection, if it is maximally full, saturated with activity and transformation, it is hard to see how and where a notion of temporality can arise. Put differently, in a philosophy which still relies on the notion of Reason comprehending all things *sub specie aeternitatis* (Spinoza 1992: *E* II P44 C), what kind of temporality can there really be? The pages in the Spinoza book devoted to themes such as duration, temporality, or even a kind of 'futurity' curiously seem like branches grafted onto an already solid and attractive growth. Yet, at the same time, it is equally apparent that from the outset, any invocation of materialism on Negri's part will ultimately have to lead to a theory of temporality which can ground a notion of change and transformation, specifically, political transformation.

5. TEMPORALITY

In contrast to philosophies with a prominent theory of time, which can usually boast a complex theory of consciousness as interiority to go along with it, from Paul to Augustine to Luther to Kierkegaard to Heidegger, materialism has traditionally been accused of being a mere 'spatialism' or at best a 'motionalism', a sheep in wolf's clothing, and we have seen that Negri does not pass up the chance at making this accusation. The question is twofold: is his materialism *really* a materialism, and how does it relate to his theory of temporality? I will try and briefly articulate the topic of temporality, then, in §6, turn back to the question of the 'powers' operative in matter, and finally conclude by reevaluating how the two relate.

What is Negri's notion of temporality, then?

In the Spinoza book, Negri still considers materialism to be a mere 'spatialism', lacking the crucial temporal categories which would be the dynamic and creative elements of being. And he speaks rather dismissively of the merely parasitical and subordinate status of materialism, unless Spinozism is integrated into it (Negri 1982a: 326; Negri 1991b: 215–16). In *Macchina tempo*, much is made of the purported reduction of time to space, in the 'Western' tradition, with an unfortunate Heideggerian manner and method: 'The hard core of the Western tradition of the idea of time and its eternal Parmenideanism consists in the spatialization of time' (Negri 1982b: 260). The spiritualist tradition reduces time to death; it is not clear whether this is part of the same error as 'spatialization', or if it is rather the reverse, at the opposite extreme. In any case, Negri wishes to contrast it with the *macchina tempo*, the machine of liberated time, which defines a new world that does not know death (Negri 1982b: 331). In this pre-Einsteinian world, there is still a *geometric* approach to time. But in fact the real problem is still declared to be the *productivity of matter* (Negri 1982b: 261). In a theme that will achieve maturity in his work of the 1990s on 'constituting power', Negri declares that only in Marx do we find a truly different notion of time, the *time of constitution*, the time of *composition* (Negri 1982b: 264).[25] Fortunately for us, Negri is also willing to grant some distinction to the 'minor tradition' of classical materialism—Democritus, Epicurus, and Lucretius share the assumption of the relation between time and *change*, so that time is defined as innovation and/or corruption (Negri 1982b: 271). The ultimate opposition, which is supposed to explain the entire history of differing views (except, presumably, that of Marx), is between the spatialization of time and the 'dynamization of space' (*dinamizzazione dello spazio*), e.g. Plato or Newton versus the atomists and thermodynamics (Negri 1982b: 316). Thinking of the quote from Deleuze which served as an epigraph, we may wonder then, is Negri an intelligent materialist or an intelligent dynamist?

The point is to distinguish between an irreversibility characteristic of ordinary time (time's arrow) and a creative potential inherent in another dimension of time. The time of creation is antithetical to the time of death. Negri distinguishes between two kinds of 'rootedness in being': the first is the strict Heideggerian variety which refers back to an empty Being, in his view, and the second kind, which Negri associates with his own project, is rooted in a transformative, productive, constitutive process (Negri 1997a: 44; Negri 1999a: 30). But shouldn't we still be suspicious of an invocation of a fundamental dynamism which is associated with our mortality, with our rushing towards death? What makes constitutive time, the time of change, so different from the time of finitude? Presumably, the arguments against existential possibility (*Möglichkeit*) hold good here as well; secondly, instead of an emphasis on mortality as that which singularizes me (death is always my death, irreducibly singular; without death nothing would *move!*), we must think instead of a more Deleuzian understanding of death as fundamentally twofold: 'toute mort est double', he says, in the sparkling reflections on the *conatus* and the Freudian *Todestrieb*, in *Différence et répétition*: 'Every death is twofold, in the canceling-out of the great difference it represents in extension, and in the swarming and liberation of the minute differences it implies in intensity' (Deleuze 1968a: 333, my translation; Deleuze 1994: 259). It is of course especially the second sense, of 'swarming and liberation of minute differences', which I wish to emphasize here. Briefly put, for Negri it is less a matter of my rushing forward to my death, according to a movement of temporality which singularizes me; temporality is indeed singularizing, but what is more, it opens up the possibility of change, 'the ontological potentiality of a multitude of singularities acting in cooperation' (Negri 1997a: 436; Negri 1999a: 333).

Negri had initially presented the case for a theory of temporality *as political* in the long text entitled 'La costituzione del tempo. Prolegomeni', included in *Macchina tempo* (apparently this was part of a longer systematic study which was lost due to 'the violence of the State'). But this text is still quite rough, leaping back and forth between Marx, Heidegger, Kant, and Hegel, with even a recurring discussion of pre- and post-Einsteinian theories of time, and the problem I have referred to as the 'spatialization' of time. For the mature statement of a theory of 'political time', or time as the constitutive trait of the political, one has to turn to the massive work on 'constituting power'. To say that time is the time of the political, that human time is the time of change, is indeed an improvement over the empty forms of time, since human time is thereby irredeemably linked to human making (fashioning and self-fashioning). Yet, and here is the rub, we come rather too close here to a configuration of Time as Labor.

In arguing for a materialism of praxis, Negri suddenly describes the dimension of temporality as 'tessuto ontologico del materialismo' (Negri 2000a: §8 *sex*, p. 32; Negri 2003a: 157), the ontological fabric of materialism; as the affirmative power of being and the subjectification of becoming. So our strands have been woven together ... but the result is a profound new theory of political time, *without a recognizable materialism*. Constitutive temporality is an acceleration of time: with, for example, the French Revolution, we are no longer in the 'long time' of ontology, but in a much 'shorter' time: 'temporality is now constitutive of constituting power. What is new is thus not the temporal rootedness of constituting power, but rather the quality of time: short time is opposed to long time, the present to memory, and subversion to tradition' (Negri 1997a: 325; Negri 1999a: 245). Aside from the sarcasm at the expense of *longue durée* history, we should understand that time is the active feature of the political.

The enduring suspicion that at the heart of materialism there was temporality, and at the heart of temporality, instead of a further concentric circle of metaphysics, there lay the hard core of 'power', of the transformation of reality through praxis, through labor, through the intellect making the world 'common', is gradually being confirmed: 'on the terrain of metaphysics, temporality means productivity, and productivity means labor' (Negri 1997a: 329; Negri 1999a: 248). Yet, since the expression 'materialism' is never abandoned, it may be worth returning to one last time, in a very different light.

6. THE OPERATOR WITHIN MATTER

We have often asked the question, Is there any matter at all left in this world of affirmation of change, of *Stoffwechsel*, the constant exchange of matters, and revolution? Need there be any matter, if desire and plenitude come first? And Negri can turn to us and respond, isn't the appeal to Nature or Matter itself the magical invocation of a first ground of productivity? Or more practically, if there indeed is only matter and its series of transformations, how can the new emerge? Nature must meet the world of machines. And if we claim that materialism has come a long way from the world of atoms and chance with the Spinozist addition of desire, then he can ask, 'Is a physics of desire sufficient to bestow upon eternity the figure of freedom? Can it imprint upon the world the discontinuity of innovation, and hence overcome the heavy and monotonous aporias of materialism?' (Negri 2000c: 168).[26]

In this view, matter is reduced to mere extension, there is no biologistic emphasis on *living* matter; instead, to relieve the monotony, an operator within matter is required, whether we call it labor, praxis, or intellect: a form of activity. Activity means two things: (1) 'materialist historians such as Thucydides and Machiavelli, like the great materialist philosophers such as Epicurus, Lucretius and Spinoza, have never negated a *telos* constructed by human action' (Hardt and Negri 2000: 470 n.23). Materialism must not forget human action. (2) The activity of the brain which is directly involved in the 'networks' of the real (and by extension in the production of the common). Negri locates himself in a Spinozist rather than a Kantian tradition : the world *can* be thought. Otherwise there could be no liberating force in constitutive ontology. Varieties of skepticism (which, for Negri, include phenomenological bracketing) deny that the world can be thought. The problem would be, can the world be thought because it is matter, or because it possesses a structure akin (or identical) to that of thought? The latter option would be closer to Negri's emphasis on 'immaterial labor' and the primacy of intellect (in the tradition of Vico's *verum ipsum factum* and the notion of the productive imagination). It's obviously this cheerful ontological confidence, *precisely*, which arouses the ire of all idealisms: 'Spinozism', 'materialism', and already 'atomism' were abhorrent because of the facility with which they give 'thought' access to the 'world'. If praxis and thus intellect are somehow 'first', then truth and being are the same; 'idealism separates the love of the truth from the passion for the real being' (Negri 1982a: 327; Negri 1991b: 216–17), whereas here being is saturated with truth 'without frills' ('la verità "senza fronzoli" è impegno nell' essere' (Negri 2000a: §5 *bis*, p. 58; Negri 2003a: 176)).[27] The real overwhelms the possibility of *Schwärmerei*, of excessive enthusiasm of the imagination.

In contrast to the philosophies specializing in the 'active powers of the mind', from Reid to Kant and Husserl, materialist thought operates with the self-imposed stricture that it can only be an articulation of *what is* (although the important role played by the imagination, in Spinoza and in Negri, seems to extend beyond this strong realism), what already is. The world precedes the thinker.[28] Contemporary naturalism speaks of the 'causal closure of the space-time world': if I want to speak suitable naturalistic language I cannot invoke powers, forces, faculties, or other causes which lie outside this causal closure. Now, if at times the usage of 'materialism' in Negri's vocabulary seems too loose, or saturated with other notions (power, action, process, praxis, ontology, and sometimes temporality), we can also venture a different explanation and say that what he really means is *naturalism*. Naturalism can be summarily defined as the position according to which 'there is no privileged standpoint, or "first philosophy", that can permit us to discover or determine the rules for natural science, for aesthetics, politics or even ethics apart from an engaged practical acquaintance with those pursuits' (Symons 2001). In contrast, materialism makes ontological claims (in the ordinary, non-Negrian sense of the term) which Negri does not have to 'commit' to, since science and the transformation of the world is itself a part of the 'making common', the movement of appropriation. Quine says it quite well: 'We are after an understanding of science as an institution or process in the world, and we do not intend that understanding to be any better than the science which is its object' (Quine 1969: 84). This is precisely the role that the 'common name' is supposed to play, for Negri: to link the power of naming with the real, without wholly subjugating our power of acting to the preexisting structures and strictures of the real. Common being is already productive being, it is already saturated with activity and transformation; common being is not being seen through a microscope.

The other way of explaining the 'operative' element in Negri's ontology is through temporality and 'constituting power' as a kind of life-force or *élan vital*, but a collective one, which is already politicized and hence not understood biologistically. This is also part of the sense in which the word 'ontology' is used here: as leverage for critique. Desire and the passions are already inscribed within the mysterious field of the 'biopolitical'. The 'biopolitical' incantation in Negri is actually bidirectional: on the one hand, it serves to demonstrate that politics already controls, or seeks to control, the most intimate recesses of humanity, deeper than conscience or individuality: the biological world itself. On the other hand, there still is an element of *bios* in the notion, after all: just when we think that politics is a matter of government and resistance, of sovereignty and contestation, of constitutions and rights, the unshakable drive or *conatus* reemerges.

If the world is what is first, along with the body, and both of these are characterized by an essential dynamism, we can start to see what the ultimate question for Negri really is. It is less a classic imperative such as 'You must act!', or its variant as a question, 'How can the multitude be free to act?' (itself a version of La Boétie's question, repeated in *Anti-Oedipus*: Why does the multitude desire its servitude?), and more the question, How can *the new* appear? What does it mean for the *new* to emerge? Hence the vocabulary of 'innovation' and the total lack of fear with regard to science and technology. There is no longer the old convenient opposition between a reductionist tendency of natural science and a 'good' *verstehende* dimension of human science, not merely because if *Geist* is now the brain, the epistemological autonomy of the *Geisteswissenschaften* is dissolved or loses its raison d'être, but (following Foucault), because the human sciences are viewed as those which inflict the worst excesses of normativity upon human life. Long live physical science, then!—and furthermore, science and technology are not to be denounced as 'spatial machines' or 'machinations' for dominating the future. They should rather be praised as the transformation of the present, the activity of making the world common; they are 'utensils of *kairòs*' (Negri 2000a: §4 *sex*, p. 41; Negri 2003a: 164).

Ultimately, the 'leap' which I do not entirely follow (both in the sense of understanding it and of agreeing with it) is that from a materialist ontology to the assertion that the true 'base' of this materialist metaphysics is 'living labor', which takes back the world from the subsuming force of capitalism. I have hinted before at the entwinement of the political and the metaphysical in Negri's thought, and this chapter might just as well have been entitled 'Materialism and Temporality: Studies on the relation between metaphysics and politics'; well, it is now clear that the transformation of the world by living labor is a hallmark of the *'nuova potenza'* of temporality. What is left of a materialist ontology? Negri himself seems to realize that a materialist might be disappointed with his 'Nine Lectures On What I Have Taught Myself' (the subtitle of *Kairòs, Alma Venus, Multitudo*), and asks, 'Why should one really want to define this field (*campo*) as materialist?' (Negri 2000a: §5 *quinque*, p. 59; Negri 2003a: 177) His response is to reiterate the old identification of materialism with a mere spatialism; he calls it a 'prisoner of extension' (ibid.). Marxist materialism stands and falls by the first part of its name more than the last.

Thus there may be a real problem in trying to articulate together materialism and temporality. Both are required for Negri's argument: matter must be animated by temporality, which gives rise to all forms of change. Otherwise there is only mere spatialism and/or scientific reductionism: only specification of what is, in the lesser sense (i.e. as opposed to constitutive ontology, the saying of what is as a moment of liberation). But is this a legitimate understanding of materialism? And doesn't the 'commitment' to temporality force Negri to be more Heideggerian than he wishes to be? In §§4 and 5, I argued that an emphasis on potentiality (power) rather than existential possibility allowed Negri to move on to the conditions of real transformation, rather than being caught in questions of the 'rootedness' of Being. But if this is to work, it is arguably best to remove (a surgical intervention, once again) notions such as *progettualità*, 'projectuality', which do not seem necessary:

> The horizon of freedom is that of absolute affirmation because freedom has traversed absolute negation. It has extinguished the void by constructing the fullness of being. *This being is the substantiality of all that subjectivity posits, constructs and determines as projectuality—subjectivity which is as*

compact and full as substantial being, seized and reconstructed in projectuality. (Negri 1982a: 264; Negri 1991b: 167, emphasis mine)

Similarly, in the midst of a rhetoric of plenitude and actuality, we still find invocations of the primary constituting power as a 'force which projects itself', along with a definition of the political dynamic of democracy as 'absence, emptiness and desire' (Negri 1997a: 21; Negri 1999a: 14). Of course, Negri might well say that this is a fundamental drive of *wanting more*, a constitutive appetite of humanity, and trace it back to Spinoza's notion of *cupiditas*; or he might be less metaphysical and state that 'hunger, pain and desire' are at the root of a will to criticize working time (Negri 1997a: 264; Negri 1999a: 198).

7. CONCLUSION

Granted that a naturalistic critique is possible, how can a materialist ontology ever arrive at the actual conditions of transformation? Exhaustively specifying the contours of the natural world is not a recipe for change, is it? The importance of temporality lies in its ability to bring a stable, balanced state of things into crisis: to bring about change, or at least to force a situation in which change does not need to provide justification for itself, faced with the weight of 'what is' (we can recall the usage of the term 'ontology' and particularly 'constitutive ontology' in this sense). Temporality combines the dynamic traits of the Nietzschean 'innocence of becoming' with other, more constructive traits. Mere materialism then appears to be restricted to an understanding of time or change as *growth*.

How can naturalism ever speak of the human world, then? Negri understands that with the best, most courageous moments of materialism, there is no longer merely the posit of the eternity of matter, but an actual infusion of teleology therein; yet 'the visibility of innovation and the ethicopolitical point of view itself are eliminated', such that even with a work he praises elsewhere for its radicality, Deleuze and Guattari's *A Thousand Plateaus*, 'we have returned to the heyday of Democriteanism and Epicureanism' (Negri 2000b: §18e; Negri 2003a: 193). If there is just Nature and its 'exchange of matters' (*Wechselwirkung*), a ceaseless process of generation and corruption, and worse, if Nature is saturated with artificiality, riddled with prostheses, to the point that one can hardly tell it apart from Labor or Intellect, how can the new emerge? How can the centaur smile? Hardt and Negri say it quite soberly:

Metaphysical monism is the one and only basis of the historical pluralism of subjects, of the life of freedom. How can we develop this life of plurality on the monistic horizon of freedom? How can we affirm freedom when nothing above it can impose an order on it? (Hardt and Negri 1994: 310)

How do we reconcile a reductionist naturalistic explanation with the question of freedom? In a way, we really have 'returned to the heyday' of Democriteanism and Epicureanism, or actually, we never left it! Faced with the divide between cosmos and chaos, between the imposition of order and the 'Baroque', 'Renaissance', 'Romantic' paeans to disorder, the latter path seems to go more naturally with the heretical dimension of our materialism; physicalist statements of reduction do not normally produce parascientific speculations on species varying to such an extent that there might be 'human polyps on Jupiter or Saturn', as Diderot says wishfully in the *Rêve de d'Alembert* (Diderot 1994: 629).[29]

In the name of 'hybridization',[30] the coming together of the natural and the political, the production of common being, Negri rejects naive naturalism and promotes the power of the imagination: we must not burrow into an idyllic Lucretianism of atoms and chance, or its modern version as alluded to above with Diderot. The ultimate concern is not to lose the political dimension, the possibility of change/innovation/transformation. Yet at the end of the first 'book' of *Kairòs, Alma Venus, Multitudo*, namely, *Kairòs*, Negri declares that our ultimate task is to think matter as eternity, with all its aporias, just as the ancients did: as *Alma Venus*, the life-giving Mother Venus of the second line of Lucretius' *De rerum natura*. But if materialism is ultimately about what is common, what does Negri tell us about the relation of this 'common' to our desires? 'In order to become real, the formal conditions of expression of the common must be tested in the ethical–political domain, and thereby verified on the eternal edge of being' (Negri 2000b: §17b; Negri 2000a: §17 *bis*, p. 80; Negri 2003a: 191–2).

Materialism is a theory of action for Negri, not a theory of science or of truth! From materialism to temporality, from physicalistic ontology to constitutive ontology, from rationality and communication to desire and the common, 'Knowledge has to become linguistic action and philosophy has to become a real *reappropriation of knowledge*' (Hardt and Negri 2000: 404).

NOTES

1. This chapter does not consider work appearing after 2004.
2. The main case of this 'reinforced' reading, in my presentation, is Spinoza; the same demonstration could be made with Marx. The exception is Heidegger, from whom Negri clearly 'borrows' or 'appropriates' certain ideas without thereby wishing to link the fate of his own thought to that of this author.

3. All citations from Negri's *Kairòs, Alma Venus, Multitudo* are my translations from the Italian edition (Negri 2000a); page references to the published English versions (Negri 2000b, Negri 2003a) follow.

4. See the excellent commentary by J.-Cl. Bourdin (Bourdin 2000).

5. F. Guattari, 'Psychanalyse et politique', quoted by R. Schérer in Schérer 1996: 29.

6. 'Even the animals are not shut out from this wisdom [sc. the ancient Eleusinian Mysteries] but, on the contrary, show themselves to be most profoundly initiated into it; for they do not just stand idly in front of sensuous things as if these possessed intrinsic being, but, despairing of their reality, and completely assured of their nothingness, they fall to without ceremony and eat them up' (Hegel 1977: 'Sense-Certainty', §109, p. 65).

7. At times one might wish for a better response to the Hegelian challenge, but it is never really forthcoming (this point was well made by J.-F. Kervégan at the conference on Negri's *Le pouvoir constituant* (Negri 1997a) held in 1998 at the University of Paris X-Nanterre). I believe Negri's response would include an appeal to *innovation* and its absence in Hegelian ontology, which makes room for change and transformation, but only over and against an inertia of the real.

8. Of course, Nature is nothing monolithic; a contemporary naturalist would say its ontology is always provisional; in a very 'French' twist on the scientific ebullience of the Enlightenment, Diderot says that Nature is 'une femme qui aime à se travestir' (*Pensées sur l'interprétation de la nature* §12, Diderot 1994: 565); not a transvestite, but a woman concealed underneath an infinite number of 'travesties': natural forms are nothing but 'masks' (*Eléments de physiologie*, in Diderot 1994: 1261).

9. All citations from Negri's first book on Spinoza, *The Savage Anomaly*, are my translations drawn from the French translation (Negri 1982a); page references to the published English edition (Negri 1991b) follow.

10. The distinction, familiar to readers of Negri's work on Spinoza, is between *potere* and *potenza* (in Latin, *potestas* and *potentia*), power as rule or authority versus power as potentiality.

11. My second and last translation remark is that 'constituting power' is a clearer translation of *pouvoir constituant* (*potere costituente, Verfassungsmacht*) than 'constituent power'. Briefly, it is the power to call together an 'assemblée constituante' and write a constitution. Thereby, quite frankly, it is the hidden source of legitimacy of all democratic constitutions.

12. A tradition which Negri does not appear to have always been satisfied with as an explanatory model, judging by comments such as this, from *Macchina tempo*: '*operaismo* is the night in which all cats are grey' (Negri 1982b: 317).

13. I will leave aside the mercifully short-lived upsurges of the 'virtual' in philosophy, with their hodge-podge of Bergsonism and media theory, and their peculiar attempts to connect themselves to a life-line of materialism.

14. See the *Oxford English Dictionary*'s entry 'Matter' and Halleux 1998: 766.

15. Even Negri is willing to acknowledge this, speaking, for example, of the 'paradox of the monstrous affinity between the mechanism of Hobbes and that of DIAMAT' (Negri 1982b: 26), and more recently, denouncing the 'historical' and 'dialectical' versions of materialism (in Negri 2000a: 60–1; Negri 2003a: 178).

16. '*Geist* is the brain' (Negri 1995b: 98). On the fundamentally social character of the brain, see Negri 2000b: §16b (16 *bis* of the Italian; Negri 2003a: 189), and already in *Macchina tempo*, the reference to Vygotski (Negri 1982b: 317). I have tried to reconstruct a 'Spinozist' tradition of the social brain, through Vygotski, Negri, and Paolo Virno, in Wolfe, 2005.

17. The Renaissance is the moment of a flourishing subjectivity which will subsequently be enclosed in the Cartesian reordering of the world. Elsewhere, Negri adds Bruno and Leopardi as key figures of this 'happy positivism' which escapes the pitfalls of the Enlightenment. This is the topic of his *Lenta Ginestra. Sull' ontologia di Leopardi* (Negri 1987a).

18. Spinoza, Letter 23 to Blyenberg (in Spinoza 1992), and Negri 1982a: 155–70 (specifically 159); Negri 1991b: 86–98 (specifically 89).

19. One may feel that Negri wrongly minimizes the role of causal determination in Spinoza: the very individuality of a body stems from its emplacement within a wider causal system!

20. Emphasis mine. Deleuze says that his final project, with Guattari, will be a 'nouvelle philosophie de la nature, au moment où toute différence s'estompe entre la nature et l'artifice', at the conclusion of his interview in the *Magazine Littéraire* (Deleuze 1988b: 25).

21. 'Living labor is the constituting power of society' (Hardt and Negri 1994: 'Postmodern Law and the Withering of Civil Society', 221; see also Negri 1997a: 348; Negri 1999a: 264–5).

22. All citations from Negri's book-length study of 'constituting power' are my translations drawn from the French translation (Negri 1997a); page references to the published English edition (Negri 1999a) follow.

23. 'Spinoza's Anti-Modernity' (Negri 1995a), first published in French in 1991, is a brilliant article which stands out from the mediocrity of the polemics on modernity and postmodernity. At times Negri views postmodernity as having a liberating role, according to the logic of the 'greatest peril' concealing the 'greatest emancipation'. Thus 'in post-modernity, that is, the era which began in the Sixties and in which we still live today, the ethical and ascetic illusion of modernity seems to have come to an end, and along with it, the metaphysical madness of transcendence and of ruling has withered away. Now the common can appear in the full plenitude of its definition' (Negri 2000b: §15; Negri 2003a: 188). There are accents here reminiscent of Reiner Schürmann's notion of the 'withering-away of principles': the cataclysms of the twentieth century have in some sense forcibly emancipated us from the 'archic' reign of principles (cf. Schürmann 1996; Schürmann 2003). Negri's argument was already present, albeit in cruder form, in his 1986 text 'Postmodern' (in Negri 1989).

24. On the distinction between power to act and power to be acted on as a constitutive trait of materialist thought, Deleuze refers to Hobbes, *De Corpore*, chapter 10.

25. One hears echoes here (but is there a real influence or merely a confluence?) of Deleuze's distinction in *Logique du sens* (Deleuze 1969) between Chronos and Aiôn, in which Chronos represents the 'chronological' division of time into past, present and future, where only the present is really 'in time', whereas in Aiôn time itself is productive. It is in the latter sense that Negri invokes the Benjaminian *Jetz-zeit* in *Macchina tempo*. In his most recent work, Negri terms this 'productive' form of time *kairòs*, a 'present temporality' which cannot be subdivided into past, present, and future (Negri 2000a: 'Kairòs, prolegomeni della dismisura', §3, p. 38; Negri 2003a: 161). In an even more explicit invocation of the permanent present or 'now-time', he speaks of a 'network of moments' (Negri 2000a: 'Kairòs, prolegomeni dell campo materialista', §7 *quinque*, p. 64; Negri 2003a: 180) using the French term *réseau*.

26. These paragraphs are apparently a revised version of 'Alma Venus. Prolegomeni del comune', Negri 2000a: §13; Negri 2003a: 187–8.

27. And for Negri, this means that constitutive ontology is political, 'il materialismo è rivoluzionario' (Negri 2000a: §5 *bis*, p. 58; Negri 2003a: 176).

28. The very same idea is expressed neatly by the late Althusser: 'the materialist trend in philosophy recognizes the existence of objective external reality, as well as its independence in relation to the knowing and perceiving subject. It acknowledges that being, the real, exists and is prior to its discovery, prior to the fact of being thought and known' (Althusser 1994: 60).

29. One commonly notes that it is a dreamer, d'Alembert, who is speaking.

30. On hybridization and monstrosity in Negri's thought, see his contribution (among others) to Fadini, Negri, and Wolfe 2001.

Bibliography

Abensour, M. (1997) *La démocratie contre l'État: Marx et le moment machiavélien* (Paris: Presses Universitaires de France).

Abse, T. (2000) 'The Professor in the Balaclava: Toni Negri and Autonomist Politics', circulated by e-mail.

Althusser, L. (1977) 'Introduction: Unfinished History', in D. Lecourt, *Proletarian Science? The Case of Lysenko*, trans. G. Lock (London: New Left Books).

Althusser, L. (1978a) 'Preface' to G. Duménil, *Le Concept de loi economique dans Le Capital* (Paris: Maspéro).

Althusser, L. (1978b) 'Marx dans ses limites', in *Écrits philosophiques et politiques*, vol. 1 (Paris: STOCK/IMEC, 1994), 359–524.

Althusser, L. (1982a) 'Le courant souterrain du matérialisme de la rencontre', in *Écrits philosophiques et politiques*, ed. F. Matheron, vol. 2 (Paris: Stock/IMEC, 1994).

Althusser, L. (1982b) 'Le courant souterrain du matérialisme de la rencontre', in *Écrits philosophiques et politiques*, ed. F. Matheron, vol. 1 (Paris: Stock/IMEC-Livre de Poche, 1994).

Althusser, L. (1990a) 'Marxism Today', trans. G. Lock, in *Philosophy and the Spontaneous Philosophy of the Scientists* (New York: Verso).

Althusser, L. (1990b) 'Is It Simple to Be Marxist in Philosophy?', trans. G. Lock, in *Philosophy and the Spontaneous Philosophy of the Scientists* (New York: Verso).

Althusser, L. (1994) *Sur la philosophie* (Paris: Gallimard).

Althusser, L. (1997) 'The Only Materialist Tradition, Part I: Spinoza', trans. T. Stolze, in *The New Spinoza*, ed. T. Stolze and W. Montag (Minneapolis: University of Minnesota Press).

Arendt, H. (1958) *The Human Condition*, 2nd edn. (Chicago: University of Chicago Press).

Arendt, H. (1963) *On Revolution* (New York: Penguin, 1965).

Arendt, H. (1968) *Between Past and Future* (New York: Penguin).

Arendt, H. (1972) 'On Violence', in *Crises of the Republic* (New York: Harcourt Brace).

Arendt, H. (1978) *The Life of the Mind* (New York: Harcourt Brace).

Aristotle (1941) *Basic Works*, ed. R. McKeon (New York: Random House).

Arthur, C. (2002) 'Capital, Competition, and Many Capitals', in M. Campbell and G. Reuten (eds) *The Culmination of Capital* (Houndmills: Palgrave).

Assoun, P.-L. (1999) 'Vie/vitalisme', in *Dictionnaire critique du marxisme*, ed. G. Labica and G. Bensussan (Paris: Presses Universitaires de France).

Badiou, A. (2000) *Deleuze: The Clamour of Being*, trans. L. Burchill (Minneapolis: University of Minnesota Press).

Balibar, É. (1992) 'Foucault and Marx: The Question of Nominalism', in T. Armstrong (ed.) *Michel Foucault Philosopher* (New York: Harvester).

Balibar, É. (1997) 'Jus–Pactum–Lex: On the Constitution of the Subject in the *Theologico-Political Treatise*', trans. T. Stolze, in *The New Spinoza*, ed. T. Stolze and W. Montag (Minneapolis: University of Minnesota Press).

Barry, A., T. Osborne, and N. Rose (eds) (1996) *Foucault and Political Reason: Liberalism, Neo-Liberalism and the Rationalities of Government* (Chicago: University of Chicago Press).

Bataille, G. (1993) *The Accursed Share*, vols. 2 and 3, trans. R. Hurley (New York: Zone Books).

Bataille, G. (1998) *Essential Writings*, ed. M. Richardson (London: Sage Publications).

Beasley-Murray, J. (1994) 'Ethics as Post-Political Politics', *Research and Society*, 7, 1994, 5–26.

Bensaïd, D. (1995) 'A la recherche du sujet perdu (Negri corrige Marx)', in Bensaïd, *Le Discordance de temps* (Paris: Éditions de la Passion).

Bensaïd, D. (2002) 'Multitude et empire', unpublished text.
Bensaïd, D. (2003) 'La Politique comme art stratégique', in *Un monde à changer* (Paris: Textuel).
Bensaïd, D. (2004) 'Multitudes ventriloqués', available on the *Multitudes* web site at http://multitudes.samizdat.net/article.php3?id_article=1739, consulted January 2005.
Bergant, D. (1997) *Israel's Wisdom Literature: A Liberation-Critical Reading* (Minneapolis: Fortress Press).
Bidet, J. (1985) *Que faire du Capital?* (Paris: Klincksieck).
Bidet, J. (1990) *Théorie de la modernité* (Paris: Presses Universitaires de France).
Bidet, J. (1999) *Théorie générale* (Paris: Presses Universitaires de France).
Blanchot, M. (1988) *The Unavowable Community*, trans. P. Joris (Barrytown, N.Y.: Station Hill Press).
Bloch, E. (1972) *Atheism in Christianity*, trans. J.T. Swann (New York: Herder & Herder).
Bloch, E. (1986) *The Principle of Hope*, trans. N. Plaice, S. Plaice and P. Knight (Cambridge: MIT Press).
Bologna, S. (1977) 'The Tribe of Moles: Class Composition and the Party System in Italy', trans. Red Notes, in *Working Class Autonomy and the Crisis* (London: Red Notes, 1979).
Boman, T. (1970) *Hebrew Thought Compared with Greek*, trans. J.T. Moreau (New York: Norton).
Borges, J. L. (1964) 'Kafka and His Precursors', trans. J. Irby, in *Labyrinths: Selected Stories and Other Writings*, ed. D. Yates and J. Irby (New York: New Directions).
Bourdin, J.-C. (2000) 'The Uncertain Materialism of Louis Althusser', in C. T. Wolfe (ed.) *The Renewal of Materialism* (*Graduate Faculty Philosophy Journal* 22:1).
Brenner, R. (1998) 'The Economics of Global Turbulence', *New Left Review*, Second Series/229.
Brenner, R. (2002) *The Boom and the Bubble* (London: Verso).
Brueggemann, W. (2002) *Reverberations of Faith: A Theological Handbook of Old Testament Themes* (Louisville, Ky: Westminster/John Knox Press).
Bukharin, N.I. (1971) *Economics of the Transformation Period* (New York: Bergman).
Burchell, G., C. Gordon and P. Miller (eds) (1991) *The Foucault Effect: Studies in Governmentality* (Chicago: University of Chicago Press).
Burke, E. (1998) *A Philosophical Enquiry into the Sublime and Beautiful and Other Pre-Revolutionary Writings*, ed. D. Womersley (New York: Penguin).
Butler, J. (1993) *Bodies that Matter: On the Discursive Limits of 'Sex'* (New York and London: Routledge).
Cacciari, M. (1976) *Krisis: Saggio sull crisi del pensiero negativo da Nietzsche a Wittgenstein* (Milan: Feltrinelli).
Callinicos, A. (1978). 'The Logic of *Capital*' (Oxford University D. Phil. thesis).
Callinicos, A. (1989) *Against Postmodernism* (Cambridge: Polity).
Callinicos, A. (1994) 'Marx and Modern Times', in C. Bertram and A. Chitty (eds) *Has History Ended?* (Aldershot: Avebury).
Callinicos, A. (2001a) 'Toni Negri in Perspective', *International Socialism* 92, 33–61.
Callinicos, A. (2001b) 'Periodizing Capitalism and Analysing Imperialism', in R. Albritton et al. (eds) *Phases of Capitalist Development* (Houndmills: Palgrave).
Callinicos, A. (2002) 'Marxism and Global Governance', in D. Held and A. McGrew (eds) *Governing Globalization* (Cambridge: Polity).
Callinicos, A. (2003a) *The New Mandarins of American Power* (Cambridge: Polity).
Callinicos, A. (2003b) *An Anti-Capitalist Manifesto* (Cambridge: Polity).
Callinicos, A. (2004) *Making History*, 2nd edn. (Leiden: Brill Academic).
Callinicos, A. (2006) *The Resources of Critique* (Cambridge: Polity).
Castoriadis, C. (1988) 'Modern Capitalism and Revolution', in *Political and Social Writings*, vol. 2, trans. and ed. D.A. Curtis (Minneapolis: University of Minnesota Press).
Cheah, P. (1998) 'Given Culture: Rethinking Cosmopolitical Freedom in Transnationalism', in P. Cheah and B. Robbins (eds) *Cosmopolitics: Thinking and Feeling Beyond the Nation* (Minneapolis and London: University of Minnesota Press).

Cleaver, H. (1984) 'Introduction, part I' to Negri, *Marx Beyond Marx* (Brooklyn: Autonomia, 1991).

Cliff, T. (1979) 'The Balance of Class Forces in Recent Years', *International Socialism*, 2, 6.

Clifford, R. (1998) *The Wisdom Literature* (Nashville, Tenn.: Abingdon).

Colli, G. (1980) *Scritti su Nietzsche* (Milan: Adelphi).

Colli, G. (1996) *Écrits sur Nietzsche*, trans. P. Farazzi (Paris: Éditions de l'Éclat).

Collins, J.J. (1998) *The Apocalyptic Imagination: An Introduction to Jewish Apocalyptic Literature*, 2nd edn. (Grand Rapids, Mich.: Eerdmans Publishing Company).

Crenshaw, J.L. (1998) *Old Testament Wisdom*, rev. edn. (Louisville, Ky.: Westminster/John Knox Press).

Crenshaw, J.L. (2001) 'The Book of Job', in J. Barton and J. Muddiman (eds) *The Oxford Bible Commentary* (New York: Oxford University Press), 331–55.

Deleuze, G. (1966) 'Humanity: A Dubious Existence', in Deleuze 2004.

Deleuze, G. (1967a) 'Conclusions on the Will to Power and the Eternal Return', in Deleuze 2004.

Deleuze, G. (1967b) 'Nietzsche's Burst of Laughter', in Deleuze 2004.

Deleuze, G. (1968a) *Différence et répétition* (Paris: Presses Universitaires de France).

Deleuze, G. (1968b) 'On Nietzsche and the Image of Thought', in Deleuze 2004.

Deleuze, G. (1969) *Logique du sens* (Paris: Éditions de Minuit).

Deleuze, G. (1983) *Nietzsche and Philosophy*, trans. H. Tomlinson (New York: Columbia University Press). Originally published in French in 1962.

Deleuze, G. (1986) *Foucault*, trans. S. Hand (Minneapolis: University of Minnesota Press).

Deleuze, G. (1988a) *Spinoza: Practical Philosophy*, trans. R. Hurley (San Francisco: City Lights).

Deleuze, G. (1988b) 'Signes et événements' (interview by R. Bellour and F. Ewald), *Magazine littéraire* 257, September.

Deleuze, G. (1990a) *Expressionism in Philosophy: Spinoza*, trans. M. Joughin (New York: Zone Books).

Deleuze, G. (1990b) *The Logic of Sense*, trans. M. Lester and C. Stivale (New York: Columbia University Press).

Deleuze, G. (1994) *Difference and Repetition*, trans. P. Patton (New York: Columbia University Press).

Deleuze, G. (1995) *Negotiations*, trans. M. Joughin (New York: Columbia University Press).

Deleuze, G. (1997) 'Spinoza and the Three *Ethics*', in *Essays Critical and Clinical*, trans. D. W. Smith and M. Greco (Minneapolis: University of Minnesota Press).

Deleuze, G. (2001) 'Nietzsche', in Deleuze, *Pure Immanence: Essays on a Life*, trans. A. Boyman (New York: Zone). Originally published in French in 1965.

Deleuze, G. (2004) *Desert Islands and Other Texts 1953–1974*, trans. M. Taormina et al. (Los Angeles: Semiotext(e)).

Deleuze, G., and M. Foucault (1977) 'Intellectuals and Power', trans. D. Bouchard, in D. Bouchard (ed.) *Language, Counter-Memory, Practice* (Ithaca: Cornell University Press).

Deleuze, G., and F. Guattari (1987) *A Thousand Plateaus: Capitalism and Schizophrenia*, vol. 2, trans. B. Massumi (Minneapolis: University of Minnesota Press).

Deleuze, G. and F. Guattari (1990) *Anti-Oedipus: Capitalism and Schizophrenia*, trans. R. Hurley, M. Seem and H.R. Lane, preface by M. Foucault (Minneapolis: University of Minnesota Press).

Derrida, J. (1967) *De la Grammatologie* (Paris: Éditions de Minuit).

Derrida, J. (1978) *Writing and Difference*, trans. A. Bass (Chicago: University of Chicago Press).

Derrida, J. (1981) *Dissemination*, trans. B. Johnson (Chicago: University of Chicago Press).

Derrida, J. (1988) *Limited Inc*, trans. S. Weber et al. (Evanston: Northwestern University Press).

Derrida, J. (1993) *Aporias*, trans. T. Dutoit (Stanford, Calif.: Stanford University Press).

Derrida, J. (1994) *Specters of Marx: The State of the Debt, the Work of Mourning and the New International*, trans. P. Kamuf, introd. B. Magnus and S. Cullenberg (New York and London: Routledge).

Derrida, J. (1997) *Politics of Friendship*, trans. G. Collins (London and New York: Verson).

Derrida, J. (1999) 'Marx & Sons', trans. G. Goshgarian, in M. Sprinker (ed.) *Ghostly Demarcations: A Symposium on Jacques Derrida's Specters of Marx* (New York: Verso).

Descombes, V. (1980) *Modern French Philosophy*, trans. L. Scott-Fox and J.M. Harding (Cambridge: Cambridge University Press).

Diderot, D. (1994) *Œuvres*, vol. 1: *Philosophie*, ed. L. Versini (Paris: Robert Laffont).

Dosse, F. (1997) *The History of Structuralism*, 2 vols, trans. D. Glassman (Minneapolis: University of Minnesota Press).

Dussel, E. (2001) *Towards an Unknown Marx* (London: Routledge).

Eribon, D. (1991) *Michel Foucault*, trans. B. Wing (Cambridge: Harvard University Press).

Esposito, R. (2004) *Bíos. Biopolitica e filosofia* (Turin: Einaudi).

Fadini, U., A. Negri, and C.T. Wolfe (eds) (2001) *Desiderio del mostro. dal circo al laboratorio alla politica* (Rome: ManifestoLibri).

Ferrari Bravo, L. (2001) 'Homo Sacer. Una riflessione sul libro di Agamben', in *Dal Fordismo alla globalizzazione* (Rome: ManifestoLibri).

Foucault, M. (1972) 'The Discourse on Language', in *The Archeology of Knowledge*, trans. A.M. Sheridan Smith (New York: Pantheon).

Foucault, M. (1977) 'Nietzsche, Genealogy, History', in *Language, Counter-Memory, Practice*, ed. and trans. D.F. Bouchard (Ithaca: Cornell University Press). Originally published in French in 1971.

Foucault, M. (1980) 'Two Lectures', in *Power/Knowledge: Selected Interviews and Other Writings 1972–1977*, trans. C. Gordon et al. (New York: Pantheon).

Foucault, M. (1989) *The Order of Things* (London: Routledge).

Foucault, M. (1990) 'Nietzsche, Freud, Marx', in G.L. Ormiston and A.D. Schrift (eds) *Transforming the Hermeneutic Context* (Albany: SUNY Press). Originally published in French in 1967.

Foucault, M. (1991) *Remarks on Marx: Conversations with Duccio Trombadori*, trans. R.J. Goldstein and J. Cascaito (Brooklyn: Semiotext(e)). Originally published in Italian in 1981.

Foucault, M. (1994) 'Cours de 7 janvier 1976', in *Dits et Écrits*, vol. 3 (Paris: Gallimard), text 193. Originally published in Italian in 1977.

Foucault, M. (1997) *Il faut défendre la société* (Paris: Gallimard).

Foucault, M. (2001) 'La vérité et les formes juridiques' (1974), in *Dits et Écrits*, vol. 1, *1954–1975* (Paris: Gallimard).

Foucault, M. (2003) *Society Must Be Defended*, trans. D. Macey (London: Penguin).

Foucault, M. (2004) *Naissance de la biopolitique. Cours au Collège de France, 1978–1979* (Paris: Gallimard/Seuil).

Foucault, M., and G. Deleuze (1994) 'Introduction générale aux Oeuvres philosophiques complètes de Friedrich Nietzsche', vol. 5, *Le Gai Savoir et fragments posthumes (1881–1882)*, in Foucault, *Dits et Écrits*, vol. 1 (Paris: Gallimard), text 45. Originally published in 1967.

Gabel, J.B., et al. (2000) *The Bible as Literature*, 4th edn. (New York: Oxford University Press).

Good, E.M. (1990) *In Turns of Tempest: A Reading of Job, with a Translation* (Stanford, Calif.: Stanford University Press).

Guattari, F. (1984) *Molecular Revolution: Psychiatry and Politics*, trans. R. Sheed, introd. D. Cooper (Harmondsworth: Penguin).

Gutiérrez, G. (1987) *On Job: God-Talk and the Suffering of the Innocent* (Maryknoll, N.Y.: Orbis Books).

Habel, N. (1975) *The Book of Job* (New York: Cambridge University Press).

Habel, N. (1985) *The Book of Job: A Commentary* (Philadelphia: John Knox/Westminster Press).

Hacking, I. (2002) *Historical Ontology* (Cambridge: Harvard University Press).

Hall, S., and M. Jacques (eds) (1983) *The Politics of Thatcherism* (London: Lawrence & Wishart).

Halleux, R. (1998) 'Matière', in M. Blay and R. Halleux (eds) *La science classique, XVIe-XVIIIe siècle. Dictionnaire critique* (Paris: Flammarion).

Hannington, W. (1936) *Unemployed Struggles 1919–1936* (London: Lawrence & Wishart).

Hardt, M. (1991) 'Translator's Foreword', in A. Negri, *The Savage Anomaly: The Power of Spinoza's Metaphysics and Politics*, trans. M. Hardt (Minneapolis: University of Minnesota Press).

Hardt, M. (1993) *Gilles Deleuze: An Apprenticeship in Philosophy* (Minneapolis: University of Minnesota Press).

Hardt, M., and A. Negri (1994) *Labor of Dionysus: A Critique of the State-Form* (Minneapolis: University of Minnesota Press).

Hardt, M., and A. Negri (2000) *Empire* (Cambridge: Harvard University Press).

Hardt, M., and A. Negri (2002) '"Subterranean Passages in Thought": *Empire*'s Inserts', *Cultural Studies* 16, 2, 193–212.

Hardt, M., and A. Negri (2004) *Multitude: War and Democracy in the Age of Empire* (New York: Penguin Press).

Harman, C. (1988) *The Fire Last Time* (London: Bookmarks).

Harman, C. (1991) 'The State and Capitalism Today', *International Socialism*, Second Series, 51.

Harman, C. (1996) 'Globalization: A Critique of a New Orthodoxy', *International Socialism*, Second Series, 73.

Harvey, D. (2003) *The New Imperialism* (Oxford: Oxford University Press).

Haver, W. (1997) 'Queer Research; or, How to Practice Invention to the Brink of Intelligibility', in S. Golding (ed.) *The Eight Technologies of Otherness* (New York: Routledge).

Hegel, G.W.F. (1962) *Scritti di filosofia del diritto*, trans. A. Negri (Bari: Laterza).

Hegel, G.W.F. (1976) *Science of Logic*, trans. A.V. Miller (Atlantic Highlands: Humanities Press).

Hegel, G.W.F. (1977) *Phenomenology of Spirit*, trans. A.V. Miller (Oxford: Oxford University Press).

Hegel, G.W.F. (1988) *Lectures on the Philosophy of Religion, One-Volume Edition: The Lectures of 1827*, ed. P.C. Hodgson, trans. R.F. Brown et al. (Berkeley: University of California Press).

Hegel, G.W.F. (1995) *Lectures on the History of Philosophy*, trans. E.S. Haldane and F.H. Simson (1840; Lincoln: University of Nebraska Press).

Heidegger, M. (1929) *Sein und Zeit*, 16th edn. (Tübingen: Max Niemeyer, 1986).

Holdren, N. (forthcoming) 'A Biopolitical Stage of Capitalism?', in *Critical Sense*.

Honig, B. (1993) *Political Theory and the Displacement of Politics* (Ithaca: Cornell University Press).

International Socialism (1985) Special issue on the 1984–85 miners' strike and its aftermath, Second Series, 29.

Jacques, M., and F. Mulhern (eds) (1981) *The Forward March of Labour Halted?* (London: Verso).

Johnson, M.D. (2002) *Making Sense of the Bible: Literary Type as an Approach to Understanding* (Grand Rapids, Mich.: Eerdmans Publishing Company).

Kant, I. (1996) *Religion and Rational Theology*, ed. and trans. A.W. Wood and G. Di Giovanni (New York: Cambridge University Press).

Kant, I. (2000) *Critique of the Power of Judgment*, ed. P. Guyer, trans. P. Guyer and E. Matthews (New York: Cambridge University Press).

Kirby, V. (1997) *Telling Flesh: The Substance of the Corporeal* (New York and London: Routledge).

Kraus, K. (1975) *Dits et contredits* (= *Sprüche und Widersprüche* (1909)), trans. R. Lewinter (Paris: Gérard Lebovici).

Lacoue-Labarthe, P. (1989) *Typography: Mimesis, Philosophy, Politics*, ed. C. Fynsk (Stanford, Calif.: Stanford University Press).

Lazzarato, M. (1997) 'Per una ridefinizione del concetto di "bio-politica"', in *Lavoro immateriale. Forme di vita e produzione di soggettività* (Verona: Ombre Corte).

Lazzarato, M. (2002) 'From Biopower to Biopolitics', trans. I.A. Ramirez, in *Pli: The Warwick Journal of Philosophy* 13: 100–111.

Lazzarato, M. (2005) 'Biopolitique / bioéconomie', in *Multitudes* 22. (English translation by A. Bove available at http://multitudes.samizdat.net/Biopolitics-Bioeconomics-a.html.)

Lefort, C. (1972) *Le travail de l'oeuvre Machiavel* (Paris: Gallimard).

Lefort, C. (1986) 'Outline of the Genesis of Ideology in Modern Societies', in *The Political Forms of Modern Society* (Cambridge: MIT Press).

Lemke, T. (2001) '"The Birth of Bio-politics": Michel Foucault's Lecture at the Collège de France on Neo-liberal Governmentality', *Economy and Society* 30, 2, 190–207.

Levinas, E. (1969) *Totality and Infinity: An Essay on Exteriority*, trans. A. Lingis (Pittsburgh: Duquesne University Press).

Losurdo, D. (2002) *Nietzsche, il ribelle aristocratico* (Turin: Bollati Boringhieri).

Löwy, M. (1996) *The War of Gods: Religion and Politics in Latin America* (New York: Verso).

Lucretius (1916) *De rerum natura*, ed. W.E. Leonard (New York: E.P. Dutton).

Luttwak, E. (2001) *Strategy*, rev. edn. (Cambridge, Mass.: Harvard University Press).

Macherey, P. (1992a) *Avec Spinoza: études sur la doctrine et l'histoire du spinozism* (Paris: Presses Universitaires de France).

Macherey, P. (1992b) 'De la Mediation à la Constitution: Description d'un Parcours Speculatif', in Macherey 1992a.

Machiavelli, N. (1996) *Discourses on Livy*, trans. H.C. Mansfield and N. Tarcov (Chicago: University of Chicago Press).

Machiavelli, N. (1998) *The Prince*, trans. H.C. Mansfield (Chicago: University of Chicago Press).

Macpherson, C.B. (1962) *The Political Theory of Possessive Individualism* (Oxford: Oxford University Press).

Magazine littéraire (1992) Special issue 298, 'Les Vies de Nietzsche'; reissued in 2001 as 'Hors série' 3: *Nietzsche*.

Manin, B. (1997) *The Principles of Representative Government* (New York: Cambridge University Press).

Marx, K. (1970a) *Critique of Hegel's 'Philosophy of Right'*, trans. A. Jolin and J. Malley (Cambridge: Cambridge University Press).

Marx, K. (1970b) 'Theses on Feuerbach', in *The German Ideology*, ed. and trans. C.J. Arthur (New York: International Publishers).

Marx, K. (1971) *A Contribution to the Critique of Political Economy* (London: Lawrence & Wishart).

Marx, K. (1973) *Grundrisse: Foundations of the Critique of Political Economy*, trans. M. Nicolaus (New York: Penguin).

Marx, K. (1975) 'On The Jewish Question', in *Early Writings* (New York: Vintage Books).

Marx, K. (1976) *Capital*, vol. 1, trans. B. Fowkes (New York: Penguin).

Marx, K. (1981) *Capital*, vol. 3, trans. D. Fernbach (Harmondsworth: Penguin).

Marx, K. (1996) *Later Political Writings*, ed. and trans. T. Carver (New York: Cambridge University Press).

Marx, K., and F. Engels (1998) *The Communist Manifesto* (London: Verso).

Mepham, J. (1979) 'From the *Grundrisse* to *Capital*', in J. Mepham and D.-H. Ruben (eds) *Issues in Marxist Philosophy*, 3 vols. (Brighton: Harvester), vol. 1.

Merleau-Ponty, M. (1949) 'A Note on Machiavelli', in *Signs* (Evanston, IL: Northwestern University Press, 1964).

Montag, W. (1999) *Bodies, Masses, Power: Spinoza and His Contemporaries* (New York: Verso).

Montinari, M. (1975) *Che cosa ha veramente detto Nietzsche* (Rome: Ubaldini).

Montinari, M. (1982) *Su Nietzsche* (Rome: Riuniti).

Mutman, M. (2001) 'On Empire', *Rethinking Marxism*, 13, 3–4.

Nancy, J.-L. (1991) *The Inoperative Community*, ed. P. Connor, trans. P. Connor, L. Garbus, M. Holland and S. Sawhney (Minneapolis: University of Minnesota Press).

Negri, A. (1958) *Stato e diritto nel giovane Hegel* (Padua: CEDAM).

Negri, A. (1959) *Saggi sullo storicismo tedesco: Dilthey e Meinecke* (Milan: Feltrinelli).

Negri, A. (1970) *Descartes politico o della ragionevole ideologia* (Milan: Feltrinelli).

Negri, A. (1978a) *Domination and Sabotage*, in *Books for Burning*, ed. and trans. T.S. Murphy et al. (London: Verso, 2005).

Negri, A. (1978b) 'Capitalist Domination and Working-Class Sabotage', trans. E. Emery, in *Working Class Autonomy and the Crisis* (London: Red Notes, 1979).

Negri, A. (1979) *Marx oltre Marx* (Milan: Feltrinelli).

Negri, A. (1981) *L'anomalia selvaggia: saggio su potere e potenza in Baruch Spinoza* (Milan: Feltrinelli).

Negri, A. (1982a) *L'anomalie sauvage. Puissance et pouvoir chez Spinoza*, trans. F. Matheron (Paris: PUF).

Negri, A. (1982b) *Macchina tempo. Rompicapi, Liberazione, Costituzione* (Milan: Feltrinelli).

Negri, A. (1987a) *Lenta Ginestra: Saggio sull' ontologia di Giacomo Leopardi* (Milan: SugarCo).

Negri, A. (1987b) *Fabbriche del soggetto* (Livorno: Secolo XXI).

Negri, A. (1988) *Revolution Retrieved: Writings on Marx, Keynes, Capitalist Crisis and New Social Subjects* (London: Red Notes).

Negri, A. (1989) *The Politics of Subversion: A Manifesto for the Twenty-First Century*, trans. J. Newell (Oxford: Polity).

Negri, A. (1991a) *Marx Beyond Marx: Lessons on the Grundrisse*, trans. H. Cleaver et al. (Brooklyn: Autonomedia). Translation originally published in 1984.

Negri, A. (1991b) *The Savage Anomaly: The Power of Spinoza's Metaphysics and Politics*, trans. M. Hardt (Minneapolis: University of Minnesota Press).

Negri, A. (1992) 'Marxistes: une approche paradoxale', *Magazine littéraire* 1992.

Negri, A. (1994) 'Wittgenstein et la douleur: quelques conséquences sociologiques', *Chimères* 22. English translation: 'Wittgenstein and Pain: Sociological Consequences', trans. T.S. Murphy, *Genre: Forms of Discourse and Culture* 37, 3–4 (Fall/Winter 2004).

Negri, A. (1995a) 'Spinoza's Anti-Modernity', trans. C.T. Wolfe, *Graduate Faculty Philosophy Journal* 18, 2 (Spring).

Negri, A. (1995b) 'On *A Thousand Plateaus*', trans. C.T. Wolfe, *Graduate Faculty Philosophy Journal* 18, 1 (Fall).

Negri, A. (1996) 'Notes on the Evolution of the Thought of the Later Althusser', trans. O. Vasile, in A. Callari and D. Ruccio (eds) *Postmodern Materialism and the Future of Marxist Theory* (Hanover, N.H.: Wesleyan University Press).

Negri, A. (1997a) *Le pouvoir constituant. Essai sur les alternatives de la modernité*, trans. E. Balibar and F. Matheron (Paris: Presses Universitaires de France).

Negri, A. (1997b) 'Reliqua Desiderantur: A Conjecture for a Definition of the Concept of Democracy in the Final Spinoza', trans. T. Stolze, in T. Stolze and W. Montag (eds) *The New Spinoza* (Minneapolis: University of Minnesota Press).

Negri, A. (1999a) *Insurgencies: Constituent Power and the Modern State*, trans. M. Boscagli (Minneapolis: University of Minnesota Press).

Negri, A. (1999b) 'The Specter's Smile', trans. P. Dailey and C. Costantini, in M. Sprinker (ed.) *Ghostly Demarcations: A Symposium on Jacques Derrida's Specters of Marx* (New York: Verso).

Negri, A. (2000a) *Kairòs, Alma Venus, Multitudo: Nove lezioni impartite a me stesso* (Rome: Manifestolibri).

Negri, A. (2000b) 'Alma Venus. Prolegomena to the Common', trans. P. Dailey and C. Costantini, in The Renewal of Materialism, ed. C.T. Wolfe (Graduate Faculty Philosophy Journal 22, 1, Spring).

Negri, A. (2000c) 'Nécessité et liberté chez Spinoza: quelques alternatives', trans. F. Matheron, Multitudes 2 (May).

Negri, A. (2001a) 'Ruptures dans l'empire, puissance de l'exode', October 27 2001, interview in Multitudes 7 (online version available at multitudes.samizdat.net/Ruptures-dans-l-Empire-puissance.html).

Negri, A. (2001b) 'Il mostro politico. Nuda vita e potenza', in Fadini, Negri and Wolfe 2001.

Negri, A. (2002a) Il lavoro di Giobbe (Rome: ManifestoLibri).

Negri, A. (2002b) Du retour: Abécédaire biopolitique (Paris: Calmann-Levy).

Negri, A. (2002c) Il potere costituente. Saggio sulle alternative del moderno. (Rome: ManifestoLibri) (2nd edn., first published in 1992.)

Negri A. (2003a) Time for Revolution, trans. M. Mandarini (New York: Continuum).

Negri, A. (2003b) Guide. Cinque lezioni su Impero e dintorni (Milan: Raffaele Cortina).

Negri, A. (2004a) Subversive Spinoza: (Un)contemporary Variations, trans. T. Murphy (Manchester: Manchester University Press).

Negri, A. (2004b) Negri on Negri: In Conversation with Anne Dufourmantelle, trans. M.B. DeBevoise (New York: Routledge).

Negri, A. (2005) 'The Political Subject and Absolute Immanence', in Theology and the Political: The New Debate, ed. C. Davis, J. Millbank and S. Žižek (Durham, N.C.: Duke University Press).

Negri, A. (2006) 'The Discreet Taste of the Dialectic', in M. Calarco and S. DeCaroli (eds) Sovereignty and Life: Essays on Giorgio Agamben (Stanford, Calif.: Stanford University Press).

Negri, A., et al. (1996) Le Bassin de travail immatériel (BTI) dans la métropole parisienne (Paris: L'Harmattan).

Neilson, B. (2004) 'Potenza Nuda? Sovereignty, Biopolitics, Capitalism', Contretemps 5, 63–78.

Newsom, C.A. (1996) 'The Book of Job', in The New Interpreter's Bible, vol.4 (Nashville, Tenn.: Abingdon Press), 319–637.

Newsom, C.A. (2003) The Book of Job: A Contest of Moral Imaginations (New York: Oxford University Press).

Nietzsche, F. (1982) Daybreak: Thoughts on the Prejudices of Morality, trans. R.J. Hollingdale (Cambridge: Cambridge University Press).

O'Connor, J. (1987) The Meaning of Crisis: A Theoretical Introduction (Oxford and New York: Basil Blackwell).

Panitch, L., and S. Gindin (2002) 'Gems and Baubles in Empire', Historical Materialism 10, 2, 17–43.

Pasquino, P. (1994) 'The constitutional republicanism of Emmanuel Sieyès', in B. Fontana (ed.) The invention of the modern republic (Cambridge: Cambridge University Press).

Pettit, P. (1997) Republicanism (Oxford: Clarendon Press).

Pinto, L. (1995) Les neveux de Zarathoustra: La réception de Nietzsche en France (Paris: Le Seuil).

Plotnitsky, A. (1993) Reconfigurations: Critical Theory and General Economy (Gainsville: University Press of Florida).

Pope, M.H. (1965) The Anchor Bible: Job (New York: Doubleday).

Quine, W.V.O. (1969) 'Epistemology Naturalized', in Ontological Relativity (New York: Columbia University Press).

Rabinow, P., and N. Rose (2003) 'Thoughts on the Concept of Biopower Today', available at www.molsci.org/files/Rose_Rabinow_Biopower_Today.pdf.

Raines, J. (2002) Marx and Religion (Philadelphia: Temple University Press).

Read, J. (2003) The Micropolitics of Capital (Albany: SUNY Press).

Revel, J. (2005) Michel Foucault: Expériences de la pensée (Paris: Bordas).

Rosdolsky, R. (1977) *The Making of Marx's Capital*, trans. P. Burgess (London: Pluto Press).
Rose, N. (2001) 'The politics of Life Itself', *Theory, Culture and Society* 18, 6: 1–30.
Ryan, M. (1982) *Marxism and Deconstruction: A Critical Articulation* (Baltimore and London: Johns Hopkins University Press).
Ryan, M. (1989) *Politics and Culture: Working Hypotheses for a Post-Revolutionary Society* (Baltimore: Johns Hopkins University Press).
Said, E.W. (1978) *Orientalism* (Harmondsworth: Penguin).
Schérer, R. (1996) 'L'usine de l'âme', *Chimères* 27.
Schürmann, R. (1996) *Des hégémonies brisées* (Mauvezin: T.E.R.).
Schürmann, R. (2003) *Broken Hegemonies*, ed. and trans. R. Lilly (Bloomington: Indiana University Press).
Skinner, Q. (1998) *Liberty before Liberalism* (New York: Cambridge University Press).
Soelle, D. (2001) *The Silent Cry: Mysticism and Resistance* (Minneapolis: Fortress Press).
Spinoza, B. (1992) *Ethics ... and Selected Letters*, trans. S. Shirley (Indianapolis: Hackett).
Spinoza, B. (1985) *The Ethics*, trans. E. Curley, in *Collected Works of Spinoza*, vol. 1 (Princeton: Princeton University Press).
Spinoza, B. (1998) *Theological-Political Treatise,* trans. S. Shirley (Indianapolis: Hackett).
Spinoza, B. (2000) *Political Treatise*, trans. S. Shirley (Indianapolis: Hackett).
Spivak, G.C. (1995) 'Translator's Preface', in Mahasweta Devi, *Imaginary Maps*, trans. and ed. G.C. Spivak (London and New York: Routledge).
Spivak, G.C. (2003) *Death of a Discipline* (New York: Columbia University Press).
Symons, J. (2001) *On Dennett* (Belmont: Wadsworth).
Taylor, C. (1975) *Hegel* (Cambridge: Cambridge University Press).
Thompson, E.P. (1978) *The Poverty of Theory and Other Essays* (London: Merlin).
Toscano, A. (2003) 'Antagonism and Insurrection in Italian *Operaismo*', available at www. goldsmiths.ac.uk/csisp/ papers/toscano_antagonism.pdf.
Toscano, A. (2006) *The Theatre of Production: Philosophy and Individuation between Kant and Deleuze* (Basingstoke: Palgrave).
Tosel, A. (1997) 'Superstition and Reading', trans. T. Stolze, in *The New Spinoza*, eds W. Montag and T. Stolze (Minneapolis: University of Minnesota Press).
Tronti, M. (1979) 'Lenin in England', trans. Red Notes, in *Working Class Autonomy and the Crisis* (London: Red Notes).
Vatter, M. (2000) *Between Form and Event: Machiavelli's Theory of Political Freedom* (Boston: Kluwer).
Vatter, M. (2001) 'Chapitre XXV du *Prince*: l'histoire comme effet de l'action libre,' in Y.C. Zarka and T. Ménissier (eds) *Machiavel. Le Prince ou le nouvel art politique* (Paris: Presses Universitaires de France).
Vattimo, G. (1992) 'Italie: aspects de la renaissance italienne', in *Magazine littéraire*, 1992.
Vattimo, G. (2004) *Nihilism and Emancipation: Ethics, Politics and Law*, trans. W. McCuaig (New York: Columbia University Press).
Virno, P. (1999) *Il Ricordo del presente. Saggio sul tempo storico* (Turin: Bollati Boringhieri).
Virno, P. (2002) *A Grammar of the Multitude*, trans. I. Bertoletti et al. (New York: Semiotext(e)).
Virno, P. (2003) *Quando il verbo si fa carne. Linguaggio e natura umana* (Turin: Bollati Boringhieri).
Vygodsky, V.S. (1974) *The Story of a Great Discovery* (Tunbridge Wells: Abacus Press).
Wolfe, C. (2005) 'Il cervello sociale', *Forme de vita* 4: 141–53.
Wood, E.M. (2002) 'Global Capital, National States', in M. Rupert and H. Smith (eds) *Historical Materialism and Globalization* (London: Routledge).
Wright, S. (2002) *Storming Heaven: Class composition and Struggle in Italian Autonomist Marxism* (London: Pluto Press).

Contributors

Alex Callinicos is professor of European studies at King's College London and a longtime member of the Socialist Workers Party. He is the author of *Is There a Future for Marxism?* (1982), *Marxism and Philosophy* (1983), *Against Postmodernism* (1991), *An Anti-Capitalist Manifesto* (2003) and *The Resources of Critique* (2006), among many other works.

Pierre Macherey was professor of philosophy at the Université de Lille-III until his retirement in 2003. He contributed to the original French edition of Louis Althusser's collective volume *Lire le Capital* (1965) and is the author of *A Theory of Literary Production* (1966, translated 1978), *Hegel ou Spinoza* (1979), *The Object of Literature* (1990, translated 1995), *Avec Spinoza* (1992) and a five-volume introduction to Spinoza's *Ethics* (1994–98).

Timothy S. Murphy is associate professor of English at the University of Oklahoma, where he edits the scholarly journal *Genre: Forms of Discourse and Culture*. He is the author of *Wising Up the Marks: The Amodern William Burroughs* (1997), cotranslator of Negri's *Subversive Spinoza* (2004) and *Books for Burning* (2005), and coeditor of *The Philosophy of Antonio Negri: Resistance in Practice* (2005).

Abdul-Karim Mustapha is coeditor of *The Philosophy of Antonio Negri: Resistance in Practice* (2005) and a member of the editorial boards of *Multitudes* and *Rethinking Marxism*. He is also the author of a forthcoming book, *Age of the Globe: On Philosophy and Periodization*, and currently teaches at Wofford College.

Mahmut Mutman teaches cultural and media theory at the Department of Communication and Design, Bilkent University, Turkey. He is the author of several publications on orientalism, Islamism, nationalism and film.

Jason Read is assistant professor of philosophy at the University of Southern Maine. He is the author of *The Micro-Politics of Capital: Marx and the Prehistory of the Present* (2003).

Judith Revel is a philosopher, Italianist and translator who teaches at the Université de Paris-I, Panthéon-Sorbonne. She specializes in contemporary thought, particularly French poststructuralism and Italian political thought since 1945, and is the author of *Foucault, le parole e i poteri* (1996), *Le Vocabulaire de Foucault* (2002) and *Michel Foucault: Expériences de la pensée* (2005).

Ted Stolze teaches philosophy at Cerritos College in southern California. He is coeditor of *The New Spinoza* (1997), translator of Macherey's *In a Materialist Way: Selected Essays* (1998), and is currently working on a book on Spinoza, Marxism and Buddhism.

Alberto Toscano is lecturer in sociology at Goldsmiths, London. He is the author of *The Theatre of Production: Philosophy and Individuation Between Kant and Deleuze* (2006) and the coeditor of Alain Badiou's *Theoretical Writings* (2004). Most recently, he has cotranslated and introduced, with Matteo Mandarini, Antonio Negri's *The Political Descartes* (2007). He is a member of the editorial board of *Historical Materialism: Research in Critical Marxist Theory*.

Miguel Vatter is associate professor at the Institute of Political Science of the Catholic University of Chile. He is the author of *Between Form and Event: Machiavelli's Theory of Political Freedom* (2000), and writes on contemporary political theory as well as on the history of political thought. He is currently at work on a book on Leo Strauss.

Charles T. Wolfe is a lecturer and postdoctoral fellow in philosophy at the Université du Québec in Montréal. He recently edited the collection *Monsters and Philosophy* (2005) and is an editor of the journal *Multitudes*. His main interests are philosophical materialism and the history and epistemology of the life sciences.

Index

Note: 'n' following a page number refers to the numbered note on that page.